Brun Cam

Brun Campbell

The Original Ragtime Kid

LARRY KARP

McFarland & Company, Inc., Publishers
Jefferson, North Carolina

Frontispiece: Artist's conception of Brun Campbell's planned marker for Scott Joplin's grave (Brun Campbell Archive).

ISBN (print) 978-1-4766-6345-6
ISBN (ebook) 978-1-4766-2383-2

LIBRARY OF CONGRESS CATALOGUING DATA ARE AVAILABLE

BRITISH LIBRARY CATALOGUING DATA ARE AVAILABLE

Front cover images © 2016 iStock

Printed in the United States of America

McFarland & Company, Inc., Publishers
Box 611, Jefferson, North Carolina 28640
www.mcfarlandpub.com

To some special friends
without whom this book would not have been written

Casey Karp
Loving son, savvy editor

Erin Karp
Loving daughter, wise counselor

Jack West
*Who from Day One understood what was important,
and thus made all the difference*

Derek Butler
*Who refuses to accept that you can't make
chicken salad out of chicken feathers*

David Reffkin
*Consultant par excellence in history,
music, and just about everything else*

Richard Egan
*Nonpareil historian, performer, and composer
of Midwestern ragtime*

"As far as doing the right thing,
go by what your heart dictates,
and I believe you will always be right."

—Brun Campbell, from a letter to
pianist Jerry Heermans, ca. 1949

Do you know what young Brun Campbell did?
Hopped a freight car, scrunched way down, and hid
All the way to Sedalia
(Or so he'd regale ya)
And became Mr. J's Ragtime Kid

—Larry Karp

Table of Contents

Acknowledgments		ix
Introduction		1
I.	When Ragtime Was Young	9
	Ragtime in the Red Light Districts	55
	"My Girl Taffy"	58
II.	When the Ragtime Kid Grew Old	64
	Interlude	64
	1943: Hal's Pal	72
	1944: Pedal to the Metal	83
	1945: A Shift in the Wind	97
	1946–1947: The Pen Is Mightier Than the Pest	116
	1948: The Kid at the Crossroads	123
	1949–1952: Last Act: Spotlight on The Kid	134
III.	Short Pieces	148
	Otis Saunders and "The Maple Leaf Rag"	148
	The Maple Leaf Rag	151
	The First Ragtime Circuit	154
	The Original Hot Men of the 90s	156
	Ragtime in the Red Light Districts	169
	How About You?	172
	Cavalcade of Jazz, or "The Two-Four Beat"	174
	It Has to Be Ragtime	178
	Not the Best-Case Scenario: Scott Joplin and His	
	"Maple Leaf Rag"	180
	Joplin Biography	181

IV.   Brun Campbell: An Appreciation   185

V.   Recalibrating Brun: The 1940s Musical Composition
       by Richard Egan   191
       The Rag   193
       The Blues   196
       The Love Songs   199
       The Love Songs of Harold A. Campbell   202
       Conclusion   204

Appendix 1: Musical Works by Brun Campbell   207
Appendix 2: Writings and Readings   213
Appendix 3: When Ragtime Was Young *and* When the Ragtime
       Kid Grew Old: *Brun's Organizational Variations*   219
Appendix 4: Transcripts of Hal Nichols' Memories 'N Melodies
       Radio Shows   223
Appendix 5: Interview of Cecil Charles Spiller by Galen Wilkes,
       January 26, 1992   231
Appendix 6: Brun Campbell Family Tree   241
Index   243

Acknowledgments

I'm beyond grateful for the help I received from two scholars of music and history who worked closely with me throughout the entire Brun Campbell project, both in the organization of the material and the synthesis of Brun's historical biography. Without David Reffkin and Richard Egan's willingness to contribute original material and field my endless questions, I could not have written this book.

David Reffkin is the director of the American Ragtime Ensemble (founded 1973), and a distinguished expert on orchestration and performance of early 20th-century popular music and the *salon* tradition. As a professional violinist, he is both a soloist and a member of a variety of groups, as well as a conductor, arranger and musical contractor. He was the producer and host of the weekly radio program, *The Ragtime Machine*, for 30 years, creating the world's largest archive of interviews with ragtimers. His research, writing and editing have earned him local and international awards, among them the Mayor's Certificate of Honor for service to San Francisco. He was associated with *The Mississippi Rag* for 34 years as a correspondent, reviewer and contributing editor, voted by readers as Best Ragtime Journalist. Among his published pieces is the Foreword for the outstanding discography *Cakewalks, Rags and Novelties*. As director of the American Ragtime Ensemble or as a soloist, he has recorded *Ragtime Chamber Music, Prestidigitations* (music by Judith L. Zaimont), and *I Love a (Violin and) Piano*. David is often called upon to work as a music curator, archivist, seminar speaker, consultant, editor and teacher. In 1974 he helped create the Scott Joplin Ragtime Festival, which presented him with the Scott Joplin Award in 2006. He is a graduate of the New England Conservatory of Music.

Richard Egan is a descendant in the lineage of the Folk Ragtime tradition that has been passed down from Brun Campbell to Trebor Tichenor, Tom Shea, and subsequent generations. He began his ragtime career aboard the Goldenrod Showboat on the St. Louis levee in the mid–1980s. Fluent in the traditional American musical language, he travels the Missouri and Illinois contra, square and barn dance circuit, playing piano in the company of string musicians. He has composed numerous Midwestern rags, some of which are featured on his three solo CDs (*From the Land of Ragtime, Lowland Forest, Missouri Romp*). In 2012, he was noted in *St. Louis Magazine*—along with fellow ragtimers Joplin, Turpin, Chauvin, and Tichenor, in addition to jazzmen, bluesmen, rockers, rappers etc.—as one who has shaped the St. Louis sound. A past president of the Friends of Scott Joplin, he helped open the Scott Joplin House in 1991, instituted the monthly Ragtime Rendezvous in 1997, and organized the erecting of a monument on the grave of ragtime patriarch Tom Turpin in 1999. Egan's publications include transcriptions of the works of Brun Campbell and Blind Boone's "Camp Meeting No. 1."

Another consultant whose work was critical to the successful completion of this project was Casey Karp. Casey, an insightful, incisive editor, read through the entire manuscript at several points in its development. I accepted almost all his suggestions, always with gratitude, sometimes with embarrassment. In addition, Casey was available at all times to consult on questions of content and relevance, and his contributions were unfailingly on the mark. Finally, as a writer primarily of fiction, my skills with graphics in word processing programs leave much to be desired, but Casey, a computer professional, stepped up here as well.

For extensive contributions regarding Brun's time in Tulsa between 1907 and 1925, I'm indebted to the late Rod Tillman and his wife Carol and Ian Swart, who went far beyond the call of duty in scouring old city directories, census records, and other resources.

The time Brun spent in Oberlin, Kansas, between 1887 and 1891 was critical to his psychological development and behavior in later life. For documents related to this time period, I thank Dr. Jay Anderson, DVM of Oberlin; Jane Anderson of Seattle; and Sharleen Wurm, director of Decatur County's Last Indian Raid Museum.

Brun lived intermittently in Arkansas City, Kansas, between 1891 and 1907. Dalene McDonald, director of the Arkansas City Public Library; Sandy Randel, director of the Cherokee Strip Land Rush Museum/Cowley County Genealogy Library; Ashley Randel of the Cherokee Strip Museum staff; and genealogists Bill and Lou Tharp of Winfield, Kansas, provided me with a tremendous number of documents that shed light on Brun's childhood and early adult life, and helped me to interpret his memoir, *When Ragtime Was Young*.

Of primary importance in demonstrating the lasting significance and influence of Brun's music were commentaries by the late Trebor Tichenor, Virginia Tichenor, Terry Parrish, Richard Egan, John Petley, the late Tom Shea, David Thomas Roberts, and Kathi Backus.

Aisha Johnson, special collections librarian at Fisk University; Mary

Nicely, program coordinator at the Kennedy-Douglass Center for the Arts, Florence (AL) Department of Arts and Museums; and Roberto G. Trujillo, head, Department of Special Collections and Frances and Charles Field Curator of Special Collections, Stanford University Libraries, were kind enough to send me information from their respective archives.

I appreciate Galen Wilkes' generosity in offering his recorded interview with Cecil Charles Spiller regarding Spiller's friendship with Brun.

Dr. Eric Peterson provided insights into significant aspects of Brun's emotional constitution.

Thanks to Robert Perry, David Reffkin, and Daniel Grinstead for their learned analyses of the two allegedly Joplin hand-played piano rolls.

I suspect Dan C. Brown's glossary of the clothing of ragtime pianists as presented by Brun will be helpful to many people other than myself. Thank you, Dan.

Others who helped me plug significant holes in Brun's story were Ann Westerberg, Betty Singer, Dr. Edward Berlin, Jack Rummel, Bryan Wright, Mark Forster, and Maggie Young.

I'm particularly grateful to Carol Binkowski for helpful discussions before and throughout the writing of the book.

Thanks to David Alff, my editor, for major help and encouragement throughout this project, and to Dr. AmyRose McCue Gill of TextFormations, an outstanding indexer.

Much of the time I was working on this book, I was also dealing with medical problems. Thanks to Derek Butler, my personal trainer, and Drs. Gary Rosen, Carl Brodie, Jack West, Humera Ali, Eric Peterson, and Ken Gross for recognizing and accepting the importance of the work to me, and helping no end to keep me moving forward on my project.

I'm indebted to the staff at Riverview Cemetery, Arkansas City, for providing me access to view Taffy (Campbell) George's crypt.

For ongoing encouragement and general advice, I thank Max Morath, Jack Rummel, Terry Parrish, Jeff Barnhart, Fred Hoeptner, and Washboard Kitty Wilson.

David Reffkin, Richard Egan, Peg Kehret, and the late Trebor Tichenor read my manuscript at various levels of development, and provided excellent guidance.

Finally, thanks to my family: Myra, Casey, Maggie, Erin, Peter, and Simon, who always put up, usually cheerfully, with someone who spends so many of his waking hours locked away in a room with people who are imaginary, dead, or both.

If I've neglected to mention anyone else who contributed to my work, it was not intentional, and I apologize. And I take full responsibility for any and all errors.

Introduction

Sanford Brunson Campbell "Brun" was born in rural Kansas in 1884. Edison's phonograph was a scientific curiosity. The idea of radio broadcasts was visionary. American popular music consisted in large measure of racist minstrel-show tunes and maudlin ballads about dead lovers, dying children, and other lachrymose subjects. In 1884, if people wanted music in their homes beyond what they could play or sing, they bought a Swiss music box.

But by the time Brun entered his teen years, big changes were in the works. In 1897, a person could go into a general store and come out carrying a small phonograph with cylindrical sound recordings to play on it. In the same year, Guglielmo Marconi founded the Wireless Telegraph and Signal Company in England. And in 1897, "Mississippi Rag," by William H. Krell, was published, the first tune whose title included the word "rag" in reference to a musical form.

Ragtime, a musical genre characterized by a syncopated melody played against a steady left-hand duple beat, had crept out of black culture, primarily in the Midwest and South, and was first heard by any considerable number of white ears at the World Columbian Exposition in Chicago in 1893. Then in 1899, Scott Joplin's "Maple Leaf Rag" was published in Sedalia, Missouri, and for the next two decades, until jazz came along, ragtime was America's popular music, a true national craze. As always, Irving Berlin said it with music: "Everything in America is Ragtime" (1915).

But the ragtime era, as Max Morath and Moss Hall named those two decades on their NET television series, was not just one big happy song and dance. As the nineteenth century gave way to the twentieth, race relations in Brun Campbell's country were disastrous. Legally, blacks might have been free, but that didn't count for much when whites were still free to mock them, disparage them, exploit them, and hang them by the neck from trees. Scientists told Americans that blacks represented a separate branch of the human race, one inferior to whites in every imaginable way, an underclass inherently predisposed to lawlessness, violent behavior, lascivious sexual practices, and gen-

1

eral immorality. Religious leaders proclaimed that the Lord had created blacks to serve whites. Not surprising, then, that a black musical form would have been anathema to most white communities. Scientists warned that music of this sort was dangerous to the nervous system; preachers proclaimed it the very music of the devil. Whether it was in fact either or both, it was also irresistible to young white people, and they embraced it (and each other) enthusiastically, as they danced to it in ever-increasing numbers.

"I'm Certainly Living a Ragtime Life" (1900) was a popular song of the day, and by any measure, Brun Campbell certainly lived a ragtime life. At 15, he ran away from home and rode a train to Sedalia, determined to persuade Scott Joplin to teach him to play ragtime piano. Joplin did, and in the process bestowed a nickname, the Ragtime Kid, on his pupil. How long the lessons continued is uncertain; it might have been no more than three weeks. But Brun was hooked, and for the next seven or eight years he rode the circuit, working as an itinerant pianist throughout the Midwest and South, entertaining customers in every bar, restaurant, hotel, brothel, amusement park, and riverboat where he could snag a gig.

Brun married for the first time in 1907. In his later years, he claimed his fiancée agreed to the marriage only after he promised to give up public performance. He and his wife settled in Tulsa, where he followed his father into the barbering trade. He married at least two other times, and with his last wife, brought up three daughters. In the mid–1920s, with the ragtime era fading into history and the Jazz Age going full blast, Brun abandoned Oklahoma for the wilder west of Venice, California, where for the next quarter-century he cut hair (reportedly very badly) at his City Hall Barber Shop on Venice Boulevard.

But in the 1940s, Brun Campbell came to live a second ragtime life. As his musical genre showed signs of reviving, the old man hopped aboard the bandwagon, grabbed the reins, and throughout his remaining ten years, worked fanatically to bring back ragtime, resuscitate the reputation of his old teacher and hero, Scott Joplin, and not incidentally, familiarize the musical world with the work and accomplishments of one Brun Campbell.

I became acquainted with Brun some ten years ago, a good half-century after his death. As I read Rudi Blesh and Harriet Janis' landmark history, *They All Played Ragtime* (1950), two things caught my attention. One was the fact that John Stark, the fifty-eight-year-old white music store owner who published Scott Joplin's "Maple Leaf Rag," had given Joplin a contract which included provision for royalties. That was extraordinary: Standard operating procedure then in music publishing would have been for the white publisher to give the young black composer a small one-time payment, and pocket all the income himself. But I found no evidence that historians had poked their heads into this curious hole in history and looked around.

Then there was that brash fifteen-year-old white boy who became so enchanted with the new American music that he ran away from his Kansas home and hopped a train to Sedalia, Missouri, determined to take piano lessons from a black man he'd never met. In those times? In that place?

To a writer of mystery novels, this cheeky kid was a godsend. I grabbed hold of him with both hands, set him down onto Page 1, sent him off on that historic train ride, and started typing. After an intensive but pleasurable year, Brun and I had worked out an explanation compatible with history for the amazing royalties contract, while helping to solve a (fictional) murder in Sedalia that threatened Scott Joplin's safety. The title of that book? *The Ragtime Kid*, what else?

I enjoyed my ragtime historical characters to the point that I didn't want to say goodbye, and decided to expand my historical mystery into a trilogy. The second book, *The King of Ragtime*, told the story of Scott Joplin's accusation that Irving Berlin had stolen Joplin's music to write "Alexander's Ragtime Band." Then in 1951, at the age of 67, Brun returned in the third volume, *The Ragtime Fool*, passionately promoting the music of his old piano teacher as he helped solve another murder. He was now an appealing figure in a different way, no longer a fifteen-year-old kid whose impetuous and foolish acts were understandable, but an elderly man desperate to face down mortality long enough to convince the world of the greatness of his one-time piano teacher and hero.

Sending my editor the final manuscript for *The Ragtime Fool* set me up for a heavy case of the blues. After six years of daily fun and games with Brun and his ragtime pals, I knew I was going to miss my friends. But I also knew the tripartite story was over, and it was time to move along. I started work on a medical mystery.

For the next year I wondered how I might get back to ragtime, but every bright notion faded as quickly as it had arisen in my head. Sometimes, though, you get lucky. Shortly after my medical mystery came out, an antiques dealer emailed to tell me he'd cleaned out the house of a reclusive elderly woman in Venice, California, and had three cartons of memorabilia that had belonged to her father ... who happened to have been Brun Campbell. When the shopkeeper Googled Brun's name, up popped my ragtime-based books. Might I be interested, the dealer asked, in acquiring his "stuff"?

Not a week later, three cartons arrived at my door. The "stuff" in them went far beyond anything I could have wished or hoped for. Imagine my excitement as I dug through manuscripts that described and detailed the life of an itinerant ragtime pianist in the Midwest a century earlier. In addition, there were a considerable number of short pieces on the history of ragtime and its pioneers, and exhortations to musicians of the time to join the Brun Campbell crusade. Some of these essays had been published during the late 1940s and early 1950s in magazines for devotees of popular music of the time, primarily *Jazz Journal* and *The Record Changer*, but to the best of my knowledge, many had never reached the public view.

It was obvious that Brun intended to publish his longer writings as a memoir, a first-hand account of his experiences during the early years of ragtime. Throughout an extensive correspondence during the late 1940s with Jerry Heermans, a young pianist in Portland, Oregon, Brun revealed his strong desire to see this work appear in book form. But the writer's slapdash modus operandi extended to his attempts to interest publishers in his book, and not surprisingly the work never was published. Brun likely gave up on the idea around 1950, when *They All Played Ragtime* came out. Not that he went quietly. He continued to pursue his goal through inquiries to *Jazz Journal*, but his comments in the letters to Jerry Heermans now lacked his customary extreme enthusiasm and certainty of success. He warned the young man to be careful about giving any information to Blesh and Janis, and complained bitterly that Blesh had appropriated his material, such that he'd never be able to get his own book published.

I seriously doubt that Rudi Blesh was guilty of any skulduggery. More likely, when Blesh interviewed him in 1949, Brun's ego compelled him to give the historian his stories, probably in the hope that Blesh might offer Brun a piggyback ride to success via joint authorship of *They All Played Ragtime*—a preposterous idea. As usual, Brun acted in haste, then had plenty of leisure time to regret his decision.

In addition to the personal and historical manuscripts, the cartons held seventy-year-old unpublished musical compositions by Brun and his brother Harold. (Appendix 1 lists these works.) There were phonograph records Brun had cut during the 1940s. Photographs. Business records. Correspondence with many notable people of the time, including Scott Joplin's widow, Lottie; W.C. Handy, the "Father of the Blues"; and noted ragtime-jazz historian Roy Carew. All this and more, a-jumble in those three cardboard cartons.

I spent several months organizing the material, and as I did, I became convinced that Brun Campbell deserved a re-evaluation. He has received only passing mention in written histories of ragtime. But no one else has left us a written account of life as a ragtime pianist in low and rough places at the turn of the nineteenth century into the twentieth. Together with a great deal of historical and biographical information I'd collected as I wrote my fictional trilogy, this new material brought Brun to life, and I had no trouble seeing what my next writing project needed to be. Brun clearly had great difficulty relating a straight, unembellished account of an event—ironic, I thought, and funny, that of all possible recipients, the work of the Great Ragtime Storyteller had found its way not to a historian or a musician, but to another storyteller, someone who would be unable to resist trying to shape it into a more readable form which would tell the story of a man who lived a consummate two-part ragtime life during complex and critical times in American history.

So what you're about to read is a storyteller's account of the life of a story-teller. The materials that had sat in a small house in Venice for sixty-some years, along with further information acquired through research in libraries and online, revealed Brun as a man with a poorly integrated personality, someone who lived in a world unrelievedly black and white. Enthusiasm to burn, but little reflective ability; persistence beyond stubbornness, with a severe shortage of common sense. When events did not go his way, he was prone to altering his accounts of them to make the story fit the occasion. Brun seems to have dealt primarily in embroideries rather than whole cloth: whatever he said at any particular moment, he believed. I think the histories he wrote and told his barber shop audiences really did happen, but details were subject to variation.

In fairness to Brun, we'd do well to keep in mind that research on the manner in which the human mind and brain set up and retrieve memories has led some investigators to wonder whether there really does exist objective reality in observation and recall. Attorneys are well aware of the pitfalls in eyewitness testimony. So are storytellers.

I'd never argue that fiction should be presented as fact—but neither would I say unprovable material should be automatically consigned to the historical scrap heap. I did my best to seek out information to confirm or question particular dubious points in Brun's accounts of his salad days and patriarchal years in ragtime, whether I thought he might have triggered the skepticism unknowingly or was consciously trying to tell a better story. In any case, and considered in the overall context, these questions contributed significantly to the narrative. Fact and truth are not synonymous. In the words of author Jessamyn West, "Fiction reveals truth that reality obscures." Given that Brun's accounts of people and events were recalled at a considerable temporal distance by a mind incapable of resolving dichotomy, speculation was at times unavoidable. But even the most assiduously constructed scholarly history is subject to correction when contradictory material is discovered.

Brun's longer unpublished manuscripts, *When Ragtime Was Young* and *The Original Ragtime Kid of the 1890s*, are a mishmash of memoir and chapters on the history of ragtime and its pioneers—personal material, historical information, and comments thrown into the work without any sort of logical arrangement or progression. Brun did do some superficial rewriting and rearranging of chapters, but none of his five versions of *When Ragtime Was Young* and two versions of *The Original Ragtime Kid* showed any reasonable coherence. In addition, some of the material turned out to have been written by Roy Carew, a first-rate jazz historian who served as Brun's mentor and editor during the late 1940s. Toward the end of his life, The Kid cannibalized some of the historical chapters for use as individual magazine articles, not a bad move.

Since Brun was unable to organize his own life story, I decided to rework it with a mind toward reader interest and comprehension. I removed non-personal historical material from *When Ragtime Was Young*; the titles of sections that Brun eventually published as articles are included in Appendix 2. Unpublished, non-personal chapters, I reproduced in the "Short Pieces" part of the book. Also included in "Short Pieces" are several unpublished articles Brun wrote in the hope of promoting the ragtime revival and converting contemporary musicians to his cause.

Then I edited Brun's memoir, combining and rearranging passages from the five manuscripts of *When Ragtime Was Young* and *The Original Ragtime Kid of the 1890s*. (See Appendix 3 for a summary of Brun's organizational variations of these two works.) To preserve authenticity, I left the great majority of the writer's verbal infelicities (and those of some of his correspondents) uncorrected, and I request the indulgence of readers for not having dotted the work with staggering numbers of sics. To address the issue of trying to clarify, extend, and/or check facts related to many of Brun's assertions, I wrote a running commentary on his memoir.

The second act of Brun's ragtime adventures, which I've called *When the Ragtime Kid Grew Old*, is an account of his final decade, his revivalist period, constructed from the range of material he saved during the 1940s and early 1950s: business and tax records, newspaper reports, photographs, musical manuscripts, phonograph recordings, personal effects, and correspondence. The great majority of the letters in his files had been sent to him, but a small number of significant notes by Brun did help considerably to clarify the "one-way telephone conversation" aspect of the collection.

In the concluding section of this book, Richard Egan, author of the folio *Brun Campbell: The Music of "The Ragtime Kid,"* comments on Brun's musical compositions.

The roots of storytelling, like those of ragtime, are planted firmly in folk art, and Brun had a knack for conveying the flavor of the times and the nature of life as an itinerant pianist during the earliest years of the ragtime era. Though his spelling, grammar, word choice, sentence structuring, and punctuation fell far short of academic standards, this tended to enhance the folksiness and increase the charm of his tales. Several of his friends during the 1930s and

1940s remarked that it took very little encouragement to get Brun to lock the door to his barber shop and spend an afternoon regaling a captive audience with stories of his colorful past, every now and again interrupting his anecdotes to pound out a ragtime tune on the upright piano he kept in his shop.

So picture Brun hanging his CLOSED sign on the door of that tiny barber shop at 711 Venice Boulevard. He opens the lid of his upright piano and pulls out a bottle of whiskey and shot glasses. (Brun's piano doubled as a liquor storage cabinet.) Settle into a chair and listen to the animated gray-haired barber reminisce about his experiences and adventures from another place, another time, when he was The Original Ragtime Kid of the 1890s. Every detail may not be strictly factual, but that's all right. Just sit back and enjoy his stories.

I

When Ragtime Was Young

by S. Brun Campbell
Commentary by Larry Karp

I was born in Washington, Kansas, the county seat of Washington County, on March 26th, 1884.

In other written pieces and in interviews, Brun said he was born in Oberlin, Kansas, which is approximately 190 miles due west of Washington. Both towns were founded prior to 1884, so either could have been the location where the future Ragtime Kid howled his way into the world. However, some strong circumstantial evidence does exist to place Brun's birth in Washington.

Why might Brun have misrepresented his birthplace? Most likely, years after the fact, he suffered lapses of tongue and mind. The ambiguity would disturb historians, and rightly so. But it's classic Brun, and it sets a proper tone for his story.

There seems to be an old proverb–Arabian, I believe—to the effect that a man's fate is hung around his neck like a collar that cannot be removed. All of which amounts to the proposition that we all have a destiny which at times seems to turn upon trivial incidents, and at other times is the result of momentous decisions.

The vocabulary and construction of the alleged Arabian proverb and its consequences for Brun Campbell sound considerably more erudite and polished than what usually came out of Brun's pen. Roy Carew was a noted jazz historian, and a friend, mentor, and occasional co-author of Brun's during the 1940s. Carew opened his interview-article on Brun, "How I Became a Pioneer Rag Man of the 1890s," (*The Record Changer*, April 1947) with the identical two sentences.

It was my destiny to become the "Original Ragtime Kid" and one of the pioneer ragtime pianists of the 1890s, of that new and exciting music called "Ragtime."

As far back as I can remember, I was raised in an atmosphere of excitement. Every time a bad wind and hail storm came up, my parents would drag me to the cyclone cellar. My grandfather, who was also named Sanford Brunson Campbell, told me exciting stories about the gold rush to California, the pioneers, the old outlaws, the Indians and the great herds of buffalo that had roamed the western prairies.

He had brought my father and mother and myself to Oberlin in Decatur County, in the northwest corner of the state of Kansas. He had been a very wealthy man and had invested heavily in Decatur County farmland years before, purchasing thousands of acres from the Government for 50c per acre. The railroad was being built west then and he built two towns along the proposed new railroad right of way. One of the towns was named Allison, Kansas. It was a proposed railroad division town, which was to have a roundhouse and machine shops and would be the end of one of the railroad's divisions. This place quickly grew to a town of about 500 inhabitants before the railroad reached it.

Then all of a sudden the heavy wind and rain storms set in and washed out the graded railroad right of way so that a new railroad survey had to be made, which missed my grandfather's two towns by about ten miles and left them inland. Next the great draughts set in and ruined all the crops in Western Kansas, causing great hardships to the people. The town of Allison remains an inland town today of about six hundred inhabitants. It stands as a monument to my grandfather, who tried to be a great pioneer.

He still had some interests in Decatur County, and had brought my father and mother to Oberlin with the intention of setting my father up in business, or on a farm. He believed that part of Kansas was the best in the state, and that it had a great future, as the frontier was rapidly moving westward. But when he tried to dispose of his holdings he found that he could sell them for very little cash. He took his loss and gave my father a few hundred dollars with the advice to stay there and grow up with the country. Broken in health, my grandfather returned to Rochester, New York, where he died a few years later.

My parents, being young, took his advice and remained in Oberlin. As there was only one barber shop in town, my father decided to take up the barber trade, and accordingly opened a one-chair barber shop. He seemed to have a natural ability for barber work. He prospered and in a short while had three other barbers working for him. His shop became the most popular barber shop in town.

My father, being somewhat of a singer, formed a real "Barber Shop Quartette" that sang at parties and civic affairs. As he prospered, he invested his money in city property and became active in the town's affairs.

Like all progressive men, he dreamed of better things. So he moved to St. Joseph, Missouri, where he thought he could get a position as a traveling salesman. However, this did not happen, so he took a job in one of the popular barber shops of the town and did very well.

Material from Decatur County's Last Indian Raid Museum in Oberlin, Kansas provides a window through which to assess the early life of Brun Campbell. It appears that Brun came honestly by both his tendency to take action without a great deal of forethought, and his inclination to dress up his life experiences. His memoirs reveal how strongly impulsiveness, ego drive, and poor judgment in matters of business ran heavily in the men of this particular Campbell clan. The "exciting stories" Grandpa Campbell told the boy as the "old man" strove to become "a great pioneer" likely played a significant part in the origin of Brun's lifelong striving after importance and fame, and his mercurial behavior in pursuit of his goals. As for impetuous behavior without consideration of consequences, it's worth noting that at the time of Brun's birth, his father, Luther Ensign Campbell, and his mother, Lulu Bourquin Campbell, were only seventeen and fifteen respectively.

Allison, Kansas, thirty-five miles from Oberlin, was founded as Toiyobe in the late 1870s, and became Allison in 1880. At first glance, an article in the June 14, 1979, *Oberlin Herald* newspaper seemed to support Brun's claim that his grandfather had been a major landowner whose equity had been wiped out by bad weather, but the author explained that when the Rock Island Railroad line came through in 1886, ten miles north of Allison, and no other railroads put tracks through the town, Allison was "broke." Seventeen years later, all that was left of the once-hopeful settlement was an alfalfa field. No mention of cause for the railway bypass was given, and adverse weather conditions were not specified until the 1890s, when there occurred "droughts, prairie fires, grasshopper invasions, hot winds and hailstorms ... along with Indian scares and hard times." So if Grandpa Campbell really did own 50,000 acres of salable land, it sounds as if he might have flat-out misread the intentions of the railroad magnates.

The *Herald* article makes no mention of any Campbell among the names of the founders and settlers of Allison during the early 1880s. The earliest documentation of the presence of S.B. Campbell and his family in Allison and Oberlin appears in 1887, the latest in 1891. The grandfather, his son Luther (Lute), daughter-in-law Lulu, and grandson Brun are all mentioned. Multiple documents show that S.B.'s actual residence was in Allison, while Lute, Lulu, and young Brun lived in Oberlin. The grandfather had been married at least twice before his arrival in Kansas, but he seems to have been unmarried during the time he and his son and grandson lived in Allison and Oberlin.

The first evidence of S.B. Campbell's presence in Allison was by way of notices in the *Allison Breeze*, dated September 2 and 9, 1887, in which "S.B. Campbell, Notary Public and dealer in Deeded Lands, School Land & Claims, also Agent for Allison City Property," offered "50,000 acres of choice Farming Land, improved and unimproved, from $5 to $8 per acre, part down balance on 3 to 15 years time. Good crops and plenty of rain. All correspondence promptly answered. I am always ready to Show Land to parties looking for a location." The notices were signed, "S.B. Campbell, Contractor and Builder."

It's uncertain whether Mr. Campbell actually did own this land, allegedly purchased at 50 cents per acre, or if he was acting as sales agent for other parties. The purchase price would have been $25,000, a prodigious sum in those days. But it's worth noting that the newspaper offers were published shortly after the Rock Island debacle, suggesting that if Campbell really had owned the land, weather-related or other bad luck did not likely figure in his losses.

Between 1887 and 1891, numerous newspaper squibs reported visits back and forth between the family members. One such piece came from the *Allison Times* on May 4, 1888: "Mrs. L.E. Cambell, and son Bunny who has been visiting at Washington, Kas, for some time passed through here Wednesday, on there way home to Oberlin."

Newspaper stories from the 1880s and 1890s often demonstrated astonishingly poor writing. Here in just one sentence we have a misspelled name, a misused homophone, an error in case, and an erroneous nickname. A pet name Brun carried in his youth was Brunnie—not Bunny. The Teacher's Term Report to the District Clerk for School District No. 1, Decatur County, of May 24, 1889, listed "Brunnie Campbell" as one of the youngest children in the class, and one of the few who had progressed to recommendation for the McGuffey Reader in the next school term.

Why might Brun's mother have taken him to visit in Washington? The 1880 U.S. Census showed twelve-year-old Lulu Bourquin(e)'s family, headed by father Adolphus, a harness maker, living in that town. In the same census, Luther Campbell, age 13, was listed as a member of his father's Washington household. A bit of routine obstetrical calculation would place Brun's conception close to the June solstice of 1883–not confirmatory evidence that Brun was born in Washington, rather than Oberlin, but together with there being no record of the family in Oberlin until 1887, sufficient for that conclusion to be drawn.

Between November 1887 and spring 1888, Luther apparently suffered from an unspecified serious illness, with multiple remissions and relapses. He finally recovered his health, and between 1890 and 1891, owned and operated a barber shop on Penn Avenue in Oberlin. Numerous newspaper squibs and ads touted his work as a "tonsorial artist" and complimented the appearance of his shop.

But on December 4, 1891, the *Oberlin Opinion* reported that "Lute Campbell left Tuesday for McCook, where he will, for a short time, work.... The family will remain in Oberlin until spring."

Lute's change of residence could have been related to a major alteration in the family situation. Brun's account of his grandfather's departure to Rochester and subsequent death came across as the passing of an old, broken man, but in fact, the *Oberlin Opinion* of May 15, 1891, reported that "L.E. Campbell received a telegram Monday (which would have been May 11), notifying him of the death of his father on Sunday morning, at his home in Palmyra, N.Y. The deceased, S.B. Campbell, formerly resided at Allison, in this county, and was an old soldier and well known in this community."

According to census records, S.B. was born in 1843, so although he was in fact a Civil War soldier, he certainly was not an old one, even by standards of that time. In 1891, he'd have been 47 or 48. U.S. government records show he had enlisted as a Private in Company G, Wisconsin 3rd Cavalry Regiment, on March 1, 1862, was promoted to Full Corporal, and finally mustered out on September 29, 1865. During his post–Kansas years in upstate New York, he acquired a third wife, Irene, who applied for a widow's pension on June 8, 1891.

S. B. Campbell's military service could well have represented another source of those "exciting stories" he told his grandson. Children of that generation were entertained and educated, for better and for worse, by tales of derring-do recounted by Civil War veterans of both the Union and Confederate armies.

The 1900 U.S. Census for Pierce County, Wisconsin, lists Sanford Campbell, age 88, born in 1812 in Wisconsin, and married for 49 years to Mary, then 71 years old. This man almost certainly was Brun's great-grandfather, given that Brun's grandfather served in a Wisconsin cavalry unit, and that the 1920 U.S. Census listed Lute as having been born in Wisconsin. Since S.B. was born in 1843, he would have been the offspring of an earlier union of the Pierce County Sanford Campbell.

S.B. Campbell's return to New York state occurred no later than 1889: the Rochester City Directory of that year showed him working as a clerk at 8 Baker Block, and boarding at 33 Manhattan, which implies he had not yet married

Irene. But that must have occurred shortly, since the 1890 Rochester City Directory lists him as having "removed to Palmyra," where he died on May 10, 1891, of tuberculosis and laryngitis. He was buried on May 12 at Mt. Hope Cemetery in Rochester.

We had not lived in St. Joseph very long before I became one of the city's "Dead End Kids." After school I would shine shoes and sell newspapers on the street. That exciting job did not last long, for my father caught up with me, gave me a good whipping, and put me out of business. That was quite a blow to me but I finally got over it.

Since Luther left Oberlin for McCook in December 1891, then took his family to Arkansas City in 1893, the move to St. Joseph likely occurred in 1892.

It might seem odd that Brun's dad punished him for showing the initiative to earn money shining shoes and selling newspapers, but during the status-conscious 1890s, Luther Campbell might well have objected to the company his son would've been keeping. "Dead-End Kids" were (mostly) boys who lived on the streets and were going to go nowhere in life except to jail and/or an early grave.

One day at the dinner table my father asked me how I would like to go through the house where Jesse James was killed, just a mile or so from where we lived. Well, I thrived on excitement and was all for it; so we went through it. The caretaker explained the shooting in detail. I was only nine years old and I imagine my eyes popped out as big as saucers as he told the story.

On April 3, 1882, while Jesse James was living in St. Joseph under the name of Thomas Howard, Robert Ford, a recent recruit to the James Gang, shot his host in the back of the head. Composers of popular songs are quick to grab hold of good stories and easy rhymes: "For that dirty little coward who shot Mr. Howard has laid poor Jesse in his grave." Ford and his brother Charles had been staying with the James family while they planned "one last" train robbery, but Robert Ford decided to kill James before the robbery took place, in order to collect a $5,000 bounty offered by Missouri Governor Thomas Crittenden. In the end, he received only one-tenth that sum.

One day my father came home all excited. The newspapers were running notices of the opening of the Cherokee Strip in Oklahoma, a strip of land about two hundred miles long by fifty wide, comprising nearly seven hundred thousand acres of rich homestead land. The people of the United States had demanded that their government open this strip of land to them; so the government decided to open it for settlement.

The government also decided that the opening of that vast strip of

Indian Territory land to the people of the United States should be in the form of a race. Each person had the right to register with the government for the right to participate in that proposed race. My father got all "hot and bothered" about entering that great race.

Therefore, we packed our belongings and moved to Arkansas City in southern Kansas, which bordered on the Oklahoma line.

During the late nineteenth and early twentieth centuries, parcels of land, many having previously belonged to Native Americans, were opened to homesteaders for settlement. Some plots were simply sold to applicants; others were distributed through either lotteries or "land rushes," also called "runs." On September 16, 1893, the greatest land rush in American history, a competition for more than six million acres, took place in the so-called Cherokee Strip territory in northernmost Oklahoma.

Eyewitness to History's 2006 article "The Oklahoma Land Rush of 1893" (www.eyewitnesstohistory.com) is an excellent first-hand account of the Cherokee Strip Land Rush. In addition, the Cherokee Strip Land Rush Museum in Arkansas City, Kansas (arkcity.org/index.aspx?ID=216), is a superb repository of information on the Land Rush.

Upon our arrival there, just four miles from the "Cherokee Strip," my father got a job in a barber shop, run by a Barber by the name of Deets. The shop was in the basement of First National Bank—on the North West Corner of 5th Ave and Summit Street. The barbers who worked for Mr. Deets was Lute Campbell (my Dad), Bill Stickler, Bert Faulkner, & Bill Roberts. The porter was Jim Johnson. All the gay blades of Arkansas City made this shop their head quarters, it was what you would call a Musicial Barber Shop. Bill Stickler played Violin, Bill Roberts played Clarinet, Jim Johnson the Negro porter & his assistant Gabe played Mandolin & Violin and sang, and many of the Customers used to meet there and do a bit of Harmonizing with their Barber Shop quartette. Phrine Hutchinson, Matt Sleeth, Geo Sipes, were just a few of the young men who used to meet there in those days. My Dad worked all day and part of the night. Those were the days of one of the most colorful eras in American history. They were the days of hardy American pioneers—the kind that have made the United States of America the best country on earth.

Brun's attraction to and regard for black musicians and their music clearly went back to the 1890s, and is one of the major themes in his life story. Could his having heard Jim Johnson and Gabe play and sing in his father's barber shop been a defining moment in the boy's life—his first real exposure to the black musical community?

Let me tell you something about Arkansas City Kansas and my kid days there. Arkansas City was a town of about seven thousand five hundred persons—a railroad and cattle town with fertile farm land and grazing ranges surrounding it. It was the division point for the main line of the Atchison, Topeka & Santa Fe and Branches of the Missouri Pacific and Frisco R.R. Whose main streets were made up of business buildings of the 80's and 90s boom days of the pioneers, with a sprinkling of old wooden buildings and wooden sidewalks of an earlier era. The residential districts set in a grove of Box Elder, Cottonwood, Maple and Lotus and Elm trees. It's four ward public schools were made of brick. It was not much different in appearance from any other town in the midwest of the same size, but now it was being overrun by hordes of people heading for the new promised land. Arkansas City was full of seething activity. Even the wooden Indians standing in front of the tobacco stores seemed to have come to life.

People came through Arkansas City in all kinds of transportation. I saw a covered wagon train fifty-two miles long, reaching from Wichita, Kansas, to Arkansas City. I saw another covered wagon train that was all ox-drawn. I saw great herds of cattle driven through the city from the north to the vast grazing lands of Oklahoma by cowboys. I saw all kinds of gamblers, old stage-coach drivers, old Indian scouts of the Dodge City days, cowboys by the thousands, and old-time gunmen who shot it out with one another in true western style. Most of them "fanned" the hammer of their guns whenever they had to go into action.

"Fanning the hammer" involves holding the trigger of a revolver and hitting the hammer repeatedly, so as to fire several shots in rapid succession. The consensus holds that this practice is damaging to both gun and finger, and also lowers shot accuracy. Cowboy-movie heroes fan hammers right and left, but old-time Western gunslingers used this technique only to entertain people.

My chums and I were having plenty of excitement by this time. I would go back and forth the four miles from Arkansas City to the Indian Territory line two or three times a day for being a youngster I did not want to miss any excitement. Hundreds of people had to stand in line for days on the hot prairie and wait their turn to register in sweltering tents, with government agents, for their right to enter the coming race. The Santa Fe and other railroads brought people in passenger coaches, box cars, flat cars and cattle cars, and unloaded them out onto the hot prairie, where they, too, got in line to register.

Peddlers sold Arkansas River water for fifteen cents a tin cupful and salt pork and biscuit sandwiches for twenty-five cents each, to the people standing in line waiting to register. Other kinds of food was very high.

The crowds of people who were in Arkansas City prior to the opening of the Cherokee Strip attracted plenty of amusement like repertoire shows, wizard oil vendors, and the like. Gambling was forbidden, but it was there—dice men, drop case operators, card sharks of all kinds, three-shell manipulators and many more games of chance. They all took the suckers.

The Repertoire Show, a type of tent show, was popular during the late nineteenth and early twentieth centuries. Small towns lacked the opera houses and performance halls of the larger cities; the gap was filled by touring troupes of actors who would set up in tents to perform comedies, tragedies, and melodramas of the time. Then the troupe would move on to the next town and put on the same show or a different one in their repertoire.

Brun mentioned Wizard Oil vendors along with Repertoire Shows because purveyors of patent medicines used to travel from town to town in wagons, and put on "medicine shows" with vaudeville-style music, dancing, and comedy to loosen up the suckers for the "doctor" to pitch his particular cure-all patent medicine. One popular nostrum of the time was Hamlin's Wizard Oil, which contained ammonia, camphor, chloroform, cloves, sassafras, and turpentine in an alcohol base, and was said to cure rheumatism and just about any other ailment afflicting humankind. Medicine shows persisted in the American Midwest well into the twentieth century. *Good For What Ails You: Music of the Medicine Shows, 1926–1937,* from Old Hat Records (CD1005), is an excellent example of medicine show music.

A drop case was a box set on a slant. Near the upper edge of the case was a hole or a slot through which the sucker dropped a marble, which then rolled down the incline to the bottom, its course determined by nails placed vertically into the lower panel of the case. Wins and losses were determined by the ultimate location of the marble. With the addition of electricity, a bunch of flashing lights, and a plunger to start the marble on its journey, the drop case evolved into the pinball machine.

Whenever a big circus came to Arkansas City in those days, they would have to give three shows a day to take care of the many cowboys and Indians who came to see the circus.

An old Indian scout, Gordon Lillie (Pawnee Bill) was Indian Interpreter for the five Civil and Indian tribes of old Oklahoma and Indian Territory at the time.

"Civil tribes" refers to descendants of the Cherokees, Choctaws, Chickasaws, Creeks, and Seminoles, who in the 1830s were removed from their native lands in the southern states, and at great inconvenience and loss of life were forced to relocate to what was named Indian Territory, and is now Oklahoma. It was presumed white settlers would never choose to live there.

There were some forty thousand blanketed Indians who would come up to Arkansas City every three months from the Indian Territory to receive their Government allotments which amounted to $70 each, paid to them through the First National Bank of Arkansas City. These Indians would start coming in to the city a couple of weeks before payday and erect their Tepees along the river banks and set up their camps. One morning we found some Indians had put up their Tepees in our backyard during the night and made it their camping grounds. They were very friendly and never bothered us. One of the old Indian squaws gave my mother a pair of fine beaded Indian moccasins and an Indian blanket. No doubt this was her way of paying us for camping in our back yard.

Indians are strange and do many strange things. One old Indian Chief by the name of "Wash-un-gha" who was over one hundred years old and a big six-footer, straight as an arrow, would always manage to get his "Fire-water" when he came to town and get thoroughly drunk, when he would always be found laying on the steps of the First National Bank, where he drew the Government allotment check. Somehow, he thought he was safe there on that account.

Brun's remark about Indians being strange probably represented no more than the cultural naïveté of an alert, curious nine-year-old white boy in 1890s Oklahoma. Lute Campbell wrote a great deal of derogatory prose and doggerel, poking heavy-handed fun at blacks, Italians, Irish, and other groups whose members would not have qualified for Ku Klux Klan membership. But his son's writings and interviews are entirely free of offensive epithets and negative judgments on members of other ethnic groups.

Washungha (sometimes hyphenated, sometimes not) was the last chief of the Kaw, or Kansa, Indians, and lived from about 1830 to 1908, so he could not have been over one hundred years old in 1893, nor at any other time. Whether Brun actually did see Washungha on the steps of the First National Bank is open to question, but it's certainly possible. The chief lived near Junction City, Kansas, some 150 miles from Arkansas City. Great numbers of the Kaw people had been relocated to northern Oklahoma during the 1880s, and Washungha was active in legislating allotment of land to individual Kaw. He was one of several Kaw chiefs who traveled to Washington, D.C., in 1902 to sign an allotment treaty. The town of Washungha, Oklahoma, on Kaw Lake, forty miles from Arkansas City, is named for him. So Brun might well have witnessed Chief Washungha, sleeping off a bender. If so, the chief would hardly have been the only political figure in history to go out of town on business and have a bit too much to drink.

Eventually it came time for that great race to take place. So some of us kids high-tailed it down to the starting point on the Oklahoma line, to see the race. Soldiers were patroling the line as far as we could see to keep order and make sure that no one crossed the line ahead of the starting time.

Considerable effort was expended both toward preventing prospective land claimants from jumping the gun, and tracking down cheaters to negate their claims. Oklahomans are still called "Sooners," the name given in 1893 to overly eager land rushers.

As those two hundred thousand people took their places in the line, in covered wagons, sulkies, buggies, on horseback and even on high-wheeled bicycles and other modes of transportation, they eagerly waited for the shots to ring out from the soldiers' rifles for them to go.

It came! And what a mad race it was! Wagons and buggies were overturned! Horses fell! Riders and drivers were killed! But that great mass of humanity was on its way to the Cherokee Strip.

The Robinson Library in Oklahoma City provides information that generally agrees with Brun's account of details, though the Library's estimate of Land Rushers is considerably lower than Brun's. Most likely, Brun's reckoning was taken from contemporary guesses, and very great crowds do tend to bring forth inflated guesstimates of their size. (More detailed information can be found at www.robinsonlibrary.com/america/uslocal/west/oklahoma/history/landrun.htm.)

So September 16th, 1893 has gone down in history as the greatest "Horse Race" ever run in the world. My father made that historical race, but he must have gotten in his own way for he never staked a claim.

After the run many people returned to their old states who were not fortunate in staking out a claim. Others stayed in the new country and worked and grew up with it.

My father decided to make Arkansas City our home. I entered school and also commenced to take music lessons. My mother and father were musically inclined. My mother picked a banjo and my father strummed a guitar, and they both sang for their own amusement. We also had an old square piano which interested me, and at an early age I learned to play a one-fingered version of "The Old Gray Goose is Dead." Here we have the ideal setup for a musicial career—musicial parents, a piano and natural aptitude.

In Brun's various manuscripts, he sometimes spelled "musical" correctly, but many other times, the word went down as "musicial." This inconsistency might have been the result of partial editing of his work by another person, or it could have represented just one of Brun's many inconsistencies. It would not be surprising to learn that in telling his stories aloud, Brun sometimes said "musicial."

The fond parents, seeing what young Brun could do with a dead goose, decided to put the matter on a more lively basis, so at the age of ten, lessons with a professor were arranged for. Well, when the professor called at the house a couple of times, and found out how much the old piano needed tuning, he refused to continue with my lessons until the instrument was tuned up. Everything was all right then and we went ahead. In a couple of years I was playing popular songs of the "gay nineties," and at the age of fourteen I could play the more difficult music.

Square pianos are notoriously difficult to keep in tune, a point in accord with Brun's account.

One day a doctor's son and myself ran away from home to Oklahoma City to a celebration that was in progress there. We became separated and I wandered into the Armstrong-Byrd music store and commenced to play over some of the popular tunes of the day. A crowd began to gather in the store and about the entrance, to listen to the music; they began to encourage me with applause and asked for more.

After a time there emerged from the crowd a young mulatto with a light complexion, dressed to perfection, and smiling pleasantly. He came over to the piano and placed a pen-and-ink manuscript of a piece of music in front of me and asked if I would play it for him. The manuscript was entitled "The Maple Leaf Rag," by Scott Joplin. I went over the piece for him and he seemed to be struck with the way I played it. He afterwards told me that I had made just two mistakes.

It turned out that the mulatto was Otis Saunders, a fine pianist and composer of Ragtime Music, a pal of Scott Joplin and one of Ragtime's great pioneers. I learned from Saunders that Scott Joplin was located at the time in Sedalia, Missouri. Saunders also told me that he was going back to Sedalia in a few days to join Joplin.

What celebration could it have been that Brun ran off to attend in Oklahoma City? The word "celebration," and the fact that it was a big enough event to entice Brun and his friend from Arkansas City, 130 miles away, suggests it might have been an early version of what evolved into Cherokee Strip Day, September 16. If Brun was fourteen at the time, as his manuscript suggests, the year would've been 1898, five years after the Cherokee Land Rush.

Ragtime historian and musician David Reffkin points out that if this was in fact Brun's first exposure to ragtime, it would have been remarkably different from anything he had ever played, seen or heard. Even if Brun had heard folk ragtime in Arkansas City bars and restaurants, Joplin's classic "Maple Leaf Rag" still would have been very different and more difficult to play, and Reffkin's observation still would apply.

In his 1945 manuscript, "Otis Saunders and the Maple Leaf Rag," Brun wrote, "When I first met Otis Saunders in Oklahoma City, Oklahoma, in the latter part of 1898, I was going on 15 years of age…. At the Armstrong-Byrd Music Co. of Oklahoma City, [Saunders] worked behind the counter as a salesman and player of popular sheet music…. At the time, Otis had a pen-and-ink manuscript of 'Maple Leaf Rag,' the cover of which read, 'Maple Leaf Rag by Scott Joplin and Otis Saunders, Sedalia, Missouri.'" This statement is in conflict with Brun's assertion in the passage quoted above that the pen-and-ink manuscript bore only Joplin's name as composer. Could Saunders have put a cover around the manuscript itself, and added his name? Was he planning to try to sell the work to a publisher, and cash in on part of the proceeds? Or do the reports simply represent another of Brun's inconsistencies in recollection?

I asked Otis Saunders if he would coach me on playing the "Maple Leaf Rag," and he did. When it was time for him to return to Sedalia and join his pal Scott Joplin, I asked him if I came to Sedalia would he and Joplin teach me to play ragtime. He said he would if I got my parents consent, which of course they would not give.

Well, after that Oklahoma episode, a roaming propensity and a newly awakened interest in ragtime prompted me to run away from home again, in the summer of 189.9–this time to Sedalia, where I lost no time in locating Otis Saunders and Scott Joplin.

Brun's memoirs indicate that he never did ask his parents for permission to go to Sedalia, but rather, one day the following summer, the boy quietly ran off and hopped a train to Missouri.

The Kid most often cited his runaway to Sedalia as having occurred during the summer or fall of 1899, less frequently as having taken place sometime in 1898. This is perhaps the single most striking example of Brun's tendency to be inconsistent in citations by one unit of time.

They were both playing piano in a tavern there. At Otis Saunders' suggestion I played the piano for Joplin. After he heard me play he agreed to teach me.

He taught me his first four rags, "Original Rags," "Maple Leaf Rag," "Sunflower Slow Drag," and "Swipsey." I was the first white pianist to play his "Maple Leaf Rag." I met all the local ragtime pianists and composers like Scott Hayden, Arthur Marshall, Melford Alexander, Jim and Ida Hastings. Joplin and Saunders had nicknamed me the "Ragtime Kid," and that name stayed with me all through my early ragtime career.

Brun was inclined to make claims of primacy in ragtime, particularly in relation to Scott Joplin. His often-repeated statement that he was Scott Joplin's only white pupil was a thick slice of baloney: Joplin had several white students during his New York years. But to give Brun his fair due, he likely was Joplin's *first* white student, and could well have been the first white pianist to play "Maple Leaf Rag."

Being a young white boy it was not so very long that the white people of Sedalia were wondering who I was and why I was always hanging around those negro pianists. They commenced asking questions, so Otis Saunders advised me to go home.

How long Brun stayed in Sedalia during his first visit there is uncertain. In 1951, *DownBeat* cartoonist J. Lee Anderson, quoted Brun as saying he had studied with Joplin and Saunders for "about three weeks."

Sedalia was known for its good interracial relations, so it's surprising to read Brun's report of those questions by white Sedalians. History is always subject to reconsideration. On the other hand, it's not beyond possibility that the slapdash youngster might have worn out his welcome with his teachers, who decided to give him a tactful sendoff.

Brun, on his sixteenth birthday. A clumsy cut-down of a well-worn original, but saved in a frame, this photograph suggests that someone, whether Brun himself or another member of the family, prized the image (Brun Campbell Archive).

Now, when I bade Scott Joplin goodbye as I left for my home in Kansas, he gave me a bright, new, silver half-dollar dated 1897; and as he handed it to me he called my attention to the date on it and said, "Carry this half-dollar for good luck and remember it is dated the year I wrote my first Rag, 'Original Rags,'" published in 1899.

Some sources indicate that "Maple Leaf Rag," was completed in 1897, and was Joplin's first written ragtime composition, though "Original Rags" found its way to publication first, by less than six months. In *They All Played Ragtime* and in Brun's article, "The Ragtime Kid, an Autobiography," (published posthumously in *Jazz Report*, Vol. 6, 1967–68), Brun made no mention of "Original Rags" being the first Joplin rag.

As he handed me the half-dollar he had a very strange and sad look in his eyes. I have never forgotten that strange look he gave me.

Brun's widely quoted comment on Joplin's "strange and sad look" is intriguing. The composer's friends described him as a very serious person, one who never smiled; it's been suggested he might have suffered from depression. Joplin did aspire to classical music status for his compositions, and was already thinking in terms of writing an extended dance suite and an opera, which he'd have known would not have been readily accepted by the white community, an essential consideration. Might he have envisioned Brun as someone he could have influenced to help gain that artistic ratification?

I had written home to my parents to soften them up some, for I knew that my father had a good whipping laid up for me for running away from home. Furthermore, I had sold my B-Flat clarinet to get money to go to Sedalia, and I knew that alone would be cause for a good licking. But when I got home and they heard me play that new music, "Ragtime," they seemed proud of me. However, my father did give me a good talking to about selling my clarinet.

This is the only mention in Brun's writings of his having raised money to go to Sedalia by selling a clarinet. In other accounts, he reported that he simply ran off; in some versions of the story, he said he hid in "blind baggage," a baggage car on a railroad train which has no opening at one end or the other. Perhaps the boy hopped a train for free passage to Sedalia, and used the money from the clarinet for food, lodging, and other expenses.

Finally, my father got to be a traveling salesman. He quit the barber business and got a position as a traveling salesman for a wholesale grocery firm. He made a fine salesman and received several salary raises, but got himself finally into some kind of trouble with the Management of the firm and was discharged. However, in a short time he got a better position as salesman for the largest wholesale grocery firm in Indian Territory at Guthrie, Oklahoma. Soon his fine salesmanship got him promoted to the main headquarters of the firm at Oklahoma City, and he was assigned to the territory west of El Reno, so we moved from Arkansas City to El Reno. I hated to leave Arkansas City and my playmates, especially my sweetheart, "Taffy." I was sixteen years old, and playing a pretty "hot" ragtime piano.

More on "Taffy" later. A lot more.

When we arrived in El Reno, I found that it was about the size of Arkansas City and a very quiet Oklahoma town, but not for long. The following year, El Reno was chosen by the government as headquarters for a new land opening to the people of the United States. This time it was to be a drawing for claims instead of a race.

The El Reno Land Lottery was another massive giveaway, this one involving some two million acres of Kiowa-Comanche and Apache land. The lottery system was adopted in an attempt to avoid the chaos and personal injuries that had marked the 1893 Cheyenne Strip run, and to do away with Sooner behavior. It is described in great detail in the Oklahoma Historical Society's Chronicles of Oklahoma (www.digital.library.okstate.edu/Chronicles/v009/v009p365.html).

In a short time El Reno was overflowing with people. The opening up of that new land was attracting people from all over the nation. Naturally, it attracted bad men of all kinds.

My father got me a position as night clerk at the Kerfoot Hotel, the best in El Reno. The government used the hotel's sample rooms, where they put in booths for people to Register for a chance to win a town lot or farm in the new country. It cost a dollar to register, so that made it a lottery and there were government laws against lotteries. But the government itself sponsored the greatest lottery ever known, then.

My mother and father registered but they never had any luck. However, a girl friend of ours who came down from our old home in Arkansas City, drew Lot #2 which was a choice business lot in what is now known as the City of Lawton, Oklahoma. Her name was Miss Mattie Beale.

You can imagine what a thrill we all got out of that event. Please imagine the crowd of people who came to that Oklahoma town of 7500 inhabitants for the drawing. It was estimated at one time that there were over one hundred thousand people there. It was about as large a crowd as had come to Arkansas City 7 years before for the opening of the "Cherokee Strip." El Reno was sure a wild town during those days, with lots of gun fights, and on top of that the soldiers from Fort El Reno would shoot up the town and the "redlight" district once in a while when they had gotten around too much liquor.

People slept in the streets, on the prairies, on vacant lots, in railroad depots, hotels, private homes, or any place they could lay their heads. Wherever you looked, all you could see was people. Indians, Cowboys, soldiers, badmen, gamblers of all kinds. Pitch men were on the corners and in the streets, "Three Shell Dealers," "Three card monte" dealers, "Spindle Wheels" of all kinds; drop case dealers and every game known to the gambling science was in operation right out in the open on the main streets of El Reno. There never was, or never will be another city in the world where gambling was conducted on such a great scale and so out in the open as it was there.

Spindle wheel: also called wheel of fortune, this was a game where the mark would pay to spin an arrow. "Where she stops, nobody knows," but where she stopped was not nearly according to chance, and few contestants came away from the game with any prize worth what they'd paid for the spin.

The Oklahoma Historical Society Chronicles and other accounts of the Great El Reno Lottery substantiate a number of Brun's observations, including the great number of people who flooded into the city to register, the open gambling on the streets, and the fact that the first booth for registrants was located in the Kerfoot Hotel, where Brun worked as a clerk. It also backs up Brun's account of the success of Miss Mattie Beal (no terminal e) in securing the second lot in the Lawton section draw, though the report stated that Miss Beal, a telephone operator, lived in Wichita, rather than Arkansas City. Still, it seems unlikely that Brun would have remembered the Number 2 winner of the Lawton (as opposed to the El Reno) District lands for no particular reason, and that he'd been previously unacquainted with Miss Beal. The Lawton Heritage Association Site (www.lawtonheritage.org/history.html) tells what became of this interesting woman.

It's interesting to read here and later in Brun's manuscript that The Ragtime Kid was in sympathy with church leaders and other persons who felt that since there existed governmental regulations against public gambling, it was improper for the U.S. government to sponsor a lottery. Several passages in his accounts show The Kid to have had some viewpoints impressively at odds with the wild, woolly image he tried to project. He went out of his way to avoid violent confrontations, and some of his comments about women sound frankly sensitive and sentimental.

And Brun meant "Fort Reno," not "Fort El Reno." A small point, but another indicator of our storyteller's sometimes careless approach to details.

One of the funniest jokes I ever saw happened in a saloon in El Reno. It was pulled by the bartender on the customers who visited his saloon for refreshments in those boom days. He suspended a twine string from the ceiling of the saloon and let it hang down so you could reach up and touch the end of it. On the end of the string he tied a lead from a .44 caliber bullet with a sign attached which read:

This is the bullet that killed Jesse James.

If you took the time to watch for a while you would see some customer slowly edge his way to where the bullet was suspended and when he thought no one was watching he would jerk the bullet from the string and sneak out the back door of the saloon, with the "bullet that killed Jesse James." The bartender told me that in one day he had replaced the bullet on the string over one hundred times. You don't happen to have one of those bullets that killed Jesse James, do you?

I saw Billie Morgan, a notorious gambler, operate a "Drop Case" and take a sucker for several hundred dollars right on a street corner in the main part of town. I saw the gambler, the original "Arkansas kid" break the Attic Gambling House at El Reno. I saw Frenchie La Britton, a high powered gambler, win ten thousand dollars on the cut of the cards. Later, Frenchie La Britton opened up a big gambling Casino at Goldfield, Nevada, during the Gold Rush there, and he made a fortune and returned to El Reno years afterwards where he died at a ripe old age.

One of the greatest sights I ever saw was at El Reno, Oklahoma. It was a

Very likely Luther Ensign Campbell, Brun's father, in his later years. The photo-card was saved in a folding frame, along with a bundle of Lute's poetic efforts and a sentimental poem, "The Great Round-Up," which speaks strongly for the identification (Brun Campbell Archive).

buckskin dress decorated with two thousand perfectly matched Elks Teeth, that belonged to a beautiful Cheyenne Indian girl. Later this beautiful dress was on display at the St. Louis World's Fair in 1904. It attracted much attention from the visitors and was a very fine specimen of pioneer Indian craftsmanship.

Everyone in El Reno seemed to be making money hand over fist, so I decided to try to make myself some easy money too. So, every saloon that had a piano in it was where I would stop and play a few ragtime pieces and pick up a few dollars from the customers. One day I was playing some hot Rags, and some barbershop chord numbers for some of the customers who had been drinking and felt like harmonizing; when in walked my Father, hotter than some of the Rags I had been playing. He and I really had a good time in the Old Wood Shed. He said it hurt him more than it did me to have to whip me. But I had heard that one before, so in a few days I would make the rounds of the saloons again and pick up some more easy money playing piano. In those days the laws were not as strict about a kid coming in a saloon or gambling house as they are to-day.

Brun would have been playing some of the popular songs of the day in the usual manner, selections favorable for singing in barbershop quartet style. These songs lend themselves to vocal lines in close four-part harmony, with the four voices being arranged from top to bottom as tenor, melody (referred to as "lead"), baritone and bass. In Brun's time, the singers invariably would have been male, but today, many women sing in barbershop quartets and choruses. SPEBSQSA, the male-only Society for the Preservation and Encouragement of Barber Shop Quartet Singing in America, was founded in Tulsa in 1938, and now has more than 20,000 members in North America. Women are represented in the activity through Sweet Adelines International.

One of my biggest thrills came to me when I played Scott Joplin's "Maple Leaf Rag" on the piano in the parlor of the Kerfoot hotel for Gordon Lillie (Pawnee Bill). I played it just as Scott Joplin the composer had taught me to play it a year or so before. "Pawnee Bill" sure liked the way I played the "Maple Leaf Rag" and 20 years later when I met him again in Tulsa, Oklahoma, he asked me to play it for him again. I don't think there ever will be a musical number written that will last in popularity as Joplin's "Maple Leaf Rag," a great monument to a great negro ragtime pioneer.

So Brun, who lived in Tulsa in 1921, played "Maple Leaf Rag" for Pawnee Bill in El Reno in 1901, then again in Tulsa twenty years later? Very interesting, in light of Brun's repeated claim during his later years that he did not play piano at all between 1908 and the 1940s. Several comments in Brun's memoirs strongly indicate that he really did play piano professionally during those years.

I met a young pianist by the name of Egbert Van Alstyne, who was the piano player for a musical show from New York City, which got stranded in El Reno. He stayed at my parents' home until he got funds to return to his home in New York. Mr. Van Alstyne in later years became one of America's popular song writers. He wrote such hits as "In the Shade of the Old Apple Tree" and those early Indian song hits "Navajo" and "Cheyenne." He told me in later years that his inspiration to write an Indian song came to him while he was watching the Cheyenne Indians as they passed through El Reno on their yearly visit to another Indian tribe. Van Alstyne was a pioneer composer of Indian song hits.

The Van Alstyne Family History (www.vanalstyne.com/family/getperson.php?personID=I11967&tree=VanAlstyne) states that Egbert Van Alstyne remembered his ragtime road show had gone broke in El Reno, and he'd stayed with the Campbell family for "several months" while he worked as a "honky-tonk ragtime pianist."

Maybe dollar signs did pop up in the young songwriter's field of vision as he watched a band of Indians traveling through El Reno. But in some versions of *When Ragtime Was Young*, Brun wrote, "There are a few legends as to how he ... happened to write 'Cheyenne'; so I don't feel that I should tell what Van Alstyne told me as to what really inspired him ... to write it." Was Brun reluctant to reveal a racy detail from Van Alstyne's personal life, or did he just not want to spoil a story the composer might have concocted?

Another small point. At the time of Van Alstyne's visit to the Campbells in El Reno, he had not yet moved to New York. He'd been born in Marengo, Illinois March 5, 1878, and did not leave the Midwest until 1901, when he and his lyricist-friend Harry Williams took off for New York to make their fortunes.

In the course of time after the drawing, people left El Reno for parts unknown, and it was not long before the city was back to normal. My father took to drink and gambling and lost his fine position with the wholesale grocery firm. He could not stand prosperity. Mother and he separated. She sold all our belongings and my fine piano and took my younger brother and moved back to Arkansas City, where she did dressmaking.

Well, being a boy who could play the piano and who had been raised on excitement, I struck out on my own. I played the piano wherever I could find a job. I played in honky-tonk saloons, pool halls, restaurants, confectionery stores, theaters, with minstrels, and for medicine shows, 10–20–30c weekly dramatic shows, steamboats.

This is where Brun's light-handed approach to time specification really begins. Just when did the family split up, Brun going on the road, while Mrs. Campbell and younger brother Harold (born in 1891) resumed residence in Arkansas City? It could have been as early as 1901.

In any case, the Campbell marital split was not permanent. In the 1904 Kansas City (Kansas) City Directory, Lute was listed as a barber, living alone at 631 S. Third Street, but the mid-decade Kansas Census of 1905 showed L.E. Campbell, age 38, back in Arkansas City with Lula Campbell, age 36; "Branson," age 21; and Harold, age 13. Lute and Brun both worked as barbers, but it's not possible to say how much time Brun spent in Arkansas City cutting hair, compared to his time on the road, playing piano. Later census records through 1940 indicate that Lute and Lulu remained together.

I met and played ragtime for George Evans (Honey Boy Evans) and Lew Dockstader the great minstrel men. These were mostly auditions. Salary differences kept me from signing contracts with them as a featured ragtime piano act with their great minstrels. I realized later that I had made the greatest mistake of my life.

Brun claimed to have had no regrets over turning down Evans' and Dockstader's offers. But if the headstrong young man really had been that foolish, it was in fact a major blunder. During the 1890s and early 1900s, Evans and Dockstader headed up two of the biggest minstrel troupes in the country, and quite possibly could have propelled The Ragtime Kid into stardom. Brun's contradictory accounts of his feelings can be attributed to his unintegrated mindset. Later in life, there probably were times when he regretted his attitude, but at other times, he likely felt the offer had in fact been insufficient, and he'd been right to reject it, perhaps in the hope of receiving a better counteroffer. And at the times he wrote both remarks, he would have believed each one.

There was an original style of dress with the ragtime pianist and male characters of the underworld. No one seems to know just where the style originated. One of the styles which seemed popular was the High Roller Stetson hat. Box back coats, generally of blue serge were worn with button cloth top shoes, tooth pick or bull dogged toes. The shirt was of loud patterns, some with stiff bosoms and detachable cuffs worn with high white or colored collars. The cuff buttons were made of two-and-a-half and five dollar gold pieces. The shirt stud was a similar gold piece, or a diamond stud was used. A Tiffany or Belcher mounted diamond ring was also worn. The vest was of the loudest patterns of silk or linen material, double or single breasted. Then there was the loud sheppard plaids and striped suits. The coat collar was made of velvet and the coat lapels were silk faced. When the suit happened to be made of black broadcloth it would be dressed up with big white pearl buttons, big as a silver dollar, the vest would be double or single breasted with a watch chain worn across the front. The tie would be a flowing bow with loud patterns or a four-in-hand cravat. Occasionally you would see some dude pianist wearing a bowler hat (derby to you). It was a ragtime age and we were dressing in a ragtime style.

Here is a short glossary of some of Brun's cited articles of clothing:

High Roller Stetson: Stetson was a Philadelphia hatmaker, known at least as well for their society furnishings as for their famous cowboy hats. You can still see Stetson hats in the Philadelphia History Museum at the Atwater Kent. A high roller was a gambler known for risking large sums on a bet.

Box Back Coat: This is a coat like the one Clark Gable wore in *Gone With The Wind*. It's shorter than a tailcoat; the tail extends just to the bottom of the hips, and is cut straight across.

Button Cloth-Top Shoes: These look like shoes with integral spats, but button shoes fasten together with a flap secured by the buttons. You must use a button hook to pull the buttons through the eyelets and fasten the shoes. The shoe tops extend above the ankles. Shoes with cloth tops were considered more elegant than ones made completely of leather.

Toothpick or Bulldogged Shoes: Narrow-toed shoes.

Belcher Diamond: Belcher was a jewelry firm comparable to Tiffany. A Belcher mount is one which features six prongs around the central gem, and often has six smaller stones mounted around it. It's very showy and flashy.

Shepherd's ("Sheppard") Plaid: This woven fabric, also known as Border Tartan because it originated in the Scottish towns just across the border from England, is a plain crossweave of small dark and light checks.

I had kept up correspondence with my kid sweetheart, "Taffy," at Arkansas City and she was writing back about things she had been hearing about my ragtime career, places I had been playing, etc. So, as my mother and young brother were living there then, I decided to pay them a visit.

This, then, would have been early in Brun's career, prior to his parents' reconciliation.

I arrived dressed in a loud checkered suit; cloth-top, colored patent leather shoes with pearl buttons, a light-colored hat with a loud hatband around it and that ever-loving loud silk shirt, together with the loud-patterned necktie, about made my ragtime dress complete. When the natives saw me in that getup, I created quite a sensation.

I thought my girl, Taffy, would faint when she gave me the once-over, and my mother stood dead in her tracks when she saw my loud clothes. But I was her darling boy and my appearance was soon forgotten by her.

Unfortunately, there were no letters between Brun and Taffy in The Kid's archive. It would be fascinating to compare that correspondence with the old man's written recollections of some forty years later. Maybe there's a box in an Arkansas City attic, full of letters tied together with a faded blue ribbon…

While I was home on a visit I met another pianist named Ted Hill who was playing in a tavern there. We became chums and one day decided to take our .22 rifles and go frog-hunting at the river nearby. We got into a friendly argument as to who was the best shot. I took a silver half-dollar out of my pocket. It was the one that my old negro piano teacher, Scott Joplin, had given me for a lucky pocket piece at Sedalia, in 1899. I put it in a crack on top of a fence post for us to shoot at to settle the argument.

We measured off so many feet. My friend fired first and missed. I shot and hit it dead center. The impact of the bullet stretched the half-dollar into the shape of a thimble. On our return to the city I went into a blacksmith's shop, placed the half-dollar on the smithy's anvil, took a heavy hammer and flattened it out; then I carried it for a pocket piece as before until one day I somehow spent it.

Given Brun's hero-worship of Scott Joplin, it seems strange he would have used that lucky half-dollar as a shooting target in the first place, then "somehow" spent the coin. Brun never did address this inconsistency. Likely, it represented the behavior of an impulsive, unreflective boy who grew into an impulsive, unreflective man, and had not yet acquired the sentimentalism that comes to the elderly as they look back over their years.

While I was visiting my mother and sweetheart, the city held a Fourth of July celebration, and at the height of the festivities the merry-go-round organ broke down. So the manager secured an upright piano, put it on the merry-go-round and hired me to furnish the music. He gave me six dollars to play from noon until ten o'clock, and believe me, that little city heard more ragtime music than they ever knew existed. I really drew the crowds. Within the week I had the townspeople talking to themselves.

The Negroes of the town got together and had a committee of their own race call on me to play for a cakewalk and dance for them. They hired the Highland Hall and advertised the ball in the surrounding towns. On the night it took place, the colored folk came in droves. The ball was a great success until the judges awarded the prize for the best cakewalk couple.

Their decision proved unpopular and a fight ensued which was terminated only by the arrival of the police.

Back to considering Brun's lack of specificity and clarity about the passage of time. Just when did his sartorial-exhibition visit take place? Did he engage in the target-shooting contest on the same stopover? How about his experience playing fill-in piano for the carousel? And the black ball at Highland Hall?

Searches for further information regarding the latter two events were fruitless. However, in her article, "Reminiscing in Ragtime," in *Jazz Journal*, April 1950, Kay C. Thompson quoted a man named Charm H. Berkey who had grown up near Arkansas City, and claimed he'd known the boy Brun and his traveling-salesman father who had sold groceries to Berkey's father. Berkey stated that Brun's life as a ragtime pianist had begun in 1899, and that he, Berkey, during a career as a waiter and a gambler, had heard Brun play in "Sporting Houses, Dance Halls, Barrel Houses and Honky Tonks." Berkey went on to verify Brun's claim of having worn impressively loud clothing, then concluded by saying he'd known pianist Ted Hill, and that Hill had in fact gone frog hunting with Brun in Arkansas City, that the shooting contest had taken place in 1903, and that Berkey had seen the half-dollar after the contest and again in Venice after it had found its way back to Brun.

So there we may have a bit of orientation in time. But trying to fit Brun's stories into a neat chronological package would be a fool's errand. Best to take The Ragtime Kid's anecdotes as what they almost surely were: rambling accounts, where he'd come to the end of one story, and say, "Y'know, that reminds me of something else."

The following morning, several preachers gave me a verbal going-over for furnishing music for the colored people. I saw that I had gotten in bad with some of the townsfolk, so I left there and went down to Guthrie, in Indian Territory, to see Buffalo Bill's Wild West Show.

Buffalo Bill's extremely popular Wild West Shows, under various names (including "Buffalo Bill's Wild West," and "Buffalo Bill's Wild West and Congress of Rough Riders of the World") toured the United States and Europe for decades, including the years Brun rode the ragtime circuit. Guthrie was bigtime in those days, and it seems reasonable that Bill's productions would have made appearances there.

On the morning of the show, I happened to be in a saloon when in walked Buffalo Bill himself, with a couple of men. I could see that he had a bit of liquor aboard; he wanted some music, so the bartender asked me to play for him. I declined at first, but Buffalo Bill insisted, and I went over to the piano and hammered out "Carbolic Rag," a new piece I had recently learned and which had quite a left hand run in it. Buffalo Bill was entranced; he came over to the piano and gave me a twenty-dollar gold piece and told me to keep playing as long as he was in the saloon. I must have played it for a full hour, over and over again—until he left the place, he by then being lit up like a new church.

"Car-bar-lick Acid," a folk rag by Clarence Wiley, is still played at ragtime festivals. The tune was copyrighted and published by the composer in Oskaloosa, Iowa, in 1901, then published by Giles Brothers in 1904, and then by Jerome Remick in 1907. So the public distribution of the music coincides neatly with Brun's years on the road.

David Reffkin states that a musician would need only a quick glance at the sheet music to determine that there is no figure in the piece that can be described as "quite a left-hand run." He, Richard Egan, and the late Trebor Tichenor agree that the ascending line of five eighth-notes at the beginning of the B section is probably the root of Brun's description. Egan thinks Brun, so hasty in so many aspects of his life, might have been careless in using the word "run" to describe those five notes, that he might have been trying to exaggerate his playing ability, and that in the late 1940s, when he wrote *When Ragtime Was Young*, he didn't imagine anyone would challenge his usage regarding a piece of music which at the time was not well known.

In addition, as with any tune from Brun's itinerant-pianist days, the young man might not have learned it from sheet music: most bar-barrelhouse-brothel pianists of the day played by ear, and new pieces of music were constantly going viral among them. Reffkin offers the possibility that Brun might have heard another pianist play "Car-bar-lick Acid" with a substantial run, liked it, and copied it.

In his letters to Jerry Heermans, Brun referred to "Carbolic Acid" as one of his favorites. As far as I can determine, though, the only rag actually named "Carbolic Acid" was composed and recorded by the Scottdale String Band during the 1920s, far too late for it to have been the piece Brun played for Buffalo Bill. But details never were Brun's thing. He must have been referring to the Wiley "Car-bar-lick" composition.

I had heard that a friend of my folks', a Mr. Angus Miller, was staying in town at the Royal Hotel, so I stopped off to see him. While we were talking in the lobby who should come in but Buffalo Bill with his friends. He at once saw me and came over and insisted that I accompany him to the parlor and play some more ragtime music. He was not to be denied, so I obliged him. Afterwards, he gave me some money and took a stickpin from his tie and gave it to me as a present. It was a beautiful elk's tooth with a one-carat diamond surrounded by smaller stones, and was engraved with some very small words which I couldn't make out.

At this time Governor Ferguson of Oklahoma came into the parlor and I played some for him. He had some business to discuss with Buffalo Bill, so I left them with handshakes all around.

A streetside plaque in Guthrie states that the Brooks Opera House was "Built in 1899 as an adjunct to the Royal Hotel," and that "the Brooks was praised in its day as the finest theater in the Southwest. It presented popular entertainments and was also the setting for many dazzling 'first nights' for territorial society."

Thomas Benton Ferguson was Governor of the Oklahoma Territory between 1901 and 1906.

That night I was admiring the stickpin and the thought occurred to me that Buffalo Bill had been a bit tipsy when he presented it and perhaps hadn't realized what he was doing. So promptly the next morning, I went back to the hotel and returned it to him. He had missed it but hadn't remembered giving it to me and was very happy to get it back, it being a present from his wife, who was then dead.

"His wife, who was then dead"? Buffalo Bill's wife, Louisa, to whom he was married for more than 50 years, did not die until 1921, some four years after the death of her famous husband. Not that Brun necessarily fabricated this point. It's easy to imagine how embarrassed Buffalo Bill could have been over his behavior—and if his wife had in fact given him the stickpin, he'd have been more than embarrassed when she next saw him. Perhaps the famous Wild West showman decided to take refuge in a whopper. Too bad Brun did not have a magnifier so he could've read and reported upon those tiny words on the stickpin.

Another point: Though Brun was impulsive and not overly endowed with good common sense, basic honesty and appreciation for proper behavior do seem to have been part of his makeup. Perhaps the night before, he'd been tempted to keep the stickpin, but in the light of day felt obligated to return it.

From Guthrie I worked my way down through the southern states. At Birmingham, Alabama, I played piano in a Negro restaurant on 19th Street because it paid the best wages. In Biloxi, Mississippi, I played for Cap Anderson at the old Biloxi Hotel on the gulf front. Then I played on a pleasure boat that ran up the gulf coast, finally stopping in Owensboro, Kentucky, where I played piano on the show-boat City of St. Louis. After a brief time on the boat I again headed northward. At Bowling Green, Kentucky, I secured a playing job in a popular confectionery store where all the college students hung out. The girls swarmed around me like bees around orange blossoms. I realized in a few days that I was "falling" for a beautiful brunette girl who often came in the store. She always was alone, and I could tell by her actions that she was going for me. So Mr. Piano Player, not desiring any entangling alliances with the fair sex at that time, pulled up stakes and headed up the river.

In St. Louis, I played at a honkytonk on Chestnut Street, and by then was commencing to get homesick for my sweetheart, Taffy. Thereupon I headed home and had a nice visit with her and my mother. While there I joined up with the Spooner Dramatic Company, one of the popular 10–20–30c shows which toured the midwest. I played with them for about three months until the season ended, then headed home again.

Apparently, Brun didn't limit his performing gigs to the ragtime circuit. The Spooner Dramatic Company was one of the repertoire groups that toured the United States during the late nineteenth and early twentieth centuries, performing in local opera houses and/or tents. The star of the Spooner Company, Alice (Allie) Spooner, began her career as a young child, and eventually became the female dramatic lead.

Brun's role with the company would have been as pianist, providing music (perhaps as a solo performer, or as part of a small ensemble) for the singers and possibly as background to emphasize dramatic moments in a melodrama.

On one visit to my home town I was in a bookstore where the boys hung out and met a little man about 45 years old. His face was pitted from smallpox, but otherwise he was quite nice looking. He had come from somewhere in Pennsylvania and was related to the young fellow who ran the bookstore—and also, I learned, to the then governor of Kansas. Everyone called him "Barney." He was a likeable fellow, and quite witty.

While I was in the bookstore I was informed that Cap White, a saloonkeeper from Newkirk, Oklahoma, was in town looking for me to play piano at his place. I met him and after we had agreed on my weekly salary I accompanied him to Newkirk. I had been playing there scarcely two weeks when in came the little fellow, Barney, and some of the boys from Arkansas City. Barney seemed to have a good supply of money, for he bought drinks for everyone in the place. While I was playing he came over and filled my pockets with half dollars, quarters, dimes and nickels. I noticed that some of the half dollars were bent, but thought nothing of it at the time.

Fed up with such a small town, I quit and returned to Arkansas City, getting off the train and at once observing that the townspeople were as excited as a hill of disturbed ants. My curiosity was soon set at ease, for I learned that the police had a bank robber cornered in an old barn. Of course I at once ran down there to get in on the excitement. The police had surrounded the place and were pumping it full of lead, and every once in a while the bank robber would shoot back. After several hours of this there ceased to be any return fire and the City Marshal started up the stairs to the left where the fugitive was holed in, and was promptly shot in the shoulder.

A consultation was then held to decide the next course of action, some of the besiegers wanting to set fire to the barn and smoke the fugitive out. A lot of talk and arguing went on, and in the midst of this a bird dog began barking in the barn. One of the officers crept up with pistol in hand to see what this was all about and found the dog pointing at a manger full of hay, like he would at a covey of quail. The officer brushed this aside and found the fugitive, fast asleep; he being none other than our little friend, Barney.

They put him in jail, but not for long. One night he dug his way out through the stone wall with a knife and fork carelessly left in his cell by the jailer. To the best of my knowledge he was never caught; and I am certain that those coins he poured into my pockets while I played piano in Newkirk were loot from the bank he had held up.

Brun's reference to the bent half-dollars seems to indicate he was relating the deformation to their having been stolen from the bank. But what might have been the association between bent coins and bank robberies? Perhaps explosives had been used to get into the vault, and half-dollars, having more surface area than any other coins, would've been more likely to be deformed by an explosion.

After the newness had worn off my visit home, I decided to hit the road again. By this time I was one of the best ragtime pianists in the middle west and had played to many notable persons, such as Teddy Roosevelt and his staff in the Parlor of the Lee Hotel at Oklahoma City while he was there with his Rough Riders.

Brun didn't specify a date—not unusual—but since Roosevelt was elected vice-president in November 1900, and succeeded to the presidency in September of 1901, it seemed unlikely he'd have been in Oklahoma at a Rough Rider reunion any time during Brun's itinerant pianist days. But history does record such a Rough Rider Reunion with Roosevelt present on July 2, 1900, at the Lee Hotel in Oklahoma City. Chalk one up for The Kid. True, there's no proof he really was there and playing piano, but there's no proof he wasn't. He might have been hired by management to entertain the soon-to-be vice-presidential candidate, but he also might have just walked up to an unoccupied piano in the parlor where Roosevelt and his men were sitting, and launched into his repertoire.

Brun claimed to have played piano for many notable persons, including a number of famous outlaws. He said he'd played for Cole Younger, and it's interesting that of the three Younger brothers, two (Jim and Bob) died before Brun's performance days, but Cole, who was released from prison in 1901, lived till 1916. Who's to say Brun did not play one night in a bar where the infamous bandit happened to be sitting, sipping a brew? Or someone who claimed to be the infamous bandit happened to be sitting, sipping a brew? On the other hand, The Kid alleged that he'd met Wild Bill Hickok, but Hickok had been killed in 1876, eight years before Brun's birth, so this event must have represented either an encounter with an imposter or a bit of carelessly embroidered whole cloth.

I played for Henry Starr, the notorious Indian bank robber, at Tulsa, Oklahoma, just a few months before he was killed at Harrison, Arkansas.

The bar in Pisco John's Bank Exchange Saloon on San Francisco's Barbary Coast. The gentleman behind the bar at the left was the proprietor, whose real name was Duncan Nicol. The two bartenders and four customers are unidentified (courtesy Society of California Pioneers).

Another statement which raises questions about Brun's claim that he did not play piano between 1908 or so and the early 1940s. Henry Starr, a criminal with a thirty-year history of armed robberies, was indeed shot to death in Harrison, Arkansas—in February 1921.

Brun is listed in the 1921 Tulsa City Directory, residing at 628 N. Boulder, and working as a barber in the Kennedy Barber Shop. No wife is specified. It seems reasonable that the now-single and still-young man might have been playing piano at a bar when Henry Starr happened to drop by "just a few months before" he was shot down.

A wry footnote to the Henry Starr story. After the bank robber's death, his mother told bystanders: "Henry has always been a trial to me, but thank God, I will know where he is tonight."

In my travels throughout the midwest up to 1908, I think I met every negro ragtime pianist of any importance, including Tom Turpin, Louis Chauvin, Al John (The Horse), Scott Joplin, Otis Saunders, Scott Hayden, James Scott, Arthur Marshall, Jelly Roll Morton (I met him first at Mobile, Alabama), and many others whom I knew only by their first names or their nicknames.

It would take long to list my great experiences as a pioneer ragtime pianist, but I can assure you that they were very interesting and I profited by them all. I always tried to be a gentleman, which was very hard for a ragtime pianist.

Though Brun was not always able to follow aim with action, that final sentence comes across as sincere. Ragtime historians generally agree that despite The Kid's inability to tell a straight, unembellished story, his efforts in later life to spread the gospel of ragtime and Scott Joplin were earnest and well-intentioned. Returning Buffalo Bill's diamond stickpin was the act of a gentleman.

In addition, Brun's aversion to situations where his physical well-being might have been at risk, his disapproval of government-run lotteries, and his frequent disparagement of pianists who overindulged in liquor and drugs would suggest that conventional attitudes of the day played a significant part in the makeup of his complicated personality.

While I am writing of the past and looking backward, I think this would be a good spot to tell you of several rough experiences I had—typical experiences of an early ragtime pianist.

I was playing piano in a billiard parlor on North Main Street in Wichita, Kansas, in 1907, a popular place which all the young blades of Wichita made their rendezvous for a game of pool or billiards or maybe a game of stud poker. Here I met a friend of mine who ran a saloon known as the

"Bucket of Blood," in the tough stockyard district of North Wichita. If there weren't four or five fights every night in the place, it would not be running true to form. He offered me fifty cents a night more than I was getting if I would play the piano for him, so I took the job.

I reported for work the next night at 7:30. The place was in an old building—a two-story unpainted one at that, of the 1870 vintage, with a wooden sidewalk out in front. On the first floor was a saloon and bar, which had seen better days. The flooring was of old wooden planks, with a few tables and chairs placed around in orderly fashion. It was dimly lighted with old coal oil lamps that had reflectors behind them; and the tough looking bartender and the characters standing at the bar, plus the general atmosphere of the place, suggested that murder might occur at any minute. The walls were full of bullet holes, and the piano with its mandolin attachment had not escaped the aim of some slap-happy gunman. I had played in many tough places, but this one took all the marbles.

I took the front out of the piano and settled myself on the stool and had just started to play a "rag" when in popped a ham actor lighted up like Haley's comet. He hurried to the bar and ordered a glass of whiskey, which he gulped down in a hurry, then took to the floor and in a dramatic way started to recite "The Face on the Barroom Floor." To add a touch of atmosphere to the performance, I started to play that old tear jerker, "Hearts and Flowers." Well, that set off the fireworks, for a disgusted customer threw a beer glass at me and then knocked the actor cold. Then everyone in the place started throwing fists, chairs, and bottles at each other. When the fight quieted down it looked as though a cyclone had passed through the saloon.

That night, when the bartender paid me, he sensed that I didn't like my job, so he said, "Kid, forget the rough-house we had tonight, for it's just our customers' way of having a little fun. Some nights here are rougher than tonight." I told him the customers played too rough for me, and their idea of fun was just a bit too rich for me, and quit. The "Bucket of Blood" was sure the right name for that joint.

After that exciting experience I decided to head west for San Francisco and the Barbary Coast.

Brun's short piece "My Girl Taffy" (included at the end of *When Ragtime Was Young*) reveals that he was back in Arkansas City not later than June 1907. So, given that his short stay in the "Bucket of Blood" took place in 1907, he would've been in San Francisco for only a few months at most.

My first stop was Hutchinson, Kansas—a good, lively Kansas town. I got a job playing piano in the old Midland Restaurant, an annex to the Midland

Hotel, the popular one of the town. I played during meal hours and for my services I received my meals only, and a few tips. The bartender in the hotel's barroom ran a roadhouse out at the edge of town, outside the city limits, and hired me to play piano nights there. It was another rough-and-tumble place. The first night I played there, the place got shot up and set on fire.

I lost no time in leaving Hutchinson, Kansas behind, and soon was on my way west again, to San Francisco. I arrived there flat broke, and walked up and down Market Street, hoping I would run into some old friend who would stake me to a few dollars. Right when I was weak from hunger and in low spirits, I ran into a boyhood chum who had a good job as brakeman on the Santa Fe Railroad, out of Richmond, California. I explained my financial condition and he gladly staked me to five dollars. We had lunch together and a few beers, and a fine visit.

After I had cleaned up a bit, I made the rounds of the night spots, looking for a job as pianist. I found that all the best jobs were taken, and the pianists were frozen on them; so I went to the Chinatown district. From the pianists I had heard in San Francisco so far, I knew I was better on the keyboard than any of them—especially when it came to playing ragtime.

The first place in Chinatown I visited was one about which I had heard a great deal. It was the famous "Pisco John's" saloon on Montgomery Street. He was known all over for his famous drink, the "Pisco Punch," made from his own secret formula. Many saloons in San Francisco had their own imitations of it. No one knew its exact ingredients, but to me it seemed from its taste (which was delicious) that it was made with powdered milk, powdered sugar, pineapple juice, lime juice, gin, rum, and Bavarian brandy. It was served in a tall glass, and three of them made you feel as though you might be the king of Chinatown or the mayor of San Francisco. That's how important you felt. As a rule, two punches were all Pisco John would serve to a customer at one time. It was a drink that you could not fool around with.

I found Pisco John's saloon crowded with people drinking his famous drink. At the back of the saloon, two wine rooms were reserved for family trade. Pisco John stood at the end of the bar, mixing his famous drink in glasses and passing them to his bartenders, who added a dash of liquor of some kind before it was served to the customers. His place was run in a very orderly fashion, and drunks were not welcome.

Brun's descriptions of Pisco John, his saloon, and his famous drink are right on with historical accounts. The actual name of the popular establishment was the Bank Exchange Saloon; it was located on Montgomery Street, at the site of the present-day Transamerica Pyramid. Its doors first opened in 1853.

During the 1870s, it was bought by a Scot, Duncan Nicol. Because the bar featured a type of South American brandy called pisco, Nicol became known as Pisco John, and the Bank Exchange became world-famous as the place where everyone went to drink Pisco Punch. Rudyard Kipling and Mark Twain were among the many notables who proclaimed the wonders of John's heavenly beverage. Nicol had a secret formula and technique for preparing the drink, and kept serving it up until 1919, when Prohibition forced him into retirement. Some years later, his bar manager spilled the beans about the recipe. According to a 2009 account in *Esquire*, the beverage is composed of Pisco brandy, pineapple, gum syrup, lemon juice, and distilled water. Not as complex as Brun's guess, but along quite similar lines.

In those times, saloons were not necessarily low dives where a customer stood a fair chance of leaving without his wallet and/or most of his circulating blood. As Brun pointed out with respect to the Bank Exchange, some were elegant establishments with posh restaurants at one end of the building and ornately decorated bars at the other; both facilities catered to the silk stocking trade, the celebrated, and persons of influence. Think whites in Harlem in the 1920s and '30s. Though the Bank Exchange was located within the Barbary

A 1903 view down Pacific Street, San Francisco's Barbary Coast. More than a century later, the scene produces nostalgia in the viewer, but in its day this block was said to be the roughest, most dangerous neighborhood in San Francisco, and perhaps in the entire country (courtesy Society of California Pioneers).

Coast, San Francisco's roughest red-light district, the saloon occupied part of a fine building, and its interiors have been described as opulent. A man could come alone and drink at the bar with his comrades, or he could bring his wife or girlfriend to enjoy a comfy evening of good food and drink, separated from any boisterous male behavior in the bar section.

While I was in his place I ran into two old friends of mine from Oklahoma and the Indian Territory. They were the original "Arkansas Kid" and the "Hominy Kid," whom I had not seen since 1900 at El Reno, Oklahoma, where the Arkansas Kid broke the Attic Gambling House and gave me a thousand dollar bill to furnish music for him and his friends at a two day celebration he put on at different friends' houses.

Was the Attic Gambling House an establishment by that name in El Reno, or was Brun using a popular nickname, perhaps denoting an undercover operation in an El Reno attic? And did the Arkansas Kid really pay The Ragtime Kid one thousand dollars to play piano? Today, that sum would be equivalent to some $25,000. Still, showy monetary extravagances were not uncommon in those times, and if truth really can be found in details, it might be significant that Brun specified the payment was in the form of a thousand-dollar bill.

The Hominy Kid probably acquired his nickname from Hominy, Oklahoma, a small city in Osage County, founded by displaced Native Americans during the 1870s. In 1907, Hominy's population was 468; the town was incorporated the following year. The discovery of oil in Hominy in 1916 resulted in a rapid and impressive increase in population and industry. Aside from the oil strike, Hominy's biggest moment came in 1927, when the Hominy Indians, the town's all–Native American football team, defeated the New York Giants, the NFL champions that year.

They were two notorious gamblers from the midwest who were making San Francisco their headquarters, and they were prosperous. They gave me a hundred dollars as a stake. They wanted to hear me play the piano, so we went up into Chinatown looking for a saloon that had a piano in it.

We found one in the middle of the block in Bartlett's Alley [Bartlett's Alley is now known as Beckett Street], one of the toughest blocks in Chinatown's redlight district with its dimly lit brick buildings that housed the "fancy dressed girls" who practiced the oldest profession known.

The "Alley" was alive with drunken sailors and men from all over the globe. Fist-fights were common affairs in the street, and almost every hour of the day or night witnessed a bouncer throwing some drunk out of one of these places of sin.

I asked the owner of the saloon if I could use the piano for a while and he said, "Tear it apart if you want to." So I started rocking the joint with my favorite rag, the "Maple Leaf," with my gambling friends buying drinks for the house as I entertained the crowd.

I had not played very long before the owner of the saloon hired me. I didn't like the looks of the place and the tough characters it attracted. I noticed when a customer bought a five-cent glass of beer and paid for it with a gold piece, whether it was five, ten or twenty dollars, he never got any change back. If he beefed about his change one of the bouncers would throw him out in the street, and if a customer ordered a drink of whiskey of any special brand, any brand, it all came out of the same bottle.

My friends and I finally left the place for uptown San Francisco. As we left I told the saloonkeeper I would be on the job the next night. The Arkansas Kid suggested that I stop at their hotel on Third Street, so that we could all be together. They were popular among the gamblers and "sports" and introduced me to Jim Corbett and Bob Fitzsimmons and other prize fighters. Now that I was sure of myself and had a cinch on my board and room, I felt secure, and things looked brighter for me.

Outside the Midway Dance Hall, Barbary Coast, where many of the popular dances of the ragtime era originated. Notice that the crowd out front is entirely male, which says a lot about what went on inside (courtesy Society of California Pioneers).

Well, on the following night I reported for work in the saloon in Bartlett Alley as their pianist. I had made a good impression on the bosses of the place and felt at ease, even if the place was tough and a short change joint. I used a common tin cup for the "kitty," which I always put on top of the piano. I had played about an hour and the kitty had some change in it, when a big lug emptied it, walked over to the bar, and bought himself some drinks with my dough. I didn't dare say a word to him, for if I had he probably would have smacked me right in the kisser.

During the first night I played there, the cops came in every few minutes with some customer who had complained to them about getting short-changed in the joint. I later found out that it was a common occurrence and that the cops were squared away with the saloonkeeper. Nobody who kicked about being short-changed in the place ever got a dime back, all the while I played there.

One night a free-for-all fight took place there. One man got killed and two others were badly wounded (so I thought). The cops pinched the joint and took the victims away in an ambulance. I was just getting ready to take off like a skyrocket when the bartender told me the fight was just a "phoney" to attract a crowd to the place, and told me to play the piano like nobody's business as long as the customers kept coming. Later I found out that phoney fights in Chinatown and the Barbary Coast were an old gag to get crowds.

One day when I was wandering around Chinatown on a side street just off Bartlett Alley, I ran into an old Chinatown character named Lem Duck, better known as "Happy Hooligan" to the tourist trade and the district. He was standing in the doorway of his dirty place of business and where he lived. Because of its filthy condition it was called the "Dog Kennel." Lem was a happy-go-lucky sort of person and none too bright. For twenty-five cents he would tell your fortune. I stopped to kid with him, and agreed to let him tell my fortune. I entered his dirty and unkempt place and he took a long glass vase from a shelf full of long bamboo sticks about an inch wide. On the ends of the sticks were words written in Chinese. Happy told me to take a stick out of the vase and hand it to him, which I did. When he read the writing on the end of the stick his face lit up. Then he said, "You live to be eighty-four years old. Pretty soon you get a lot of money." And then he made some signs over my head with his hands and jabbered something in Chinese, as though he were driving away evil spirits. I took it as a joke, but he proved to be quite a prophet—as regards the money, at least. I'll tell you later on.

Lem Duck's trans-ethnic nickname originated with Happy Hooligan, an extremely popular cartoon character drawn by Frederick Burr Opper in a strip that ran in newspapers from 1900 to 1932, and served as the basis for a number of early slapstick movie shorts. Happy was always smiling, was constantly in some sort of trouble, and wore a red tin can on his head. Perhaps the cartoonist thought the little caps that Chinese men wore at the time resembled tin cans.

Brun describes Lem as "happy-go-lucky," though in Herbert Asbury's 1933 book, *The Barbary Coast: An Informal History of the San Francisco Underground*, the author mentions that Lem was subject to a good deal of harassment and practical jokes. (According to Asbury, two assailants sneaked into Lem's quarters one night while he slept, and extracted and stole his prized gold tooth. The *Oakland Tribune* of November 20, 1910, also mentioned the nocturnal theft of "Lem Duck's gold-filled tooth.")

Asbury also wrote that Lem Duck's living quarters, at least prior to the 1906 earthquake, were located in "an underground chamber known as The Dog Kennel, on the east side of Bartlett Alley." Much of Asbury's description of Lem Duck agrees with Brun's report—perhaps just a little too much and too closely here and there. Brun wrote that Lem was "none too bright," while Asbury remarked that the man was "not so bright as he might have been." According to Brun, Lem was "better known as 'Happy Hooligan' to the tourist trade and the district"; Asbury wrote that Lem "was better known to the tourists as Happy Hooligan."

The quotations from Brun and Asbury do bear a remarkable resemblance. But whether or not plagiarism needs to be added to the list of Brun's alleged storytelling sins, The Kid's detailed description of the fortune-telling encounter is thoroughly believable, and can easily be accepted at face value. Lem was in fact a widely known character (Asbury's words) in Chinatown during the time Brun was playing piano there, and it wouldn't have been at all remarkable for the two men to have met.

Anecdotally interesting—an 80" × 66" oil painting from 1961 by Michael Goldberg is titled "Lem Duck Happy Hooligan," though there's no evidence of Lem's actual appearance on the abstract, dark canvas work.

As I told you, Bartlett Alley was one of the toughest blocks in Chinatown. At the head of the alley on a side street were the "cribs" and hop joints with their dark stairways.

As described in *California Babylon*, by Kristan Lawson and Annali Rufus, "cribs" were small cubicles with cots, usually in basements, and were the most horrific of the places where prostitutes plied their trade. Chinese slave girls—sick, opium-addicted, and starving—were allowed to go only so far from their cribs as to allow them to expose themselves to passers-by, and chant, "ten-cent lookee, twenty-five-cent feelie, fifty-cent dooee."

"Hop joints" were opium-smoking parlors.

The dimly lit alley and side streets were generally blanketed with fog, which made it a dreary scene to behold. I became depressed playing piano in that atmosphere, though I made good money. I decided to quit, and began playing relief for different pianists in cafes in downtown San Francisco.

Another instance of Brun's restlessness of mind and body, and sensitivity to his surroundings. Did he have any specific idea of just what he might have been searching for?

Playing relief gave me a chance to visit many of San Francisco's notorious places of sin. It was while I was down on Pacific Street on the Barbary Coast, that I heard the best ragtime piano player I believe I ever heard. He was a little black negro about twenty years of age who played piano in a tough negro joint named Purcell's, right next door to Spider Kelly's Saloon and Dance Hall. While I was in there he played a rather long ragtime composition of his own—one of the best "rags" I believe I had ever heard. I asked him what name he had given it and he said, "I calls it 'No Name Rag.'"

I told him I played piano some and he asked me to play for him, so I played Scott Joplin's 'Entertainer Rag,' and I really played it, for I knew he was tough competition. When I had finished, he and the colored girls who worked there, as well as the customers, gave me a big hand. I played several more "rags" and became solid with the crowd. The negro bouncers kept busy throwing customers out into the street when they slowed up in buying drinks.

Joplin's famous rag, composed in 1902, was titled "The Entertainer." "The Entertainer's Rag" was a popular composition from 1910 by Jay Roberts.

At different times, Brun specified different pianists as the best ragtime piano player he'd ever heard. Most frequently, he named Louis Chauvin, but on the vinyl disc *The Professors, Volume 2* (reissued as a CD titled *Brun Campbell, Joplin's Disciple*, Delmark DE-753), Brun seemed to go out of his way to specify Charley Thompson as the prizewinner. However, Richard Egan points out that Chauvin died in 1908, and Thompson did not start playing professionally until 1910 or 1911, so Brun could not have compared them head-to-head. Egan believes that in the recorded interview, Brun was working his way through a number of the top players of the earlier era, but the interviewer cut him off to ask about Thompson. At that point, Brun, possibly thinking about a famous 1916 cutting contest won by Thompson, said Thompson "was the best of all of them," but didn't elaborate about specific time periods.

Brun sometimes told newspaper reporters that Scott Joplin had been the greatest on the keyboard, though in the recorded Affeldt interview, he said, "[Joplin] was a good piano player, but he wasn't nothin' to set the world on fire." But in the context of some of those newspaper interviews, Brun's claim for his hero's primacy would have been consistent with his promotional efforts.

In any event, it should not seem strange or be unexpected that The Kid's assessment of different players' skills might have varied from time to time. Neurological research amply confirms the common perception of how frequently people do change their opinions.

So, who might have been Brun's San Francisco-based all-time best ragtime pianist? On his CD, *Chestnut Street in the 90s* (Rag-Time Records RR CD-002), pianist Adam Swanson played a tune he called "No Name Rag," attributed to "Piano Price" Davis by Glover Compton in Blesh and Janis' *They All Played Ragtime*. Prior to Swanson's CD, the tune had been recorded only by Compton, and on that recording, the pianist identified the work as "Price's Rag.... Price's No Name Rag." Compton further described the work to Blesh and Janis as "a popular and very different piano number of his [Davis'] own that he called 'Piano Price Rag.'" Compton had met Davis in Louisville, Kentucky, in 1904, and described him as a tall man, 30 years old, who was the "acknowledged leader of Louisville ragtime," and who went to Pittsburgh four years later and died there.

Could Brun's acquaintance have been "Piano Price"? The Kid recalled the pianist as a "little black negro," but that memory might have originated in his having seen the man sitting on a piano bench. U.S. Census records for 1900 list a Price Davis in Louisville who was 22 years old, compatible with both Brun's and Compton's estimates of age. San Francisco resident David Reffkin writes, "I've never seen the name [Price Davis] in any descriptions, programs, or catalogs in my San Francisco research. Hardly seems like he would have been here at all, given his Midwest-northeast orientation, though the question remains open."

But the association of "No Name Rag" with a tune referred to as unusual or different is a teaser, as are the two references to the pianist(s) as having been outstanding. Ragtime pianists of that day truly were itinerant, and at some point, Davis could have made a trip to the West Coast, perhaps between his stints in Louisville and Pittsburgh.

As Brun wrote, Purcell's was located next door to Spider Kelly's, which according to author James R. Smith, as stated in his book, *San Francisco's Lost Landmarks*, "was considered at the time to be 'the lowest, most rotten dive in the world.'" Smith also claimed that the famous Texas Tommy and Ballin' the Jack dances were first performed in Purcell's. There is considerable evidence that the "animal dances" and other scandalous gyrations of the day originated in one or another of the dance halls of the Barbary Coast, then were transported eastward by patrons and performers who'd been "doing the Coast." In "Ragtime in the Red Light Districts," Brun's short account of houses of prostitution during the early twentieth century, The Kid wrote:

On San Francisco's Barbary Coast, in such dance halls as the Thalia, the Midway, The Diana, and Purcell's Negro Dance hall and Saloon, were originated such dances as the Grizzly Bear, Bunny Hug, Pony Prance, Turkey Trot, Texas Tommy, and other close-semi-acrobatic dances which swept the country during the ragtime craze. Pacific Street was a real ragtime street during that period, and it saw some ragtime piano playing fools.

Brun further specified:

None of the early ragtime pianists played ragtime the way it was written. They played their own styles. Some played "slow drag" style, some march time style, others fast, slow, or blue styles; and if you were acquainted with the player and heard him playing a block away you could name him.

In his book, *The Wicked Waltz and Other Scandalous Dances*, Mark Knowles mentioned that Purcell's was situated in a Barbary Coast building on Pacific Avenue that had been constructed shortly after the 1906 earthquake. This, along with the fact that Brun definitely was back in Arkansas City by June 1907, would further date his San Francisco experience to early 1907.

It seems odd that Brun made no mention of the famous earthquake and fire, or the construction that followed it. Could the building housing Purcell's have been put up so "shortly after" the disaster? In those days and in that place, there were far fewer regulations to follow and less red tape to untangle. A little money in the right palm would have gone a long way.

It was while I was in a gambling house upstairs on Powell Street that I won fourteen hundred dollars playing at roulette. I felt as important as Emperor Norton, a famous character of San Francisco and the Barbary Coast, who imagined that he was the Emperor of the United States and who went around dressed in an old uniform with phoney medals pinned upon his breast, and called everyone his subjects, and issued orders and proclamations to the people of San Francisco every so often. People considered him a harmless nut and humored him—but was he a nut? One day he ordered his subjects to build a bridge in 1869 from San Francisco to Oakland. What a laugh that was at the time. But the bridge was built seventy years later, in the exact place where he had ordered it built. He died in 1880.

With my new wealth I paid my debts and bought myself a wardrobe. One suit of clothes I had made was a loud color with small reddish squares. The cloth was of fine worsted material; the pants were made "peg-top" and the style of the coat was long and form-fitting, with large pearl buttons. The collar was velvet and the coat lapels were faced with black silk. With that suit I wore patent leather button shoes with red spats, a loud silk shirt and tie, and a derby hat. The "Ragtime Kid" was stepping high now. I don't think the San Franciscans had ever seen such a ragtime dress. People turned around to take a second look at me as I passed them on the streets. As I felt that roll of money I had in my pocket, I recalled what the old Chinaman, Happy Hooligan, had said when he told my fortune; that I would get a lot of money pretty soon. Naturally I did not think he was as nutty as people thought he was, for in my case he had called the turn.

Fourteen hundred dollars—thirty-five thousand in present-day purchasing power. That must have been some wardrobe and some pile of IOUs. But in any case, the one sentence reveals two major conflicting aspects of Brun's personality—profligacy and responsibility. Brun might justifiably have echoed Walt Whitman: "Do I contradict myself? Very well, then, I contradict myself. I am large, I contain multitudes."

In addition, the fact that Brun played roulette and consorted easily with gambler-friends indicates he harbored no particular negative opinion about gambling per se, and that his objections to government sponsored lotteries might just have represented an aversion to hypocrisy.

Unfortunately, Lem Duck's prediction regarding Brun's longevity was not nearly as accurate as his financial prognostication. In 1952, when The Kid left us, he was 16 years short of Lem's promised eighty-four.

I made the rounds of the Barbary Coast's resorts and became disgusted with the sights I saw. I commenced to yearn for the middle west. I told my friends, the Arkansas Kid and the Hominy Kid, that I was going back there.

San Francisco was beginning to recover some from the earthquake and fire, and was a lively city when I left it.

Finally, at least a mention of the famous Shake and Bake, and another indication that Brun's time in San Francisco was during early 1907.

The Arkansas Kid and the Hominy Kid hated to see me leave; they liked ragtime music and liked my playing. So I bought a railroad ticket for Colorado Springs, Colorado, and bade them goodbye and boarded the train, leaving San Francisco and the Barbary Coast to their own fate.

As I was traveling first-class with a substantial bank-roll in my pocket, when I arrived in Colorado Springs I decided I would "put on the dog." Accordingly, I stopped at a fine hotel there—a very expensive place and the best in town. I intended to spend a few days just as a tourist. On a sight-seeing trip around there I went to see the old ghost town of Colorado City, which the natives called "Old Town." It stood about as it had many years before with a couple of blocks of old wooden buildings and wooden sidewalks. The old stores and shops were empty except for the barber shop and one or two saloons with their bar, glassware and furniture and old coal oil lamps. All the old store rooms were open for inspection and the barber acted as a guide, telling fascinating stories about them.

I have forgotten the year he said the town was built, but it was there that a notorious badman and gambler made his headquarters in those roaring days of the Western Frontier. His name was the "Coyote Kid."

According to ragtime enthusiast Ann Westerberg of Littleton, CO, "if he [Brun] were staying at the best hotel, odds are it was The Antlers, rebuilt, but still in existence. And 'Colorado City' is now Old Colorado City, as we have another Colorado City down the road. It was founded in 1859…by General William Palmer, who founded Colorado Springs later."

The Ghost Town Museum (founded in 1954, www.ghosttownmuseum.com), gives some idea of what Brun might have seen in Old Colorado City/Old Town. There is no mention of the notorious Coyote Kid, but it's interesting that the two most important figures in Ute Indian mythology are Wolf the Creator and his brother Coyote the Trickster. Perhaps the tour-guide barber was using a bit of imagination, or the tourist barber, who seemed to have a strong affinity for Kids of various persuasions, misunderstood, or at a remove of some forty years misremembered the remark.

Old Town's main street with its wooden buildings and wooden sidewalks and old shade trees had a certain beauty about it that is hard for me to describe; but it was very enchanting and picturesque, to say the least. It was located between Colorado Springs and Manitou, on the street car line which ran to the foot of Pike's Peak.

Between 1890 and the early 1930s, the Colorado Springs & Manitou Railway Company, later the Colorado Springs Rapid Transit Railway, and later still the Colorado Springs & Interurban Railway Company, transported passengers the short distance between Colorado Springs and Manitou.

Within a few days after my arrival at Colorado Springs I got a job playing piano in a tavern at the edge of Colorado City, where I worked for about a month. It was a good paying job, since its customers were mostly tourists.

One day I went over to Manitou to take a trip on the railroad that ran to the top of Pike's Peak. It cost five dollars for the round trip. On the day I made the trip the tourist trade was very heavy, and the ticket sellers were swamped. I noticed an old gentleman wearing a Prince Albert coat, standing on the depot platform with a tall silk hat in his hand. People were giving him five dollar bills which he crammed into his hat, and he made them stand in line for their turns to board the trains. I found out that he was the owner, and the man who opened up the famous Independence Gold Mine at Cripple Creek, Colorado, which produced millions of dollars for him and started the gold rush to Cripple Creek in the '90's. His name was Stratton.

Winfield Scott Stratton made his fortune as a prospector, opening and developing the Independence Gold Mine in Cripple Creek. Stratton was also a major philanthropist who gave aid to many individuals and groups; he provided food and housing for innumerable people affected by the Cripple Creek Fire in 1896. Eventually, he became eccentric and reclusive. In 1900, he sold his mine to a British Company for ten million dollars, and in 1901, he acquired the Colorado Springs-Manitou railway system. After his death, his will provided for the establishment of the Myron Stratton Home (named for his father) for the elderly or infirm, and needy children.

But there are twin flies in Brun's narrative ointment. First, Stratton died in 1902. Second, he did not own the Pikes Peak Cog Railway, which carried passengers out of Manitou to the top of the famous mountain. At the time of Brun's visit, that operation was the property of one Zelmon Simmons (the same Simmons who founded the mattress company of that name). Simmons had originally bankrolled the project, which began operations in 1891.

So, who was the man with the top hat full of five-dollar bills? One certainty is that it was not Stratton. Though it seems unlikely that any millionaire owner of a railway would put himself out to collect fares, I suppose he might've been Zelmon Simmons on a lark, and was misidentified to Brun as Stratton by a less than fully informed bystander. Perhaps he was a tourist trade stand-in for Stratton, a ticketseller costumed as one of the region's most notable persons. He could have been an imposter who collected money from tourists, then made off with his ill-gotten gains. And he might've been a figment of Brun's imagination, an invention to make the story of his little excursion just a bit more striking.

As odd as Brun's bare mention of the San Francisco disasters is the fact that he made no mention whatever of the magnificent view from Pike's Peak, a sight that inspired so much awe in the mind of Katharine Lee Bates one day in 1893 that she sat down that evening in Colorado Springs and wrote "America the Beautiful." (Ms. Bates did not ride up the mountain in a rail car, though;

she went by carriage, drawn part way by horses, then by mules. Not long thereafter, the success of the cog railway caused the carriage road to be shut down.) Brun wrote impressive descriptions of rough bars, but he did say the natural beauty of Old Town's Main Street was hard for him to describe. Perhaps his focus on ragtime was so single-minded and intense as to push storage and retrieval of lovely scenery beyond operational tolerances.

After that trip to the top of Pike's Peak and back, I stopped in the Silver Dollar Saloon in Manitou for a glass of beer. I had a few glasses, and on my way out I stopped at the cigar counter for a pack of cigarettes. I happened to look down at the floor and saw a silver dollar. I stooped to pick it up, but found it was cemented into the tile floor. I had been in many "Silver Dollar" saloons with their floors bordered with silver dollars, and in some places the silver dollars were embedded in the bars, also; and why I fell for that one I can't answer. But anyway I had to buy a round of drinks for every one in the house. That was customary. So that time the joke was on me.

But while I am speaking of saloons and bars, the smallest saloon and bar I ever saw—and I believe it was the smallest in the world—was in the Santa Fe depot at Pueblo, Colorado. It was a neat little place. I think three customers was a crowd, and the bar was just big enough for the bartender to work behind. It was shaped like a half circle, and not over five feet from end to end;—no place for a bar fly.

Well—I finally quit my piano playing job at Colorado City, checked out of my expensive hotel, and bought a railroad ticket for Denver. A few days after my arrival there, I was playing piano in the Lemps Rathskellar on Curtis between 15th and 16th Streets. I played there for a while and then went to a piano job on Market Street.

One morning I woke up and found the weather twenty-six degrees below zero, which was too cold for a hot piano player. So I lit out for Kansas City, Missouri, where I ran into about the same zero weather. I went to work in a saloon at the corner of 9th and Walnut, and while I was playing there, I met Charles Johnson, who had composed "Dill Pickles Rag" in 1906.

A 1907 flyer, perfectly timed to Brun's travels, invited men to bring their wives and sweethearts to Lemp's Rathskeller to hear the finest piano orchestra ever. The Rathskeller was an outlet for The William J. Lemp Brewery of St. Louis, founded by John Adam Lemp in 1838. The Lemps became fabulously wealthy, and have been described as local royalty. One of Adam Lemp's granddaughters married Gustav Pabst of Milwaukee, a union comparable to a European royal marriage in that it connected two of America's most prominent brewers.

Unfortunately, though, the Lemps were also, to say the least, an unstable bunch. Adam Lemp's son, William Lemp, Sr., and three of William Sr.'s children all committed suicide by gunshot. William Jr.'s divorce in 1909 from Lillian Handlan Lemp, a railroad heiress known as The Lavender Lady because of her fanatical partiality to that color, was a cause célèbre both at home and abroad. Mrs. Lemp claimed her husband was chronically unfaithful and enjoyed killing cats for amusement. Mr. Lemp replied that the only cats he ever shot were those who'd been keeping him awake at night. He charged his wife with public drinking (an odd complaint for a brewer) and smoking.

Today, the restored Lemp Mansion on DeMenil Place in St. Louis is known as the Lemp Mansion Restaurant and Inn. Ghost hunters claim it to be heavily occupied by spirits, primarily those of family members who had departed this world by other than natural means.

By 1907, things had become a little tough for pianists, as a kind of reform wave was on. One day the saloons would be allowed to have music and the next week the pianos would be dead. So I went back to Wichita and played there for a while. Eventually Wichita and all towns in the midwest passed reform laws barring piano players from performing in public saloons and in the "districts." And the uncanny thing of this is that it was in Wichita where Carrie Nation and her Temperance Crusaders started the reform wave in the 1890s which spread all over America.

I commenced to see the handwriting on the wall for the ragtime pianist, so in 1908 I gave it up as a profession. Several of the crack ragtime pianists went into vaudeville and others were absorbed in the new nickelodeons, but most of those who played in the first picture houses were just average piano players. Others like myself took up other means to make a livelihood.

Since I had saved a few hundred dollars, I thought this would be the time for Taffy and I to get married. I called her on the phone and proposed to her. She accepted, and after five years' absence from Arkansas City, I returned to find that my girl, Taffy, had grown up to be the most beautiful young woman I had ever seen.

Had Brun really not been back to Arkansas City for five years? For one thing, as mentioned earlier, he was listed in the 1905 Kansas mid-decade census as living with his parents in Arkansas City and working as a barber. For another, his boyhood friend Charm H. Berkey dated his target-shooting episode involving Joplin's half-dollar to 1903, which would establish a maximal absence of four years.

She had a heavy growth of natural blonde hair which she wore very becomingly dressed, blue eyes and a clear peachy complexion, and pearly teeth, evenly matched. She was about five feet and five inches tall, solidly built, with a figure that was all curves, and a smile that would knock you out.

While I had been away, the local gossips had told her all kinds of stories about me and my ragtime career, the places in which I had played, and other poisonous gossip. Some of it was true, but most of it was not; but Taffy never let it bother her.

Her father was the Santa Fe Railroad yard master. He and I had a fight one time because he had forbidden me to go with his daughter.

In his short personal narrative, "My Girl Taffy," Brun specified that the father "beat me up." That stands as the one declared exception to Brun's pattern of avoiding physical conflicts with other men. Perhaps another testimonial to the power of Taffy's charms?

Taffy's mother was determined that she should marry a young doctor of the town, but Taffy and I had become engaged, and while the gossips were still "frying me on the pan," we were married with the understanding that my ragtime days must come to an end.

The wedding was held in her parents' home and we immediately left for Tulsa, Oklahoma, where I went into business. We lived together for five years. Then one day we had a quarrel over nothing and separated. She went home to her parents, where she died about a year later.

Years afterward I was married again to a fine girl. We have three beautiful grown daughters, two of whom are married. We live in California.

Mine was an exciting life and I have no regrets, and I do not offer any apologies for the exciting life I led in my youth. For if I did, I would be a hypocrite.

* * *

Among the short historical and promotional compositions Brun wrote during the 1940s were two unpublished personal essays that recounted activities from his itinerant-pianist years. Logically, then, they should be included in *When Ragtime Was Young*.

The manuscript from which the first story has been excerpted was titled "Ragtime in the Red Light Districts." The initial portion of the piece, Brun's account of American sporting districts and houses during the early twentieth century, furnished material for the article "Looking Backwards–Round the 'Houses' with Brun Campbell," which was published in the June 1949 issue of *Jazz Journal*. The second half of the manuscript, though, is an entirely separate, unpublished, work, the tale of young Brun's encounter with the beautiful, beguiling Madam Lillian.

Ragtime in the Red Light Districts

Many stories have been told about the generosity of the people who resorted in these places, and along this line is a tale of a young and beautiful brunette who ran a dance hall and bar in Indian Territory during the oil boom. Her name was Lillian, and her place was out at the edge of town. It was very popular, owing to the beautiful girls who worked for her. She never stood for any rough stuff in her establishment, and would not tolerate drunks. She kept the men at arm's length, for to her the business was just that: "Business."

I had occasion to visit her place one night with a bunch of young fellows who had hired me to go along and play piano for them. One of those boys was the son of a millionaire oil man and threw away his dad's money as though it were water. Of course he was welcome in the saloons and gambling houses of that booming oil town.

Lillian had a fiddler and a piano player who were very good at dance music but didn't play much ragtime, and the young fellows I accompanied were crazy about ragtime. Upon our arrival there, the millionaire's son asked if I might furnish the music for them to dance to. Lillian agreed on condition that he bought the place for the night—which he proceeded to do, at a cost of one thousand dollars.

Another casual thousand-dollar payout? Did wealthy people go around then handing out the equivalent of $25,000 for a night or two of piano playing? Maybe they did. Those times didn't become known as The Gilded Age for nothing. And if a piano player could pull in a thousand-dollar fee for a night's work, the same payment for rental of an entire establishment comes to sound pretty credible.

During the evening's festivities, Lillian and I became friendly, she leaning on the piano and singing in a liquidly beautiful soprano while I played. The party finally broke up, and as we were leaving she said to me in a low voice: "Come back again; I like your playing."

Several nights after that Eddie Leonard, the minstrel singer, who made the song "Ida" famous, was in town with a minstrel show. He and I went out to Lillian's place. Eddie fell for her without success, and even sang Harry Von Tilzer's old song to her: "I'd Leave My Happy Home For You." She invited us into a private parlor where there was a piano, and she and Eddie sang some of the popular tunes of the day. They really performed beautifully together. She was dressed in blue velvet and her diamond rings and necklace brought out all the radiant loveliness in her. I thought: What a beauty for some man! She came over and sat beside me on the piano bench and whispered in my ear, "I'm awfully blue. Get rid of your friend and come back as soon as you can."

Eddie and I went up to his hotel and had a few drinks and then bid each other good-bye. (I never saw Eddie after that). I at once called a cab and went right back to Lillian's place, where she was waiting for me. I asked what was on her mind and she said, "Kid, I want you to help me spend $80,000, and we'll start right now by going out to the Gambling Club. I'm fed up with this place and the kind of life I have to lead. I've got to get away from it or I'll go crazy."

Eighty-thousand dollars? A cool two million in today's purchasing (or gambling) power. Even in oil boom times, could an Oklahoma madam in the early 1900s really have put away that much money?

Eddie Leonard was a first-rate minstrel. Though people of later generations associate Eddie Cantor with "Ida," it was in fact Leonard who popularized the tune, which he composed in 1901.

I was stunned. I could hardly believe what she had said. She told me she had a buyer for her place and was going to sell out, and would give me the full details of what she had planned on the way to the club, which was seven miles out in the country. With that she called her car, and by the time she was dressed it had arrived. She told the driver where to take us, and on the way, she started to tell me where I fit into the picture, but didn't get to finish her story.

I had heard that she was quite a gambling woman, but didn't realize what a plunger she was until the next morning. When we arrived at the club the dance hall was crowded, and people were standing at the gaming tables trying their luck. We danced a few times and then Lillian made a bee-line for the roulette wheel. She gave me $500 and told me to spend it. So I went over to the crap table where it was soon gone. Lillian broke the club and also won the deed to it, which she later turned over to a committee of citizens for an orphanage home, with her best wishes. In the course of a few days she made me this proposition: She said, "I like you; you're good looking and play a fine piano, and you're swell company. I want you as my manager and nothing more to help me spend every cent I have. We will travel on the same pullman trains and stop at the same hotels, but we'll occupy separate sleeping quarters. As long as my money lasts, I'll pay you $2,000 per month and expenses. What do you say?"

For a moment I couldn't speak. Finally I told her that I loved her, and I couldn't understand why she wanted to spend all of her money. She said she loved me in a way, too, but we could never be more than friends and when the time came she would tell me why. I agreed to her proposition, and at times during our trip around the country I thought she was falling in love with me, but how wrong I was! For in Denver one morning over breakfast she said, "Here's where you and I separate. What money I have left I am giving to you, for I just received a telegram from the man to whom I am engaged, and I am going to join him in Maricopa, California. He's a millionaire oil man and my first kid sweetheart."

They were married in Maricopa and later moved to Fort Worth, Texas, where he had extensive oil interests. I saw her nine years later and she looked as beautiful as ever, the only difference being that her hair had turned snow white.

In Paul Affeldt's article, "The Saga of S. Brun Campbell," published in the January 1988 issue of *The Mississippi Rag*, the author wrote that Brun had told him privately "he'd essentially stopped playing professionally about 1908 and became the favorite of a famous madam. Though he didn't say who or where, the locale intimated seemed to be around New Orleans. Apparently, the lady didn't really want him performing publicly on piano, preferring to keep him as something of a pet, and including him on her travels (all expenses paid) for some time. His reticence as to writing about this part of his missing history may be understandable, considering his home life during the time I knew him (not allowed to play ragtime on his own piano, in his own house). I firmly believe that Brun, faced with this negative attitude from his family, passed over 30 years in his autobiography for the sake of conjugal harmony."

But that's not quite the way Brun tells the story. Though he did not specify the name of Lillian's establishment (if Lillian really was the lady's name), nor the name of the town whose edge harbored the place, or the name and location of the gambling club, he does give us some specifics: he and Lillian split up in Denver; she went to Maricopa to meet her fiancé; they eventually settled in Fort Worth; and nine years later, her hair was "snow white." It would be interesting to know where and how Brun happened to run into her, nine years after the joint excursion, and specifically whether the reunion might have been the consequence of a piano-playing engagement.

Brun's reference to Lillian's club as having been located in Indian Territory is consistent with his adventure having antedated his first marriage, which took place in June 1907. Oklahoma, patched into existence from Indian Territory and Oklahoma Territory, became a state in November of that year.

It's striking that Lillian referred to her fiancé as her "first kid sweetheart," the same term Brun used repeatedly to refer to his first wife, Taffy. This might have been a widely used figure of speech at that time, or Brun could have been engaging in a bit of verbal laziness, possibly misquoting what Lillian actually had said.

Might Brun have tossed a bit of embellishment into the tale here and there? Any storyteller would have been sorely tempted, and most would've given in.

* * *

From the halls of prostitution to the solid home of the desirable but very respectable hometown girl. At different points in *When Ragtime Was Young*, Brun told us his first "kid sweetheart" in Arkansas City was nicknamed Taffy, and according to a short article in *The Arkansas City Traveler* and a marriage certificate, she was also his first wife. Brun confirmed this in "My Girl Taffy," a short narrative I found among his papers. In the process of writing the brief but heartfelt piece, Brun revealed a good deal about himself. Taffy clearly was the love of Brun's life, and though he did marry her, he eventually lost her, under disturbing circumstances. The tone and content of "My Girl Taffy" suggest he never really got past that loss.

"My Girl Taffy"

It was at the Second Ward School [in Arkansas City] that I attended, and met my first kid sweetheart when I was about fourteen. She was a beautiful natural blond with blue eyes and peachy complection, and a figure that was all curves. She was the 'beauty' of the Second Ward and the Belle of the town when she was sweet sixteen, and believe me I had plenty of competition among the young men of the town. Every one called her "Taffy" on account of her beautiful blond hair. Taffy knew how to keep the young men guessing who courted her. When she was eighteen she had developed into a most beautiful creature of the fair sex, and it was at this period of her life that I commenced to get uneasy about me being 'head man' with her. Her father was the yard master of the Santa Fe RR and her mother was determined that Taffy should marry a doctor there. But she was true blue to me for I was the apple of her eye. Regardless of my playing ragtime piano in taverns through the country, and the gossip among the long hairs of the home town about me and my career, and believe me those old gossips sure dished it out. Some of their scandalous gossip was true, but most of it was false. But my girl Taffy let it all go in one ear and out the other, and all through my early ragtime days she stood by me through all the gossip and trouble I had. I was snubbed by the long hair church people of the town, and her father beat me up at one time for seeing her, and tried every way he could to break up our courtship. The younger generation of the old home town were for us but the older generation was not as broad minded, and my ragtime career was to much for them. I was the 'Campbell Kid' to them, who was sure to wind up in the penitentiary leading the life I was. So while the gossip was still 'red hot' we decided to get married. So I bought Taffy a wedding ring and we finally got her parents consent to the marriage. We were married June 6th, 1907 at her parents home, and when the word got around that little village about our marriage, 'That Done It.' Tongues commenced wagging among those old long hairs. Our marriage was the talk of the town and when those old hypocrites met us any place, they were all smiles and wished us a long and happy married life with a shake of the hand that reminded you of a piece of ice or a dead fish. Well, Taffy and I left the old home town and moved to Tulsa, Oklahoma and I gave up my ragtime career completely. We were very happy for about four years when I noticed a change come over her; she became extremely jealous of me without any foundation whatever. We commenced to have our first quarrels. In one of those quarrels, she packed her things and went home to her parents. I saw her several times after that. We tried to patch things up but it was no go. We still loved one another but it was not made for us to get along. At our last meeting we parted with tears in our eyes. I never saw or heard from her again after that.

I went to San Francisco, California and it was there that I learned of her death through a boy-hood chum that she had died of a broken heart in 1914, two years from the time I last saw her. On her death bed she had asked for me. Some years later I married again to a fine girl and we have three fine grown daughters. Naturally at times I think of Taffy who stood by me when the going was 'ruff.'

This piece was written during the 1940s, some forty years after the events, and the regret and longing in Brun's tone are unmistakable. It's interesting that despite Brun's penchant for chronological inaccuracy, he reported the date of this marriage down to the day. The marriage certificate and a newspaper account bear him out.

However, Brun told several interviewers during the late 1940s that he had married in 1908, and given up public appearances at that time. Was this a straightforward failure of memory, or was it, for some reason known only to Brun, a willful misrepresentation? Odd that his remembrance was off by one year in so many interviews, but was right on in "My Girl Taffy."

There's an intriguing aspect to the Taffy story. Brun wrote that he'd met his "first kid sweetheart" at school, when he was "about fourteen." Brun was born in 1884, so he would have turned fourteen in March 1898. And although both he and Taffy (whose real name was Ethel Bertha George—no wonder they called her Taffy) were recorded as being 23 on the marriage affidavit and the marriage certificate, this clearly was not the case as regards the bride. According to multiple sources (Taffy's obituary, 1910 U.S. census records, ancestry.com genealogical records, and records at Riverview Cemetery in Arkansas City, where Taffy is interred), her birth date was April 29, 1889. So why was she recorded as being five years older on the official marriage records? Even at eighteen, she was not only legal, but by standards of the time, she might have been considered by some to be creeping up on old-maidhood.

Was Brun's "first kid sweetheart" really only nine when he met her? And eleven when Brun's family moved to El Reno, and the boy, to his great regret, was compelled to leave her? And all of fourteen during Brun's visit in 1903, when he and his friend took potshots at the Scott Joplin silver half-dollar? It certainly looks that way.

Brun did seem to have a taste for younger females. His second wife, Lena Louise Burrough, whom he married in 1913, was eighteen at the time. (Brun would've been 29, but is recorded on the marriage certificate as being 27.) And his third wife, Marjorie May, whom he married on March 29, 1921, was thirteen years younger than he.

There are other inconsistencies in the Taffy story. The squib in the *Arkansas City Traveler* states that the newlyweds went off to live in Oklahoma City, but Brun wrote that they relocated from Arkansas City to Tulsa, and multiple documents exist to place Brun in Tulsa between his first marriage and 1925. Also, the *Traveler* reporter wrote that Brun's hometown was Joplin, Missouri, and the marriage license carries the same piece of misinformation. Though The Kid well might have played piano in Joplin during his wandering years, no record exists to prove or suggest that Joplin was ever his official residence. Very likely, he talked about Scott Joplin then as much as he did in his later life, which was constantly, and the *Traveler* reporter and the clerk who wrote the marriage license might have misunderstood.

It appears that Brun's and Taffy's marriage lasted less than three years. The 1910 U.S. Census has two listings for Brun in Tulsa, in different, though nearby, locations. The first listing has "B. Sanford Campbell" and "G. Ethel Campbell (wife)" as lodgers, with B. Sanford being 26 and G. Ethel, 21. A second listing includes only S.B. Campbell, roomer. In the same year, the census records for Arkansas City list Taffy as both Ethal Campbell and Ethal George, married, and living with her parents and sister.

On April 24, 1911, Taffy (as Ethel B. Campbell) filed for divorce in Cowley County, Kansas, District Court. The papers are distressing both in content and execution; it's difficult to believe a legal document could have been so carelessly written. The plaintiff claimed she had been "a faithful, chaste, and Affectionate wife," but that "the defendant, although an able body man and well calculated to support her, has failed, negated, and refused to supply this plaintiff with the necessities of life, and has squandered his money on riotous living and upon him self, and that during all said time plaintiff, together with the aid of friends and relatives, has supported herself." A second cause of action specified that the defendant had "been guilty of extreme cruelty toward the plaintiff ... to wit: That he has cursed her and applied to her word epithet which should not be placed in this plaintiff's petition and has frequently assaulted and chocked and beaten her; has threaten to kill her, frequently, and that his conduct was such that she was compelled to leave him for fear he would either maim or kill her, and that such conduct has continued for many months prior to the time she was compelled to leave him." Brun did not appear at the hearing, and the divorce was granted on September 8, 1911.

In such a situation, it would be a mistake to give full credence to the assertions of either side. Given the attitudes of the time, when wives were considered to be pretty much the property of their husbands, it might have been necessary for Taffy's attorney to state charges in as extreme a manner as possible, both to obtain any judgment at all, and to maximize the terms of that judgment in favor of his client. But it would be hard to believe the claims of physical violence were totally without foundation. A man who seemed to have gone to lengths to avoid physical disputes with men turns out to have been a wife-beater? Not an unheard-of association.

But so much for Brun's assertion that their problems were rooted in Taffy's becoming "extremely jealous of [him] without any foundation whatever." He did claim to have left Bowling Green to avoid any "entangling alliances" with the beautiful brunette in the confectionery store, then found himself "homesick for [his] sweetheart, Taffy," so he hauled himself back to Arkansas City for a visit. On the other hand, there's the story of Miss Lillian, but all in all, and especially considering the mores of the time in regard to the ways young men might reasonably sow their wild oats, there are no indications of wandering eyes either in Brun's writings or in any pieces that were written by others about him. True, he might have consciously omitted such details so as not to put them before the eyes of Marjorie May and his daughters, but considering the way he bragged about his pianistic talents, he probably wouldn't have been terribly reticent to report, perhaps in a wink-wink manner, an adventure or two he might have enjoyed as a stud. His frequent references to missing Taffy suggest he was faithful to her, at least in his fashion—which in the end might have clashed with her fashion, but therein lies the problem. How much really is known about Taffy's fashion?

Not a whole lot beyond Brun's claim that she was drop-dead gorgeous and a faithful correspondent. Brun didn't even mention her real name in his short article. But she had been the Belle of Arkansas City, the daughter of an important man, quite possibly someone we would now call a princess, and despite her claim in the divorce papers that there had been "no fault on her part," it's easy to imagine that her ideas about what might constitute the "necessities of life" could have differed significantly from Brun's opinions on the subject. She married at eighteen, moved away from her family and friends to another state, and found herself living in a rooming house as opposed to a fine home in a prestigious neighborhood. Perhaps she became homesick, even depressed. She could've decided that Brun up close and working as a barber was not nearly as entrancing as he had been, leading a romantic life as a piano player in low places. In a serious life dispute, a claim of no fault on the part of one of the parties is rarely justified. It's interesting that the marriage of Taffy's younger sister, Marie, to an Arkansas City contractor, also ended in divorce.

For all Brun's famous garrulousness in his later years, he seems never to have told anyone about either Taffy or Lena Louise, or even that he'd been married to anyone other than Marjorie May. Was he trying to convince his (at the least) third wife, that she had been his One and Only? But if so, why would he have put "My Girl Taffy" into any form of tangible evidence? Perhaps Marjorie May might have been complaining about the time and money he was spending on his ragtime revival work, and Brun, in a moment of pique, scribbled the story down, telling himself he didn't care whether or not she knew about Taffy, that Taffy had been his first and real love, and he'd been unfortunate to have lost her.

The divorce papers further illuminate a probable explanation for Brun's characteristic storytelling inconsistencies. The fact that he likely did resort to physical violence of some sort against his wife would cast considerable light on his overall behavior, specifically his impatience, inability to effectively organize a complex project, and perhaps his way of relating to his family in later life. Billy Bigelow, in Rodgers and Hammerstein's *Carousel*, is a prime example of such a man, to whom people and events appear in black and white, and are either good or bad, one or the other, *at that moment*. These men often claim, with great shows of remorse, "I *love* her–I don't know what happened. That wasn't really me." Which probably is a sincere comment, at least for that particular moment. Such men usually demonstrate considerable narcissism, feeling they are somehow special and entitled.

Brun wrote that he heard of Taffy's death in 1914, while he was in San Francisco. He makes no other mention, written or in interviews, of a second trip to the City by the Bay, but there's no reason to disbelieve the statement.

As only one possibility, Brun might have wanted to expose his second bride to the wonders of California. But in any case, history does not bear out Brun's friend's attributed cause of Taffy's death, which occurred on August 2, 1914. In the midst of a long hot summer, where both heat-related fatalities and the presence of typhoid fever were mentioned in the *Arkansas City Traveler*, Taffy succumbed to a moderately prolonged illness with periodic recoveries and relapses, the characteristic story for typhoid, a very dangerous disease in those pre-antibiotic days. Four years of heartbreak might have been a contributory factor, but no more than that.

Taffy was interred in the community mausoleum in Arkansas City's Riverview Cemetery; her parents rest in adjacent crypts. It happened that my visit to Ark City (as the residents call it) in 2012, to look into details of Brun's early life, took place during the first week of June, right after Memorial Day, and most of the crypts in the mausoleum were still decorated with one or two white and/or yellow flowers. Taffy's crypt, however, sported a magnificent display of red and white blossoms, held together by a ribbon with "Remembrance" across it. Ninety-eight years after her death! Who ordered this unique tribute? And when? According to cemetery authorities, there is no mechanism for ongoing or permanent tributes; displays are placed privately by families and friends. There's *got* to be a story here.

* * *

When a man trades a piano for a wife, there are going to be major changes in his existence. The Campbell men thought big, and settling down in Tulsa to cut hair is not exactly the stuff from which fame and fortune spring. Beyond his marital troubles, the energetic twenty-three-year-old groom was in for a number of surprises—most of which he did not handle terribly well—in the years to come. But that's no reason to dismiss his importance and accomplishments in ragtime.

Let's take a closer look at Brun Campbell and his activities after 1907.

II

When the Ragtime Kid Grew Old

Interlude

We know little about Brun's activities between his first marriage and his all-consuming re-entry into the ragtime world during the 1940s. His written statements in *When Ragtime Was Young* answer some old questions, but replace them with at least as many new ones. The Kid told many people that when he married Taffy, he stopped playing ragtime, and did not so much as "touch a piano" between then and the early 1940s, let alone play professionally. But if—as he wrote—he really did play for both Gordon Lillie ("Pawnee Bill") and the outlaw Henry Starr around 1920 or 1921, he hardly could have been totally inactive on the keyboard during that quarter-century. And if he actually was in San Francisco in 1914 when he heard of Taffy's death, he most likely would have been supporting himself by playing piano there. In any case, it's difficult to reconcile either the supercharged young itinerant pianist or the frenetic elderly ragtime revivalist with a guy who spent some thirty-five years quietly cutting hair and trimming beards.

Various records place Brun in Tulsa between 1910 and 1925. The 1910 U.S. Census included two entries for Brun at residences not far from each other, one as a married man, one as a solo boarder. Both entries listed Brun as a barber. Also in that census, Ethel Bertha George Campbell was listed as living in her parents' home in Arkansas City. There is no evidence of children born of this marriage.

The 1912 Tulsa City Directory showed Brun working at the Congress Barber Shop and living at Shields Rooms, no address specified. The 1913 City Directory had "S. Brun Campbell" working as a barber at Hodges and Clement, with rooms at 119A East Second.

On May 14, 1913, Brun married Lena Louise Burrough of Fort Smith, Arkansas. This marriage apparently lasted about five years, since the 1914 and 1918 City Directories included Lena in Brun's listings: in 1914, the couple lived at 119A East Second, and in 1918, at 50 N. Gillette Ave.

In 1917, all the Campbells must have been in Tulsa. Lute, Lulu, and younger-son Harold were living at 119A East Second, the same address Brun and Lena occupied at least through 1914. Harold's draft registration form, filled out in Tulsa on June 5, 1917, specified that he worked as a salesman for L.E. Campbell and that he was married. However, no wife for Harold was mentioned in the 1917 Tulsa City Directory.

Brun registered for the draft in Tulsa in 1918. The certificate specified he was a barber and married, but his wife's name was recorded only as "Mrs. Sanford B. Campbell." Considering the 1918 City Directory entry, the wife must have been Lena.

There is no entry for either Brun or Lena in either the 1919 or the 1920 City Directory, but in the U.S. Census of 1920, taken in Los Angeles in early January, Brun was listed (as "married"), along with his mother, father, and brother. However, according to City Directories, in 1921 and 1922, The Kid was back in Tulsa, working as a barber, first at the Kennedy Barber Shop, then at C.W. Hodges, and living at 628 N. Boulder. In neither year was a wife listed.

In 1923, "S. Burnson Campbell," at the same residence, was again working at the Kennedy Barber Shop, and had acquired a wife named Marjorie M. The couple was further listed in 1924 and 1925, first living at 219 E. Seminole Avenue, and with Brun working at the Gill and Rubottom barber shop. The following year, they lived at 303 West Zion, and "S. Branson" worked in Paul Rubottom's barber shop.

Marjorie May Gibson, probably Brun's third wife, was definitely his last. The U.S. Census records of 1930 and 1940 stated they were married twelve and twenty-two years earlier, respectively, which would indicate their wedding had taken place in 1918. Also, according to the U.S. Census, their eldest daughter, Dorothy, was born in 1918, then Louise in 1923, and finally Yvonne Patricia in 1925, all births having occurred in Tulsa.

But these waters are more than a bit muddy, and at least some of the mud had to have been intentionally stirred. No marriage records for Brun and Marjorie May have turned up, but Brun's entry in the 1951 edition of *Who Is Who In Music* included the information that he married Marjorie May Gibson on March 29, 1921, and that the couple had two daughters. In addition, Dorothy's daughter's birth record stated that her mother's maiden name was Johnson. This, along with the five-year interval between the births of Dorothy and Louise, the evidence that Brun's marriage to Lena lasted until at least 1918, and the fact that Marjorie May did not appear in the Tulsa City Directory in conjunction with Brun until 1923 make it likely that Dorothy was Brun's stepdaughter. In an e-mail to me, Dorothy's daughter stated, "I'm not related in any way to the Campbells. He just happened to be married to my grandmother. I did not know him and I do not have any information about him." There's a lot more between those lines than there is in them. It's interesting that near the end of *When Ragtime Was Young,* Brun wrote that he and Marjorie May had "three beautiful grown daughters," but the *Who Is Who in Music* volume specified the number of daughters as two. Perhaps whatever caused the apparent Campbell-Johnson schism occurred between the writing of those two articles.

To further confuse the matter, one of Lute Campbell's poetic ventures which he seems to have submitted for publication specifies Miss Dorothy Campbell, not Miss Johnson, at Brun's Crestmore address, as contact person for the author. Did Brun at some point adopt Dorothy, and give her his surname? And why did Brun and/or Marjorie May apparently falsify census information as to their wedding year?

The last Tulsa City Directory entry for Brun was for 1925, and it appears likely that he and his family left Oklahoma for California in the latter part of that year or in early 1926. A 1951 feature article in the *Venice Evening Vanguard* included the information that Brun had come to Venice in 1926, and had been the proprietor of the City Hall Barber Shop for all those twenty-five years. In a 2009 conversation, Yvonne Patricia Campbell said her parents had moved to the West Coast on the advice of a doctor who suggested that the better climate would cure their youngest child's asthma. Patty (as she said her father had called her) also mentioned the drying-up of jobs in Oklahoma as a secondary reason for the move. In 1930, voter registration records (Brun registered as a Republican, Marjorie May as a Democrat) showed the Campbells living at their long-term residence, 715C Crestmore, in Venice, a multiplex constructed in 1924, with some 750 square feet of living space per unit plus a separate garage in the rear. Not a great deal of elbow room for five people, but only a short, pleasant walk to Brun's barbershop.

Venice has a fascinating history. The city formally opened on July 5, 1905, after extensive preparation by founder Abbot Kinney, a New Jerseyite who, like Patty Campbell, had come west for relief of asthma. Kinney envisioned his city as a center of high culture and uplift, and the stage he set was impressive and unprecedented, including the building of a scenic lagoon and six miles of canals, construction of lovely villas, and setup of a carefully planned business community. Before long, though, it became clear that public taste dictated a culture somewhat lower on the scale than Kinney had planned. Ever the pragmatist, he yielded to the inevitable, and before long, Venice boasted a major Amusements Pier and a midway composed of exhibits from the 1904 St. Louis World's Fair. The city became a center for the early movie industry; many of those silent entertainments were filmed in Kinney's city.

By the time Brun and his family arrived, though, Venice had begun to deteriorate. Sanitation was poor, and the streets had not been designed to accommodate the progressive influx of motorized vehicles. To accommodate the new mode of transportation, the city filled many of its canals and the lagoon, and constructed streets and parking areas. In addition, southern California politics were becoming increasingly complex, raising various civic management problems. After oil was discovered in Venice in 1929, deterioration accelerated, and before long the once-magnificent urban monument to high culture had become a sleazy, slummy little burg, devoid of any pretense to art-consciousness. So it remained until the 1950s, when writers and artists of the Beat Generation took over the place, paving the way for Venice to become what it is today, a center for the post-sixties crafts and art crowd.

Of course when a desirable location goes to hell, rents plummet, and this could have been at least part of what drew Brun to settle his family in Venice. But he must have felt right at home in the Venice of the 1920s, 1930s, and 1940s. Delores Hanney put it well in her 2012 book, *The Lure of a Land by the Sea*: "Even in a place as well-stocked with eccentrics as Venice, Sanford Brunson Campbell stood out as a character."

Brun's claim that he spent his days between his first marriage and 1943 cutting hair and shaving faces, and never even thinking about ragtime and piano playing is not supported by memories of some of his friends during those times. According to Paul Affeldt, as written in his 1988 *Mississippi Rag* article, "The Saga of S. Brun Campbell," "Norm Pierce of Jack's Record Cellar wrote that he first ran across Brun as early as 1932 and even then Brun had a piano in his shop and played exceptional ragtime. The same comment has been made by at least a couple dozen other friends of Brun through the years." In a 1971 article in *The Rag Times*, Floyd Levin recalled that ragtimers who lived in the Venice area came regularly to Brun's barber shop to listen to him go on and on about the old St. Louis ragtime pioneers. Levin made mention of how vivid Brun's memories were of the performers who entertained clients in the pre–1900 St. Louis sporting districts.

Over the years, Brun told and retold an elaborate story about a customer who came into his shop one day in 1930, and paid for his haircut with the very same silver half-dollar Scott Joplin had given his Ragtime Kid in 1899. Here's the way he wrote up that story in some of the versions of *When Ragtime Was Young*:

I had forgotten all about ragtime and the old days, when on May 1st, 1930, a customer came into my place of business, made a purchase and paid for it with the half-dollar that Scott Joplin had given me back in 1899 and that was used as a target back in Kansas when I went frog hunting in 1903.

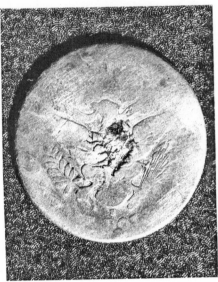

The upper two images represent Brun's lucky 1897 half-dollar, showing evidence of the alleged shot from Brun's pistol. Some authorities point out that the marks do not line up front to back, which would invalidate Brun's claim that the deformation resulted from a bullet. However, I think it's likely that the half-dollar was not secured in place before the shot was fired, such that the force of the bullet might have rotated it sufficiently to cause an oblique entry-to-exit path. Or, in hammering the coin at the blacksmith shop, Brun might have reshaped it such as to separate the entry and exit marks (Brun Campbell Archive). The lower two images show a less-worn and undefaced 1897 Barber half-dollar (courtesy Randall P. Holder, Rare Coins).

My half-dollar lucky piece had returned to me! I could hardly believe my eyes, but there it was. As I kept looking at it and turning it over in my hand, the panorama of my life as a ragtime pianist unfolded before me. That half-dollar seemed to say to me:

"Why don't you write some stories about Scott Joplin and early ragtime history, and sell them to magazines and newspapers?" It seemed to say: "Don't you think it would be nice to make a recording of Scott Joplin's Maple Leaf Rag just as he taught you to play it back there in Sedalia, Missouri, in 1899, and use the revenue from these sources to erect a memorial over his grave for what he did in the field of American music?"

Maybe so, but historians have questioned the authenticity of both the coin and the story, to the point of labeling it baldly outrageous. At least one interviewer wrote that Brun told him a customer in Oklahoma had returned the coin, but in many other interviews and articles, The Kid specified Los Angeles and 1930. Certainly, he could have faked it—hunted up a twin to his old good-luck piece, fired a bullet through it, then hammered it flat. In any case, it's worth noting that Brun's alleged homing-pigeon coin was in fact of the proper design for 1897, a "Barber Half-Dollar" (note that bit of irony), designed by Charles E. Barber, and produced from 1892 to 1915.

In the last analysis, the story is neither provable nor disprovable, nor is it critical to any subsequent events. There's no evidence that Brun took any action on Joplin's behalf until some thirteen years later. If we give credence to his own running account, his serious work as a ragtime revivalist began in 1943, likely fueled by the ragtime and trad jazz performances and recordings of bandleader Lu Watters and pianist Wally Rose. This is Brun's description of the defining moment in his crusade for syncopation, from the final passage of *When Ragtime Was Young*:

It was in February 1943, thirteen years later, that a little incident happened on a musicial program on the Hal Nichols Radio Station KFOX, Long Beach, California.... It was a recording of Scott Joplin's Maple Leaf Rag that Mr. Nichols played on his 6:30 p.m. program. I happened to hear it, and I didn't like the way it was played, and wrote and told Mr. Nichols so. He wrote me back a nice letter agreeing with me that it was not played as it should be. I had explained to Mr. Nichols who I was and he invited me over to Long Beach to spend the day with him. He was a most gracious host and we spent some very happy hours going over the old Ragtime Days. I give my friend Hal Nichols, the owner of KFOX, credit for the encouragement he gave me.

While I never erected a monument of granite or bronze [over Scott Joplin's grave] I did much better than that.

I have memorialized him in a more lasting and useful way. I have accorded him a place of honor in the Library of Fisk University at Nashville, Tennessee, beside George Gershwin and other notable men of music; for I have turned over to them the finest collection of Scott Joplin's musical works and other items pertaining to his life's work in the world: namely, thirty-eight of the forty ragtime hits he wrote, his picture, a picture of his piano, his opera "Treemonisha," pictures of the old building at 119 East Main Street, Sedalia, Missouri, that housed the Maple Leaf Club named after his "Maple Leaf Rag."

Was the Club in fact named for the Rag, or was it the other way around? It's not possible to say with certainty. There's no evidence that the Maple Leaf Club existed before November 1898, and if Brun really did sight-read from a pen-and-ink manuscript titled "Maple Leaf Rag" earlier that year, that would speak for the Rag's primacy. Tom Ireland, a reliable reporter, also claimed that the Club was named after the Rag. But Arthur Marshall and Sedalia newsman W.H. Carter stated the opposite. Ragtime historian Ed Berlin brings up a third possibility: maple trees were plentiful in Sedalia, and many place names in the city included the word, "Maple." So the names of the Rag and the Club might have originated independently and coincidentally. A less romantic idea than either of the other two, but probably more accurate.

In early 1943, Brun was 58, getting to that point in life where people begin to think more seriously about the meaning of their time on earth. *Brun Campbell: Joplin's Disciple* was right on as a title for the CD reissue of Paul Affeldt's landmark recording of Brun at the piano. Recognition was always of prime importance to The Kid, and he might well have realized that the sole hope for Brun Campbell to be esteemed, whether ante- or postmortem, would involve a ride on Scott Joplin's coattails.

Brun had a tough row to hoe. To say that in 1943, Scott Joplin was forgotten would be a serious understatement. Though the composer received significant mention in Charles Edward Smith's 1942 publication, *The Jazz Record Book* (including the comment, "his work is the best tribute to the ragtime era..."), he was otherwise severely ignored by music critics and historians. His compositions were not even cited in scholarly works by black musicologists, and he received only brief mention in the 1930 book, *Tin Pan Alley*, where author Isaac Goldberg claimed Joplin should be remembered for carrying on the work of Ben Harney, a (white) popular entertainer of the 1890s who claimed to have

Opposite: **Brun, probably in his early to mid-forties, in a photo that was stored with the license for his barber shop (Brun Campbell Archive).**

originated ragtime. Goldberg further thought Joplin's music would only "find completion in the [novelty ragtime] of Zez Confrey." Erno Rapee's *Encyclopedia of Music for Pictures*, published in 1925, contains titles of thousands of musical pieces for theater pianists, organists, and orchestras to use to accompany silent films. Under "Rags" are sixty-two titles, some genuine classic or folk rags, but even though—ironically—Hal Nichols' "Black and Blue Rag" is among those present, not a single listing of a work by Scott Joplin is included. The first significant, scholarly commentary on the composer did not appear until the latter part of 1944, when *The Record Changer* published an article with the apt title, "Scott Joplin: Overlooked Genius."

Whatever his motivation, Brun Campbell was clearly and prominently in the vanguard as he labored to persuade the world that Scott Joplin was among the greatest of American composers. Joplin's work helped educate and inspire a chain of performers and historians, from Ann Charters to Joshua Rifkin, who put out landmark recordings and kept the genre current until movie producer George Roy Hill used the music in his 1973 film, *The Sting*. At that point, popular and classical performers and audiences went wild for Joplin. He was the hottest composer in the United States. Honors rained down, culminating in an award of a Bicentennial Pulitzer Prize for his lifetime of accomplishment in American music. And ragtime established a lasting base of operations among music lovers around the world.

But did Brun really believe his donations to Fisk would memorialize Joplin (and maybe Campbell) more effectively than a monument in a cemetery? No way to know, but careful consideration of a situation was never Brun's way. Probably a combination of pressure from people who'd sent donations for the statue, and persuasion on the part of Brun's friends and writing mentors finally convinced The Kid he had no choice but to accept the unavoidable, and make the most of it.

Let's see what came to pass as The Ragtime Kid grew old.

1943: Hal's Pal

The defining moment in Brun Campbell's ragtime revivalist decade appears to have occurred directly after the 1942–1943 holiday season. The specific impelling factor was a man named Hal Nichols; the catalyst was radio.

Today, even among ragtime enthusiasts and fans of early twentieth century American popular music, Hal Nichols (1885–1953) is virtually unknown. But according to his obituary in the *Long Beach Independent*, in 1943 he was "as well known as their next-door neighbors to listeners throughout Southern Cali-

Brun in later years at the piano, his hat at the rakish ace-deuce angle he favored. Friends at the time remarked that Brun was rarely if ever seen playing piano without his fedora. His face, viewed in profile, is a study in quiet concentration and enjoyment (Brun Campbell Archive).

fornia." A one-time band musician, dance instructor, and composer of popular tunes, Nichols picked up early on the potential of commercial radio. In March 1924, he founded station KFOX in Long Beach, then supported and furthered his venture by selling radios. He remained active in broadcasting until his death in 1953, at age 68.

Nichols' long-running golden oldies music show, which aired at 6:30pm, was variously called "The Memory Room" and "Hal's Memory Room," and was co-hosted by Nichols' cats, Nosey and Barty. In 1942 and 1943, with war anxiety at its zenith, the music of a generation past was emotional comfort food for an older Southern California audience. Brun never made it clear whether he was a Memory Room regular or just happened to tune in one particular evening, but in any case, he heard a recording of "Maple Leaf Rag" that displeased him, and he sent a letter to let Hal Nichols know of his displeasure.

Nichols' reply was dated January 11, 1943, and referenced Brun's letter of January 6; when Brun wrote in *When Ragtime Was Young* that he'd heard the offending performance in February 1943, he was off by a month. Nichols began his letter by sympathizing with Brun: "…nowadays it's indeed hard to find anyone who knows the history of Ragtime, not alone playing it as it should be played or even talking about them. I know how you feel about the 'Maple Leaf Rag.' The recordings that I am able to get are played too fast by the orchestras and very few of them know the type of syncopation that was used in the old time Ragtime Tunes."

The radio host went on to make sure Brun knew that he, Nichols, had written "quite a number of rags myself" (the actual number published seems to have been three), that he had known such ragtime luminaries as Charles L. Johnson and Egbert Van Alstyne, and that he was in possession of "a tremendous library of old sheet music and a very large library of orchestra music." He went on to say that when he was writing songs, "George Norton was my lyric writer, and I was there when he wrote … 'Melancholy Baby.'" (The music for that enduringly popular tune from 1912 was written by Ernie Burnett; it's not clear just what Nichols meant to imply by his having "been there.") He sent Brun copies of two of his "new songs," "Gee, Ain't The Roses Sweet," published by Nichols Music in 1942, and "I'll Await You, Dear," both copyrighted in August 1942. (A 78 rpm recording of the two tunes, played by Hawaiian steel guitarist Sol Hoopii, carries on its printed label the message "Compliments of Hal's Memory Room.") Nichols closed his letter by saying he'd like to meet Brun and talk over "some of those old tunes and their writers."

According to Brun, that Long Beach meeting did take place, though the date was unspecified. Nichols, a "gracious host," gave Brun considerable encouragement in the direction of re-popularizing Scott Joplin's music and reacquainting the world with the composer's genius. Apparently, the two old-timers decided to meet again, but on May 10, Nichols wrote Brun a short note, apologizing for having been too busy to come to Venice.

In 1943, Income Tax Day was March 15. Brun's Form 1040 for 1942-based taxes showed a gross income of $2,505.90, which netted him $1,989.51; his tax payment was $102.90. His rent for the year on the small space at 711 Venice Boulevard was $180, and his only two listed dependents were his wife, Marjorie May, and his youngest daughter, Patricia, who would have turned seventeen in July 1942. Apparently, the older (step)daughter Dorothy, 24, and the middle child Louise, 19, either had moved out by then or were earning enough money to disqualify them as dependents.

Preserved along with the tax return form were several unbound sheets categorizing Brun's month-by-month barbershop expenses, including city and state taxes, water and electricity, newspapers, trash collection, scissors-grinder fees, and supplies such as soap, powder, antiseptic, and various brands of hair tonics, from Fitch's to Wildroot to Lucky Tiger. Between October 1942 and the end of his life, more than ten years later, Brun also kept day-by-day and week-by-week records in small pocket notebooks, documenting his income and expenses to the penny. The loose sheets and notebooks verified his usual income to have been about fifty to sixty dollars a week, sometimes as much as seventy, but sometimes as little as twenty. Such compulsive record-keeping was conspicuously at odds with Brun's overall helter-skelter approach to life. Since in 1943 he wrote and copyrighted a tune titled "That Hard-Hearted Revenue Man," it's possible he'd been subjected to some rough treatment by an IRS auditor at about that time.

In early spring, Brun was off and running on another correspondence front. He contacted Lottie Joplin, probably in the belief that his hero's widow would be a valuable ally in his budding campaign. Whether Lottie actually had been married to Scott Joplin is still open to question; no one has ever been able to find a marriage certificate. But she was certainly a shrewd businesswoman who routinely presented herself as Mrs. Scott Joplin, and between the composer's death in 1917 and her own in 1953, she was in possession and control of a great deal of Joplin's work, published and unpublished. Many black entertainers of the time boarded at Lottie's brownstone home on West 138th Street in New York City; the house also functioned with little attempt at concealment as a brothel and a resource for old-time musicians looking for party girls.

Ragtime historians tend to regard Lottie as a less-than-reliable informant, and review of her correspondence with Brun suggests that at least to some extent, The Kid's reputation for playing fast and loose with reality came from his having taken questionable information from Lottie on faith, then passing it along in his own articles and interviews. In her letters, Mrs. Joplin comes across as a skillful wheedler and cajolery artist whose approach to a mark was more effective than Brun's frontal sledgehammer assault. They both pursued the same goal—revival of Scott Joplin's reputation—but in the pursuit of capital for that venture, Mrs. Joplin clearly had had her eye out for dollars that might happen to come her own way in the process. And while Brun certainly craved recognition and acclaim, he did not profit personally. Throughout his quest, he repeatedly put his own financial situation on the line.

The first letter to Brun from Lottie Joplin came in an envelope dated March 18, 1943, and read:

Dear Sir,

I am Mrs. Scott Joplin, regarding your letter about Mr. Scott Joplin's Numbers and Photograph, I wish you would make your point more definite then I would know what it is all about. I also have an opera, in three acts. Would like very much to have it Produced.

Thanking you in advance,
Respectualy,
Mrs. Scott Joplin
P.S. Pardon the delay. I have been sick.

Mrs. Scott Joplin
212-W. 138thSt.
N.Y.C.

In her next correspondence, dated April 7, Mrs. Joplin promised to mail Brun some of Joplin's rags, but did not specify whether she intended to send original manuscripts, copies of manuscripts, or commercial sheet music copies. Mrs. Joplin went on to say: "The Opera I spoke to you about, is a Ragtime Oprera in three acts. Words and music by Scott Joplin. The Whole Opra is orchestrated. [She did not indicate whether that meant the score included separate instrumental parts, or instrumental parts were merely notated in it]. If you can get some one to produce it, I am sure it will be a money making proposition because it is beatiful. Thanking you in advance."

A third letter, written on April 16 (which arrived postage due, one cent), confirmed that Mrs. Joplin was sending Brun commercial music sheets, not original manuscripts: "The 'Euphonic Sounds' that I spoke to you about, I went to the Publisher but was unable to get it…. They were out of copies."

Then, on June 26, Mrs. Joplin wrote: "sorry we couldnt make any deal's with the Studio's, the only thing we can do is to keep on plugging. The 'Maple Leaf Rag' is turned over to the Melrose & Co.

I will try and get a more complete story of the life of Scott Joplin…. I am sick, and anything you can do will be greatly apricated."

More, on July 23: "I am sory about the delay of answering your letter, but I have not been well…. I went down to the Office of Mr. Simons, and he said you had wrote to him regarding the 'Maple Leaf Rag.' Of course you know he has that number and he said if you know where you can make money with it go ahead and he also said he would get in touch with you at once have you heard from him?"

Another letter in Brun's collected correspondence, dated December 8, 1943, clarified Mrs. Joplin's references to Melrose and "Maple Leaf Rag." George Simon, vice president of Melrose Music Corp., wrote Brun: "In reply to your letter of December 4th, please be advised that any usage of "MAPLE LEAF RAG" would have to be handled by Melrose Music Corp. with the producer of the film. We could not put ourselves in a position to permit anybody to negotiate for any of our copyrights." Here we have the first in what was to be a long series of negative responses to Brun's naïve and clumsy inquiries.

During the summer of 1943, Brun began to cast a wider net. A letter dated July 15, from California State Senator Jack B. Tenney, professed enthusiasm for the "very excellent idea" Brun had proposed in his letter of July 6. But the senator apologized for not being "in a very good position to undertake this very worthy project," since he did not then hold "any official position in the Musicians' Union other than being a member of Local 47." He suggested Brun redirect his inquiry to the president of the Los Angeles Musicians' Union, and added the assurance, "I certainly am in full sympathy with what you have in mind and will be very happy to lend my support in any way possible." A short, handwritten note on September 20 from Edward W. Bailey, president of the Los Angeles Musicians' Protective Union, promised "a letter soon ... regarding 'Joplin,'" but there was no such letter in Brun's preserved correspondence.

Later in the summer, Brun launched a campaign directed at the Common Man and Woman, which clarified his goal considerably. Among his received correspondence were fifteen letters mailed in Venice between September 27 and November 4, 1943, all indicating that Brun had sent requests with suggested boilerplate to his friends and neighbors for them to use in support of his efforts to construct a monument in Scott Joplin's memory. Respondents who wrote to endorse the idea of memorializing "the old Negro musician, Scott Joplin" included a retired auto dealer, beauticians who operated a shop next door to Brun's barber shop, a past president of the Woman's City Club of Venice, a liquor dealer, the owner of a variety store down the street from the barber shop, an employee of the Los Angeles Department of Health who had been a musician at the Lasky Studios, a police captain, a postman, a physician, and two accountants, one of whom had once been The Great Kellerman, Novelty Magician.

Brun likely hoped to squeeze a bit of operating capital from his correspondents, but most of them sounded comfortable with providing no more than moral support. Only one of the signatories, Paul J. Naas, is listed in Brun's ledgers of advance subscribers for his embryonic book and purchasers of his Memorial "Maple Leaf Rag" and "Twelfth Street Rag" recordings. Naas, a druggist whose shop was at 701 Venice Boulevard, down the street from Brun's barber shop, bought a Memorial Record for two dollars.

It's interesting that among Brun's business papers is a prospectus from Mr. Naas, describing a work of art "in watercolor portraits, pen and ink sketches, and text, ALL DONE ENTIRELY BY HAND." Naas specified the creation to be "a complete and concise illustrated history of the 19th century, covering the important events in every field of human endeavor, chronologically arranged on large cards, each recording the happenings of about six years' time." It included "more than seventeen thousand (17,000) names of people prominent during the nineteenth century..., ninety-five (95) wars in detail; all important inventions, discoveries, natural phenomena, disasters, great undertakings, etc." The artist happened to be a Mr. Alphonse Naas, of Mulhouse, France, "who spent the waking hours of three (3) years' time in completing this extraordinary work, which to be fully appreciated, MUST BE SEEN." Paul Naas closed by setting the value of the piece at $10,000. Perhaps the druggist was proposing a 1943 version of Win-Win, offering Brun a commission if he could get ten thousand dollars from a third person.

During the early fall, Brun moved to capitalize on his association with Hal Nichols. Between September and early October, Nichols wrote several letters, all begging off a visit to Venice but thanking Brun for sending materials to be used in a radio show which would focus on W.C. Handy, the Father of the Blues, and composer James A. Bland and his best-known work, "Carry Me Back to Old Virginia." Nichols promised Brun recognition for his contributions, and thanked him for sending a photo of Scott Joplin that Brun had received from Lottie Joplin.

Nichols' letter of September 30 contained a paragraph which indicted Brun had by then become serious indeed about financing his promotional activities. The radio host wrote: "I note what you say about black opals and other semi-precious stones. You must have had a very fine collection. I am indeed sorry that you had to dispose of them because from experience, I know that these things become almost alive and each and everyone is like a friend. I know I would hate to dispose of my collection. Practically all of mine are mounted in tie pins."

October brought a spate of correspondence from Nichols, culminating in a letter sent special delivery on October 16, with a copy of the script from the *Memory Room* show of October 14. The middle third of the script (which is reproduced in Appendix 4) consisted of a "Story Behind the Song," in this case, the song being "Carry Me Back to Old Virginia" (also referred to in the script as "Virginny,") by James A. Bland. Nichols noted that this tune had been

Bland's "first published song, and a great hit from the beginning. In 1902, Bland was honored by having that song chosen as the state anthem of Virginia." Nichols thanked Brun, "a musician himself, having specialized in ragtime piano in the old days, for providing information about the song and its composer," then added, "Mr. Campbell is at this time actively engaged in a movement to erect a memorial to Scott Joplin for his many contributions to the field of music, and we wish him all success." In his accompanying letter, Nichols wrote, "As a rule, I do not use a script of this kind, but in as much as you wanted it, I did write this one up in advance and used it." The radio host autographed the script, with the message, "I dedicate this script to my friend B.S. Campbell." A Freudian analyst would have something to say about that inversion of Brun's initials.

On the last page of the script, Brun wrote in pencil:

Mr. Nichols was raised in the music business. His parents, having owned the leading music store in Denver in the early day, Hal himself is a thorough musician, and composer and wrote such old hits as 'Harmony Rag,' Blue and White Rag, etc., and was a very popular orchestra leader on the Pacific Coast and in Denver Colo. Mr Nichols is a close friend of Paul Whiteman having both grown up in Denver, where Paul's father gave Mr Nichols his first violin lessons, and I thank Mr Nichols for this autographed script.

Why Brun wrote this and how might he have intended to use it are open to question. Possibly it represented the basis of a plan to impress some deep pockets that Nichols, a writer of musical hits, a popular orchestra leader, and a close friend of the famous Paul Whiteman, had used Brun's material on the air and praised his efforts to memorialize Scott Joplin.

Brun sent a petition (not specified as to how many signatures it included or whose) to Nichols, asking that the host repeat the Bland Song Story on a subsequent broadcast. Nichols put him off gently, replying that he might do that, but not "too soon."

Another indicator that Brun was scrambling for money came in a letter from Nichols on October 18: "I have your letter of October 13 telling me about the violin. I appreciate the interest you have taken in this, but I am not in the market for violins anymore. I have several very fine ones in my own collection."

Brun must have looked to Nichols for help or advice regarding publication of the songs he was writing at the time: on October 27, the radio host wrote to Brun, "it is quite a problem to get a number published by any of the first rate publishing houses, but I'm going to loan you a book ... entitled 'So You Want to Write a Song...' it is strictly on the up and up. I wish you would read it and then return it to me.... If I were you, I would not attempt to deal with anyone outside of the legitimate Music Publishers or legitimate recorders and I would copyright the numbers before releasing them to anyone. This only costs $1, but it gives you a world of protection." Since Nichols wrote again to Brun on November 3–all of six days later—that he had received back his book, Brun's reading of the material had in fact been prompt, but very likely less than thorough and thoughtful.

In autumn, with his campaign gathering steam, Brun wrote to W.C. Handy, the "Father of the Blues," who was based in New York City. The composer of such hits as "Memphis Blues" and "St. Louis Blues," Handy was just short of seventy years old, the head of Handy Brothers Music Co., Inc., (whose slogan was "Genuine American Music"), and a major figure in American music and the world of black art. As such, he was a natural target for Brun. Throughout a long, extensive correspondence, Handy's letters show him to have been highly egotistical and a tireless self-promoter whose favorite subject, far and away, was himself. He was at times bristly on the matter of race relations, understandable in that he was a member of the first generation of freeborn southern blacks, and during his younger years had suffered considerable social and financial damage at the hands of whites. His letters to Brun show gratification at Brun's professional regard for him; he often addressed the barber as "Friend," and in October 1944, inscribed a copy of his book *Unsung Voices Sung* "To San Brunson Campbell, with sincere appreciation." But he did not come across as sincere in any inclination to support Brun's campaign: he admittedly retained a suspicion of white men who wanted money from him. In addition, black musicians had long looked upon Scott Joplin, the man who'd first opened the door for black composers to attain respectability, as seriously outmoded. If he was remembered at all, he was considered something of an embarrassment.

Handy's first letter to Brun was dated October 16, 1943, and began, "I have been a very busy man as you will see by the clipping from the 'Memphis' paper … so that I have not given attention to the matters uppermost in your mind…. I hope in 1944 to be able to give some attention to memorialize Scott Joplin." Handy wrote that he had recently finished correcting proofs for his upcoming book, *Unsung Americans Sung,* and specified that "while this book does not include Joplin it is a very necessary piece of work, so necessary in schools and libraries and for programs during Negro History Week and Music Week."

Handy next wrote on October 27, enclosing a letter from Dave Elman, formerly his colleague and at this time the host of the highly popular *Hobby Lobby* radio show (and later, an author and teacher of medical hypnosis), urging widespread radio recognition for Handy's upcoming 70th birthday. Handy's accompanying letter to Brun thanked him for "the many good things you have to say about myself and my people," and implied that the activities leading to his upcoming birthday celebrations "will enable me to enlist more names in your efforts when the time comes." Though Handy went on to say he felt "so keenly the desire to serve you in Joplin's case," there was no evidence in any later correspondence that the time for that particular desire to evolve into action ever did arrive.

Lottie Joplin's next letter to Brun, on October 27, reported that she'd been sick and "had to go away, for my health." She thanked Brun for "itercieding about the medal for my husband," and requested Paul Whiteman's address so "when he make's the broadcast about my husband, I would like to have a copy of it."

Mrs. Joplin followed up this letter with another on November 10, telling Brun: "I think your doing a wonderful job. The review of the broadcast was very good, and the way things are going I think we'll get some results very soon. I wrote to Mr. Whiteman thanking helping in the broadcast." Then she thanked Brun "for all you have done," and closed by asking, "Have you heard any thing more from Mr. Roosevelt's secatary about the medal?"

There's no evidence of any involvement by Paul Whiteman in the October 14 *Memory Room* broadcast, or in any broadcast to honor Scott Joplin. It's possible Brun stretched a point for Mrs. Joplin's benefit, or that she misunderstood something Brun wrote or said during a telephone conversation. Considering what he scribbled on the script for the October 14 show, he might have told her he intended to try to capitalize on Nichols' supposed close friendship with Whiteman. But the only letter in Brun's files from the famous bandleader was written on September 27; it reads, "Thank you for your letter of the 22nd.... I will be glad to keep your originals in mind and will be glad to write you again should I find at any time that I can make use of them." The context of the letter suggests The Kid had mailed the self-proclaimed King of Jazz copies of popular tunes he'd written, hoping that might open doors to big-time publishing houses.

As to the mention of the president's secretary and the medal, the fact that a particular individual was of high standing in music, politics, business, or society never did seem to give Brun pause. His mail campaign included many prominent persons; in 1945, he sent a (complimentary) copy of his "Maple Leaf Rag" Memorial Record to President Truman. He could well have written to Roosevelt to seek support for the graveside memorial, then received a pro forma reply from the president's secretary, and been unable to resist sharing his hope and enthusiasm with Mrs. Joplin.

Shortly after writing his October 27 letter to Brun, Handy suffered a fall and sustained a severe head injury. Brun apparently inquired after Handy's condition, which brought a reply on November 4 from the composer's brother Charles. Charles Handy wrote that his brother had "improved immensely" but was "still critical." Brun must have inquired as to whether Dave Elman might be of help in the Joplin campaign, because Charles Handy replied, "Relative to

Mr. Elman, I know that he is very busy with his own business, and just through share of mutual friendship of my brother for the last twenty odd years is the main reason why he wrote the letter to the radio stations in behalf of my brother. Mr. Elman is not a musician nor a composer, and I doubt if he has ever heard of Scott Joplin, and inasmuch as I am more acquainted than my brother of what Mr. Elman has done I can candidly say, I would not want you to bother him using us for your entree."

Whether Brun respected this injunction is uncertain, but he did write a birthday tribute to Handy, which he sent to Elman, who acknowledged it as "beautiful," as did Charles Handy in a November 22 letter. In that letter, Charles Handy also wrote that his brother, who was recovering well, would "be pleased to receive a record of the broadcast of your friend Mr. Nichols."

Brun's campaign widened progressively as he sought help from prominent Americans in many walks of life. His files contain three polite letters from Wendell Willkie, the Republican presidential candidate in 1940; two of these were dated November 11 and December 3. In one, Willkie thanked Brun for "the radio script and original poem," and added, "Your offer to be of service is indeed gratifying. You may be sure I will keep you in mind."

On November 19, Nichols wrote to Brun to report that he'd received Brun's poem, "The Father of the Blues," and had thought it was "very good." Nichols went on to ask, "How did you enjoy Don Blanding Wednesday night? Everyone here thought he was great. At any rate, he is a very fine fellow and a very likable man."

Don Blanding was a popular American poet during the early twentieth century. *Vagabond's House*, his book of rhymes published in 1928, was a bestseller. Nichols' praise seemed to have inspired Brun's muse; on the back of the envelope in Brun's handwriting was written:

> I liked to hear Don Blanding recite his poetry with such grace ["such" was crossed out].
> But somehow, I think he is out of his place
> I believe he should be in the pulpit
> Learning sinners how to say grace.
> Of course he could slip in his poetry in the right place.
> And watch the sinners raise up their faces.
> And hear them say: ["say": was crossed out and replaced by "shout":]
> Keep on brother
> We're going places. And before his sermon is through.

Both Brun and his father wrote doggerel with rhyming schemes only approximate at best, and metrical patterns that had the feel of a potholed dirt road. In a November 26 letter, Nichols thanked Brun for his "very clever" poems, and said that he had sent "the one that you enclosed for Blanding on to him."

Throughout the year, Nichols' letters indicated that Brun continued to try to interest him in material for Song Stories, including one for "Alexander's Ragtime Band." The radio host put his new friend off with tact, all the while assuring him that his letters and inquiries were always welcome.

Lottie Joplin's last 1943 correspondence to Brun appeared at first to be no more than unsigned Christmas greetings, but opening the card revealed the message, "Thank you for the bit of dough. Mrs. Scott Joplin." Brun's gift likely reflected both Mrs. Joplin's skill at squeezing dollar bills from turnips, and the tender heart of an outwardly crusty old piano player; it stood as an indication of future developments in the relationship between the two.

On December 21, W.C. Handy dictated a letter to Brun, thanking him for his concern, and letting The Kid know he had "received letters from all over the world and especially in the United States from all races and creeds stating that they were praying for me; their prayers were answered, as I am on the road to recovery…"

So 1943 came to an end on a hopeful note for both Brun and Handy.

1944: Pedal to the Metal

As Allied Forces took Anzio Beach, Brun Campbell moved his operations into high gear on a number of fronts. The outcomes of the early encounters, though, must not have gone to the old ragtimer's liking. A January 6 letter from Hal Nichols informed him that there was no piano in *The Memory Room*, there was "no open time whatever," and "every minute was sold to some sponsor," so he'd have to say no to Brun's offer to play ragtime on the radio show. Then, on January 13, W.C. Handy, still recovering at home, wrote to "My dear friend" to say he had not received "the record that you made," told Brun how pleased he was at having received recognition on both Hal Nichols' recent radio programs and another broadcast from Florence, Alabama, Handy's birthplace. The composer also complained that people were plotting to take advantage of his illness to steal his music, then provided a lame excuse as to why he and his brother had not responded to Brun about the two tunes The Kid had sent them for possible publication. Handy's daughter Lucile told Brun he could check back with her father after his return to the office later that spring.

But on January 26, Lucile Handy sent back Brun's songs, explaining that her father was still under doctor's orders to rest, and that the office was overloaded, so that "you would be done an injustice to keep your manuscripts there until he returns to the city."

Also on January 26, Nichols wrote, "I had the record made ... a very fine transcription made on glass, and when we were packing it to send to Mr. Handy we had an accident while we were putting this record in the regulation record box. We got the wrong pressure on it some way and cracked it which, of course, ruined the whole thing. I thought.... I was going up to the record studio and do another one, but I didn't have the material and I knew I couldn't get in the mood to ever do another one as well as I had the first.... I wish you would tell Mr. Handy exactly what happened as I would not deceive him for the world."

The recording in question probably was of the *Memory Room* show in which Handy had been mentioned. However he might have felt about Nichols' buck-passing, Brun followed through. On February 16, Handy wrote Nichols a fawning letter of thanks, saying, "S.B. Campbell was kind enough to send me your letter relative to the broadcast and transcriptions." The composer enclosed an autographed picture of himself, and sent a cc to Brun.

On February 6, a letter came from an editor at *DownBeat*, with the proof for a short article Brun had sent, titled "Monument to Negro 'Rag' Composer Urged." The article, scheduled for the February 15 issue of the magazine, did not carry an author byline, but described Brun's efforts to memorialize Joplin, and stated "he has received letters of encouragement from W.C. Handy, Paul Whiteman, Hal Nichols of Station KFOX, Wendell Willkie and the Duke of Windsor." Interestingly, Brun wrote, "After leaving Sedalia in 1899, Joplin had his first hit, 'The Maple Leaf Rag,' published." Another example of carelessness, since others of Brun's writings reveal that he knew the first small number of copies of Joplin's breakthrough tune had been published in Sedalia before John Stark finalized his relocation to St. Louis and put out a different edition with a different cover; copies of this "Sedalia 'Maple Leaf'" today bring more than $1,000 from collectors of sheet music. Moreover, Joplin's decampment from Sedalia to St. Louis did not take place until 1901–*after* publication of "Maple Leaf Rag."

A letter from Nichols dated February 15 was no more encouraging than his January 6 message: "I don't know as I can put on an entire night of ragtime any more." But Nichols promised to "include one of the old ragtime numbers now and then." In the envelope were two membership cards, one certifying that S.B. Campbell was a listener to "Melodies 'N Memories from HAL'S MEMORY ROOM." The other card, bearing a photograph of Nichols' cat and "co-host," Nosey, certified that S.B. Campbell was "a member of the KFOX KUTE KITTEN KLUB, NOSEY NICHOLS, Chief Purr." Nichols also wrote that he was sorry to hear of an accident that had left Brun with a sprained wrist and arm, and wished his friend a speedy recovery.

On March 1, Nichols told Brun he did not yet know the date of the "Scott Joplin story," for his radio show, and wished his friend luck in interesting "one of the big [music] publishers ... in your dream, because even if you do not make any money off of your numbers, it ... would help a lot toward building the memorial for Scott Joplin." Two days later, Nichols wrote further that he was "working on the Scott Joplin story," but was hampered by "the fact that the material is quite limited and I don't have a lot about him in my books." Nichols went on to say he'd let Brun know how to obtain a recording of the Joplin broadcast, that it would cost him ten to twelve dollars, and that "the cheapest way would be to have it on a 33–1/3, but you probably don't have any way of playing it, as phonographs run at 78."

At the bottom of that letter, Brun wrote in ink, "PS I gave all the story after I recieved this," and on March 7, Nichols answered, "Thank you very much for the added material which I just received from you this morning about Scott Joplin ... the material came in very handy." The radio host promised to use it two weeks later.

Nichols kept his promise. On March 20, he sent Brun a three-page transcript of the second half of his March 17 program (Appendix 4), devoted entirely to the history of Scott Joplin and his music, and Brun's efforts to pay homage to the composer. Nichols clearly drew heavily upon the materials his friend had sent him, noting that Brun had received encouragement in his project from W.C. Handy, Paul Whiteman, "and even such personages as the Duke of Windsor and Wendell Wilkie." The host read over the air, "Oddly enough, as Mr. Campbell tells me in a recent letter, 'Maple Leaf Rag' was not Mr. Joplin's favorite number. For his own amusement, the composer used to play his 'Easy Winners' and his 'Fig Leaf Rag,' numbers quite different from the famous 'Maple Leaf.'"

Nichols then spoke an amazing line: "Mr. Campbell ... at one time had a complete collection of all [Joplin's] compositions, including the original pen and ink manuscript of 'Maple Leaf Rag.' But in 1922, Mr. Campbell's mother accidently burned these ... valuable manuscripts which, because of the death of the negro composer five years before, can never be replaced. Among these selections were copies of the more than thirty ragtime hits written by Scott Joplin and the music to a three act operetta written entirely in ragtime."

Could that possibly have been true? Aside from a brief mention in a subsequent letter to Brun from Nichols, and an offhand comment by jazz historian Roy Carew in a letter later in the year: "Too bad you lost your collection of Joplin's rags, and those manuscripts," there is no other reference to the tragedy in any ragtime anecdote or historical account. If it really did happen, why did Brun never mention it in anything he wrote or in his interviews? It's the kind of story The Kid would have relished passing along to anyone who'd listen. But it's extremely unlikely that he could have made off with any of Joplin's original manuscripts during the time of his association with the composer, and in later years, Lottie Joplin famously guarded her husband's works. Most likely, Brun fed Nichols and Carew a whopper and then decided it might be wise to limit further distribution of the story. Perhaps a family member or a knowledgeable friend called him on it. In any case, aside from the material, the three-page transcript of the show is impressive, giving a good deal of information about Scott Joplin's early days, claims and facts confirmed later that year by Carew and Fowler in their *Record Changer* articles.

A March 2 note from Lottie Joplin told Brun she was "glad you heard from Mr. Handy, and I think with his help and Mr. Whiteman's and others we will get very good results.... I am still on the sick list."

March 15 brought a change in definition from the IRS: The Individual Income Tax Return was now The Individual Income and Victory Tax Return. In other words, failure to file or evidence of cheating might be taken as evasion of support for the war effort, a serious charge at that time. Brun's 1943 income had been up from the previous year: $2,926.55 gross, $2,328.32 net. His rent remained at $180 for the year, and he paid taxes of $165.59.

On March 22, Nichols responded to Brun's letter of two days earlier, that "came zooming into my office," to say, "The letter you got from the Melrose Music Corporation seemed to open the way for some cooperation, and if they are smart, they will give you a lot of help because there is no doubt but what the 'Maple Leaf Rag' is due for another hit period and you are the boy who can do it if they will just give you the chance." Nichols further offered any help he could give Brun in his work on the Joplin memorial. A day later, he wrote to say he thought Brun should get a business card to let "people know you are the originator of the Scott Joplin Memorial idea," and that "you should adopt the phrase 'Father of Ragtime,'" both ideas to make sure "someone else" would not "grab the glory" from Brun. But on March 28, in answer to Brun's "very nice letter of March 25," Nichols wrote that Brun should not use Nichols' name with his own on the business cards and letterheads, since "it is utterly impossible to join you in this worthwhile project because I am so terribly busy and have so many things to do.... You are entitled to all the glory as it is your idea." Brun did follow through by making up letterheads and envelopes, but unfortunately he let a key misspelling slip by: "sponser."

In an April 11 query letter returned to him by a representative of the recipient, the old barber's ambition, hustle, sincerity, and naïveté are laid out in equal, large amounts. Writing in longhand, using his characteristic green ink, Brun nearly strained himself trying to interest Cecil B. deMille in making a "picture around the life of the negro, Scott Joplin." Brun gave deMille some historical background regarding Joplin's life, and explained that if not for Joplin, "there would be no jazz, swing, Boogie Woogie or Blue Music today," and that Joplin's "ragtime opera in 3 acts … inspired Geo Gershwin to write *Porgy and Bess*. He also inspired Irving Berlin to write 'Alexander's Ragtime Band' in 1911." The third claim was probably true; the first claim, partially true; the second claim, almost certainly not true.

Brun went on to describe his efforts to honor the composer: "I have the memorial sketch which is beautiful, and have progressed to the realization of its erection, but the government will not release the bronze metal [until] after the war." Finally, Brun assured deMille he was certain Melrose Music, holders of the Maple Leaf copyright, would cooperate in any efforts to make a movie, and closed with reference to his letters of support from Willkie and Handy.

Unfortunately, but not in the least surprising, all the material came back promptly, with a curt letter dated May 24, from Sidney Justin of the Paramount Pictures Legal Department. Justin wrote, "This studio has made it an invariable rule that neither it nor its employees read or consider unsolicited literary material, gags, jokes, ideas, or suggestions of any nature whatever."

On April 14, Nichols wrote to tell Brun, "The best place to get recordings made … is at Eccles, 6235 Hollywood Blvd., Hollywood, California. They do most of my recordings and all the recording for the station. There are numerous others, but Eccles is very reliable."

Grass never grew under Brun's feet. He must have contacted Eccles instantly. On April 18, C.R. Alford of that company provided him quotes for 10-inch and 12-inch recordings, single-sided and double, single copies, duplicates, and "great quantity." On April 20, Brun wrote to Nichols to tell him he'd recorded "Maple Leaf Rag." Five days after that, Nichols wrote a letter of thanks for the copy Brun had sent him, praised Brun's piano work, and promised to play the record in a couple of weeks as part of an upcoming *Memory Room* show.

On May 10, Nichols followed up with a letter telling Brun to listen to his "'Maple Leaf Rag' story Friday night (which would have been May 12). It is quite a buildup for you personally." Mr. Alford assured Brun that Eccles would "record the song and the story and handle everything in proper order as per our conversation." An Eccles invoice of May 15 for recording and dubbing "The Story of Brun Campbell and 'The Maple Leaf Rag,'" and express-shipping copies to Brun, Paul Whiteman, and Lottie Joplin came to $10.09. (Brun sent $10.90, so Mr. Alford mailed him a check for 81 cents, with a polite letter of thanks.)

A May 5 letter from Lottie Joplin informed Brun that she had heard from "Mr. Brennier of the N.B.C. broadcasting Co.," and that he had "had a letter from you telling him about…. *Treemonisha*, and he wants to broadcast it … he said he wanted to rent the opera, and how much would I charge. I would like you to advise me what to do."

Unfortunately, in another longhand, green-inked letter, dated May 10 and sent to "Mr. Brenner" at NBC, The Kid again showed how poorly equipped he was for the task he'd set himself. He told Brenner that Lottie Joplin had just sent him "two of the books of her husband's opera *Treemonisha* to read and broadcast," and that Brun had advised Lottie to "deal with you on your terms," and that he "would not muddy up the water, for Scott Joplin was my friend." But then he proceeded to stir up at least a bit of muck by telling Mr. Brenner he had "written a story about Scott Joplin that no one else can write, because they never knew Scott as I did. I will give you this story if you Buy the rights from Mrs. Joplin for use in broadcasting *Treemonisha* or for a movie." Brun asked Mr. Brenner to listen to the Hal Nichols broadcast two days from then, to hear "about me and the 'Maple Leaf Rag.'"

On May 17, Handy wrote Brun to tell him that extreme work demands precluded his taking on Brun's two songs, and that the overload was primarily related to the upcoming publication of his book, *Unsung Americans Sung*. Handy was thoughtful enough to enclose a promotional circular for his book, which asked, "Why not order today? Introductory price $3.50."

Handy's next letter, dated May 29, was chockablock with complaints about the workload that a sick man needed to shoulder to properly promote his book, and "hoping that next week I can write a better letter to you and Mr. Nicholas." Handy enclosed a newspaper clipping of an unqualifiedly reverent recent piece from the *New York Daily Mirror* about Handy's life and work, which concluded with a quote from the composer's father, a minister: "Son, I'd rather follow your hearse than see you follow music."

Hal Nichols wrote again on May 31 and made several interesting comments. The radio host asked for clarification regarding the letter Brun requested him to write "about the network broadcast November 16 to 25 which is to pay tribute to W.C. Handy and Scott Joplin on November 24." Then he went on to thank Brun "for the 'Memory Room Rag' which you sent. I treasure it very much and it will remain in the front page of my MEMORY ROOM recording album."

This recording of "Memory Room Rag" seems to have vanished, along with the manuscript—if indeed there ever was a manuscript. Brun did not notate or even give titles to most of his compositions, and if Paul Affeldt had not recorded and titled them, they would likely have vanished from recognition long before Richard Egan transcribed them from the recordings.

On June 8, Handy wrote to tell Brun he was "feeling fit as a fiddle," and was grateful for Brun's friendship and "interest in me." He'd been listening to radio reports of the D–Day invasion, had performed "St. Louis Blues" on the trumpet for two admiring New York audiences, would shortly receive an award at the American Negro Music Festival in Detroit, had sold $1,460,000 in war bonds the year before, and was working at getting reviews and advance sales for his book, *Unsung Americans Sung*. Then he tossed in a brief apology for "not really answering your letter," presumably having to do with the songs Brun had been trying to get him to look over. But as if in compensation, if unintentional, for his extravagant self-absorption, Handy told Brun, "I hope you have heard from my friend Arna Bontemps at Fisk University..."

In fact, as of that date, Brun had not heard from Bontemps, but just a few days later, he'd receive a letter written June 12 that would prove highly important. Arna Bontemps (1902–1973), was librarian at Fisk University, Nashville; he was then working with Jack Conroy on a book about the black migration from the south that would be titled, *Any Place but Here*. Bontemps was a well-recognized scholar, historian, and writer of poetry, plays, fiction, and children's books, and a major figure in the Harlem Renaissance of the 1920s. Shortly after receiving his master's degree in library science in 1943, he was named librarian at Fisk, an institution known for its interest and involvement in black American roots music. He wrote to Brun:

Dear Mr. Campbell:

I am deeply grateful to you for your prompt reply to my inquiry about Scott Joplin. All that you said will be of help in my effort to piece together the story of this interesting and important composer. I'm returning herewith the two enclosed items which you were good enough to let me read, "Memories 'N Melodies" and "The Father of Ragtime Music."

"One other set of questions I would like to ask you before I go to work on my chapter. Can you tell me anything about Joplin's personality, his appearance, his manner of speaking, his dress, his general interests other than music? In short, what I lack now is humanizing data. Was Joplin fascinated by the colorful St. Louis life of the 90's? Did he like a good time? Did he wear the gay clothes which Mr. Handy tells me were the rule for musicians of the period? Or was he aloof and absorbed only in his music? Is it known what led to his insanity and what type of insanity it was?

I'll be doubly grateful if you can supply any of this information from your own memory of the musician. I would also like to know where Joplin is buried and what relatives, if any, survive him.

In a postscript, Bontemps added that he would be "glad to mention you in connection with the Joplin story," and requested "a page of material on your life, your experience as a ragtime pianist, and your acquaintance and association with Scott Joplin and others of his period."

The fact that a scholar of Bontemps' background and standing would have known so little about Joplin stands as an exclamation point to the degree to which the composer had been forgotten. In follow-up letters of June 21 and August 1, Bontemps thanked Brun for "the sketch of your own experience as a ragtime musician," and remarked, "If others had cooperated as well as you, I am sure my comments on Scott Joplin would have been adequate."

J. Russel Robinson was a prolific composer of ragtime and Tin Pan Alley popular tunes, including such hits as "Dynamite Rag," "That Eccentric Rag," and "Margie." In 1944, he was living in Los Angeles, and Brun approached him by mail regarding the making of a movie based upon the life of Scott Joplin. On June 17, Robinson replied that if Lottie Joplin would send the book for *Treemonisha*, he would see whether George Waggner, (a producer at Universal), might be interested, or at the least, might recommend it to another producer at the studio. Robinson mentioned that the wartime gasoline shortages prevented him from coming out to Venice for a visit with Brun; this might explain, at least in part, the extensive mail correspondence in those times between people living in the same city.

June 19 brought a letter from Sam Fox, of the Sam Fox Publishing Company, acknowledging receipt of Nichols' script of October 14, 1943, signed to Brun, and two of Brun's compositions, "Mama's Little Baby Doll," and "You Are the One I Want." Fox mentioned his friendship with Nichols, and the fact that he had published Nichols' "Harmony Rag" and "Black and Blue Rag" many years before, but the publisher was not optimistic about accepting Brun's music, because "we publish so few popular songs ... perhaps I could suggest some other publisher who might be interested."

On June 20, Nichols wrote Brun, "I am returning the letter which you received from Arna Bontemps which was very interesting. I know you can be of great assistance to her in the collaboration, [which] 'deals with Negro migration in the United States,' and especially that about Scott Joplin." As well-known and well-regarded as Bontemps was in the black arts world of the time, it wouldn't be out of line to question the depth of Nichols' familiarity with the field, given his reference to Bontemps as "her." But Nichols did assure Brun that he had "quite a program" planned around the recordings Brun had sent of "Maple Leaf Rag" and "Fig Leaf Rag," and that he was sure Brun would like it.

Lottie Joplin wrote to "My Dear Mr. Campbell" on June 23, thanking him profusely for all his work, and apologizing for not writing sooner because she'd had "a sick spell and had to go away." She also said she'd not yet heard from "Mr. Brenill of the N.B.C."

agreement + Contract. June-26-1944

Between Mrs Lottie Joplin of 212 West 138th St new York City N.Y. and mr Sanford Brunson Campbell of 711 Venice Blvd. Venice California, County of Los angles.

If the efforts of mr Sanford Brunson Campbell of 711 Venice Blvd, Venice California County of Los angeles are successful in promoting the life story of my late husband Scott Joplin. I mrs Lottie Joplin his widow of 212 West 138th St New York City N.Y. agree to pay said mr Sanford Brunson Campbell twenty five per cent (25 percent) of all moneys I recieve from the proceeds of said life story of Scott Joplin

Signed this day.____ date

Sanford Brunson Campbell

x mrs Scott Joplin

Brun's handwritten contract with Lottie Joplin to represent her interests in the sale of Scott Joplin's life story (Brun Campbell Archive).

On June 30, the Executive Secretary of the Song Writers Protective Association sent Brun a letter "on behalf of our member, Mrs. Lottie Joplin, with regard to the agreement you sent her dated June 26, 1944." The official wrote that "before Mrs. Joplin would agree to have you act in her behalf insofar as trying to sell the life story of her late husband, she would like to know if you are an authorized agent ... can furnish her with references ... and the usual percentage for an agent is 10 percent."

Brun must have been persuasive. On July 6, Lottie sent by air mail special delivery, at a cost of eighteen cents, a signed "Aggrement & Contract" (written longhand, in green ink), stipulating that she would "pay said Mr Sanford Brunson Campbell twenty-five percent (25 per cent) of all moneys I receive from the proceeds of said life Story of Scott Joplin."

A copy of the script for the July 12 *Memory Room* program came to Brun with the letter in which Nichols explained why he had not played Brun's "Memory Room Rag" on the show. Nichols wrote "just five minutes before going on the air I put the MEMORY ROOM RAG on the turntable and due to a very shallow cutting on the record and also due to a very light head on the phonograph, the needle skidded across the record and put a scratch all the way across which meant that there would have been a click clear through the record if I had played it. I ad libbed myself out of the situation ... as you can see from the original script I am enclosing.... I intended to play the number and talk about it.... I am very sorry this happened, but it is just one of those things."

In the script (Appendix 4), Nichols referred to Brun as "an accomplished musician" who had "learned ragtime piano playing ... from the originators of the music themselves," and that Brun's efforts to memorialize Joplin were "going very well ... and that a suitable monument to Scott Joplin will be erected as soon as materials are available after the war." Then the host mentioned Brun's "complete collection" of Joplin's manuscripts that had been destroyed by fire.

Later in the script is the passage Nichols had to ad-lib his way out of reading: "This recording is played by Mr. S. Brunson Campbell personally. It isn't an old number—in fact, it was written especially for this program—but it is done in exactly same style as the original ragtime. It is called the 'MEMORY ROOM RAG.' In the 'MEMORY ROOM RAG' you may notice a passage familiar as a passage in the '12th Street Rag.' This was originally written by Mr. Campbell in 1903 and later became a part of the other number. Just for old time's sake, Mr. Campbell incorporated it in the 'MEMORY ROOM RAG.' And, here it is a ragtime number composed especially in honor of the MEMORY ROOM program by S. Brunson Campbell and played by him, the 'MEMORY ROOM RAG.'"

Though "Memory Room" remains a lost work, Richard Egan suggests that another of Brun's compositions, "Reminiscences," could be a version of "Memory Room Rag," since the third strain of "Reminiscences" contains a familiar passage from "Twelfth Street Rag."

Finally, Nichols talked about Brun's quest to memorialize Joplin, "a serious musician of great talent." He mentioned Joplin's "three act opera, based on

Negro music and having as its theme the negro's struggle against superstition and ignorance," then went on to say that "with the consent of Mrs. Joplin, Mr. Campbell is in the progress of completing arrangements for this opera to be made into a motion picture. The name of the opera is *Treemonisha*..."

On July 26, Nichols sent thanks in advance for a double-sided recording Brun was going to mail to him. The radio host said he'd "be glad to use 'Dallas Blues' on the program in the near future." Two days later, Nichols told Brun he'd "received the recordings of 'Dallas Blues' and 'For Your Sweet Mama's Headin' for Another Town.' [a Brun original, copyrighted in 1943]. Both recordings are fine and they will be used in a program at a later date."

However, on August 4, Nichols wrote, "I'm sorry to tell you that I will be unable to run the recording of your song. I would like to but the policy of the MEMORY ROOM is ... iron-clad... and it would not be right to run any new tunes in it. At first, I thought I might be able to run your song in as an oldie, but on second thought, I find it not advisable. If you wish, I can return the recording to you and you could let Sophie Tucker run it on her own phonograph or you could go there and see that she actually listens to it. I know this is disappointing to you and believe me, I am sorry but the policy of the MEMORY ROOM comes first."

Reconsidering the omission of "Memory Room Rag," also a new tune, from the July 12 program—was that really due to a scratch on the recording? If so, could the scratch have been other than an accident? With an inflexible Nothing-New Policy, why didn't Nichols think of it a week before, when he promised enthusiastically to play Brun's tune on the air? In addition, in his letter to Brun of April 14, Nichols had mentioned that a woman from Santa Monica had brought in "the most wonderful recording of the 'Maple Leaf Rag' I have ever heard ... played note for note as the original 'Maple Leaf Rag' was written." Nichols added that the record had been cracked, "but I don't believe it will be noticed on the air," and "I will ... be playing it most any night now, and I hope you don't miss it." Unless the damage was limited to the edge of the record, outside the run-in groove, it's hard to imagine that a crack in a 78 rpm record would not produce an easily audible rhythmic click, at least as distracting as a scratch.

Apparently, Brun did try to sell the tune directly to Sophie Tucker. Ms. Tucker handwrote Brun a short letter, dated August 4, on stationery of the Beverly Wilshire Hotel:

My Dear Mr. Campbell,

Thanks for song and manuscript am returning same to you. Regret so much I cant use the song at all. Too tame as compared to songs I sing in nite clubs. Will try to listen in so will Mr. Shapiro if we are not tied up. [Ted Shapiro was Sophie Tucker's accompanist and music director, from 1921 throughout the rest of her career.]

Thanks

Sincerely

Sophie Tucker

Poor Brun. Having the Last of the Red-Hot Mamas reject his song as too tame for her act must have felt like a very low and well-aimed blow to the old Original Ragtime Kid's ego.

More than a month passed before another letter came from Nichols, this one dated September 8. It was a heartfelt appreciation for an act of kindness on Brun's part. Nichols' feline co-host Nosey had died the week before, and Brun had sent his friend a letter of sympathy.

This was followed by an envelope from Nichols, postmarked September 19, which contained only a one-page typed sketchy biography of Scott Joplin. On the envelope, in green ink, in Brun's hand, was written "Joplin's Biography," and at the top of the page, in blue ink, "Given to me by Mrs Scott Joplin June 11, 1943." This probably represented some of the material Brun had loaned to Nichols for the July 12 broadcast. (The biography is reproduced in the Short Pieces section of this book, as part of "Not the Best-Case Scenario: Scott Joplin and His 'Maple Leaf Rag.'")

September brought Brun his second important contact of the year, one even more significant than Arna Bontemps. Roy Carew (1883–1967) was a ragtime and early jazz historian who wrote prolifically on his subjects of interest. He lived in New Orleans between 1904 and 1919, the most glorious of the glory years, after which he relocated to Washington, D.C., to work at the Internal Revenue Service. Carew was a close friend and admirer of both Jelly Roll Morton and the great New Orleans pianist-composer Tony Jackson, and founded the Tempo-Music Publishing Company as a vehicle for Morton's work. In a letter postmarked September 21, and addressed to Mr. S. Brun Campbell, Venice, California, Carew told Brun he'd sent along a copy of The Record Changer which contained "the first installment of a little series on SCOTT JOPLIN, one of the greatest composers of genuine American music, as you know." (Carew was referring to the "Overlooked Genius" pieces.) The historian went on to say, "You must know a great deal about Joplin's early days, and I believe it would be of interest to the RECORD CHANGER'S readers if you would give them the benefit of your knowledge." He encouraged Brun to either submit an article to the magazine, or send the material to him, and he'd write it up. Like Bontemps, Carew also asked whether Brun could provide him information about Joplin's personal and professional characteristics. "Anything about his personal life and doings would be interesting."

Brun's many short and long written pieces dating from the mid- to the late-1940s can be attributed in great part to Roy Carew's encouragement and active participation. On October 4, Carew wrote that he'd received Brun's "several letters" and the articles, "The Father of Ragtime Music" and "Down Ragtime's Memory Lane." He promised to ask the editor of *The Record Changer* to publicize Brun's "efforts toward a memorial for Scott Joplin." He also asked Brun to "get together more information about Sedalia, about Joplin and Otis Saunders, and any other players there, more about the tavern where Joplin played…. Write about those boys, and if they played for entertainments, dances, etc.–little interesting items about the early days." Carew thought the readers of *The Record Changer* "can be interested in early ragtime players, particularly negroes. You see, the reason why Turpin, Chauvin, Tony Jackson, Jelly Roll and others are mentioned is that they got their names on published music. They [readers] never heard about the others."

Carew said he "collected a great many of the Stark firm's numbers, but never knew any of their writers. Was James Scott a negro? … Was Arthur Lamb a negro? He wrote some very fine rags, which Stark published." The historian sympathized that Brun had "lost his collection of Joplin's rags, and those manuscripts," and encouraged him in his efforts to get a movie company to do a film based on Joplin's life, and to persuade the American Society of Composers, Authors and Publishers (ASCAP) to do a Joplin memorial over the radio.

It's disorienting to read that in 1944, Roy Carew did not know the race of James Scott, who shortly became one of the "Big Three" of classic ragtime composers. In addition, the historian apparently merged the identities of Arthur Marshall, a black Joplin protégé in Sedalia and St. Louis, and Joseph Lamb, a white man who lived in Brooklyn, New York, who did indeed compose some very fine rags that John Stark published. Lamb's identity was not discovered until 1949, when Rudi Blesh and Harriet Janis tracked him down.

On October 7, Lottie Joplin wrote to thank Brun for having "the magazine" sent to her. This would have been a copy of *The Record Changer* with the first installment of the Carew-Fowler work on Joplin.

Though Handy had promised in a letter dated June 30 "to do the little things that might have a bearing on what you are trying to do with Joplin," his next letter, written on August 10, contained the comment, "The public draws on my time so heavily, that I do not have time to get around to see Mrs. Joplin as I had planned." With this letter, Handy enclosed a flyer for *Unsung Americans Sung*. And on October 16, he sent Brun an autographed copy of the book. (It's unclear whether the copy was complimentary, or Brun had paid the sales price of $3.50, plus shipping.) Handy also asked Brun to remember him to J. Russel Robinson (to whom Handy had also sent a copy of the book) and then concluded, "I would appreciate all the help you can give us in the matter of publicity on the book."

In a letter dated October 28, Handy launched a veiled assault on Brun's wallet, informing the barber that *Unsung Americans Sung* "is making for better racial understanding," and that "the thought comes to me that our book ... will make a delightful Holiday gift. You and your friends may be of the same opinion when you read the enclosed reviews."

Also on October 28, John te Groen, vice president of the Musicians Mutual Protective Association, wrote to Brun, thanking him for sending a copy of his Scott Joplin history, and explaining that "it is impossible for us to play records at our celebration," but "we are also enclosing an invitation for you to attend our FIFTIETH ANNIVERSARY CELEBRATION as our guest." This probably was a response to a request from Brun that they play his recording of "Maple Leaf Rag," and perhaps read his Joplin story.

In Roy Carew's next letter, written November 17, the historian told Brun that the December issue of *The Record Changer* would carry information about The Kid's promotional work, as well as the third installment of the Carew/Fowler series on Joplin. He asked whether Brun knew "anything about Scott Hayden, Arthur Marshall or Louis Chauvin.... I believe they were all negroes, and Hayden and Marshall must have been with him in Sedalia, at least part of the time. You ought to be able to get quite a bit of information about Sedalia from that old negro 'Moon,' who used to be a chum of Joplin's." (Extensive efforts have failed to turn up any record of Moon's presence in Sedalia, nor any historical reference to him.) Carew urged Brun to work up a narrative "to show that Sedalia was a sort of 'cradle of ragtime,' and tell a few anecdotes about the old town. You have already written me quite a bit of interesting material, and I will be glad to help on an article."

On November 27, Handy filled a page with exclamations of pleasure at the many tributes he'd received on his seventy-first birthday. Then he told Brun, "I donated all of our publications to the Fisk University, a Negro University– GEORGE GERSHWIN MEMORIAL." This thrown-off comment would later act as a seed planted in Brun's mind.

The next letter from Nichols was dated November 29, and referred to a letter from Brun written November 24. Nichols wrote, "I was glad to hear from you but don't think for one minute I am peeved about anything you have done because such is not the case at all. The fact of the matter is I was sick for quite a long time and I laid off my broadcasts for over two weeks and didn't think I would ever go back to doing them again but am feeling better now and I am up and at 'em. I would like to have the complete story of Scott Joplin in the *Record Changer* when it is finished."

Nichols went on in his letter to tell Brun he had acquired a new cat, Barty, for his show, and that "I also have a little boy named Johnny Caldwell that I use in the act. He is a very clever little fellow. I had to revamp the MEMORY ROOM somewhat to get Johnny and Barty in there, but it was essential that I have someone to work with." According to ragtime historian "Perfessor" Bill Edwards and other sources, Nichols was ill for approximately the last decade of his life, and needed to perform *Memory Room* shows from his home. This, together with Nichols' refusal to play Brun's new compositions on his show, probably accounted for the sharp falloff in correspondence between the men after 1944.

On December 11, Roy Carew wrote to tell Brun he'd shortly be receiving the December issue of *The Record Changer*. He asked whether Joplin had played "for white parties in Sedalia, do you know? I met a lady many years ago, who used to live in Memphis, and she told me when they gave parties they got Scott Joplin to play for them" and "if they could get Joplin, the piano was all the music they wanted. I believe that was in Memphis, but might have been in St. Louis." The historian also promised to "go over everything that you have sent me pretty soon now, and work up what I can on 'Sedalia, the Birthplace of Ragtime,' or something of that sort." ("Sedalia, Cradle of Ragtime," by S. Brunson Campbell and R.J. Carew, appeared in two parts in the May and June 1945 issues of *The Record Changer*, and was the first published material to carry Brun's byline.)

1945: A Shift in the Wind

1945 saw a major change in the direction of Brun's efforts to promote ragtime and Scott Joplin. He might have picked up on the message that his mail blitz for contributions to a Joplin Grave Monument Memorial Fund was costing him more in postage than he was receiving in contributions. In addition, he probably ran out of likely marks. The volume of incoming letters fell sharply during the final months of World War II, and, largely in response to Roy Carew's urging and encouragement, Brun began to put together short histories of the early years of ragtime music and its pioneer performers and composers for publication in jazz periodicals. Though his approach changed, it seems clear that at least for the time being, his goal remained the same. Perhaps he hoped that increased name recognition might bring in additional and larger contributions.

The first letter of the new year, dated January 4, came from Roy Carew. The substantiveness of Carew's letters stands in impressive contrast to Hal

Nichols' breezy superficiality, and W.C. Handy's all-consuming self-absorption. In that January 4 letter, Carew offered brief holiday greetings, than thanked Brun "for the information about Sedalia; I see that it was quite a town. As near as I can figure these young fellows that like hot music want to hear about the places the old boys played, the kinds of folks that went, and like something that sounds like adventure.... The most interesting part of his [Joplin's] story so far seem to be in Sedalia and St. Louis.... His actual life story or a story written around him would be good. For a picturization, I believe a story written around him would be better, because there are several points that aren't so well known about his actual life. It is strange that there wasn't more written and published about him before. There is another thing about picturization ... these pictures about early jazz, blues, etc., have to be mainly about the white players. If that is the case, the story based on Joplin would have to be written from that angle." Carew then promised to get to writing the collaborative Sedalia story shortly.

A particular comment from Carew deserves attention: "Well, if Mrs. J. doesn't tell you exactly when they were married it wouldn't make too much difference. Your idea may be right, negroes didn't worry too much over formalities. It doesn't matter a great deal."

This could be interpreted as racist and/or demeaning, but it was simply matter-of-fact. Both Brun and Carew knew of the longstanding custom among blacks wherein a man and a woman would jump over a broom in the presence of family and friends, which act constituted official recognition of marriage. Neither Brun nor Carew ever expressed anything but admiration for black musicians, nor did they ever speak about blacks in derogatory terms. It would have been peculiar for Brun to have spent the final ten years of his life and all his personal resources in a single-minded attempt to memorialize a man he regarded as anything short of a full-fledged hero.

In a later article, "From Rags to Ragtime and Riches," (published in *Jazz Journal* in 1949), Brun cited June 18, 1910, as the date Scott Joplin married Miss Lottie Stokes, but in an interview published in the October 1950 issue of *The Record Changer*, Lottie told Kay C. Thompson that she and Joplin had been married in 1907. She must have seen the advisability of presenting herself as having been Scott Joplin's legally married wife, but couldn't quite keep details straight.

Meanwhile, Brun's connection with Nichols was fading. After receiving fifty-two letters from the radio host during 1943 and 1944, he got only eight in 1945, all between January and May. The first was written on January 8, and was no more than belated holiday greetings and thanks for Brun's having sent a copy of one of his letters from Carew, along with the loan of three copies of

The Record Changer, presumably the issues with the "Overlooked Genius" articles. Nichols also enclosed a snapshot of Barty, his new cat, stretched out along a tree limb. Two brief letters followed, on January 12 and 25, the first thanking Brun for sending three more copies (probably for Nichols to keep) of *The Record Changer*, the second enclosing Brun's membership card, certifying him as "a Listener of Memories 'N Melodies from Hal's Memory Room."

The 1945 W.C. Handy Lecture Series got off to a flying start on January 15. The Father of the Blues told Brun in great detail about his recent triumphal tour of the southland, then launched into a lengthy diatribe concerning the way people of all races, but especially whites, hustled him endlessly for support for various projects, never thanked him when he did provide aid, violated his copyrights, tried to take his publishing company away from him, and claimed to have composed blues tunes before he did. "Here I am with my sight almost gone," he wrote, "and they are stealing, infringing and pirating on every hand. I am seventy-one years old and blind." Then he launched into a general condemnation of racial prejudice in America, including federal restrictions that forbade black women to serve as nurses in the war effort. "It is this kind of mess that drove poor Joplin insane; he is the uncrowned ragtime king, but you know who is called the ragtime king. But I am hinting to you that any mis-step on my part will mean the loss of my business, or the loss of opportunities for its success.... My mother has no tomb-stone; my father is buried in a strange town with no mark over his grave.... Charity begins at home, Mr. Campbell." Finally, Handy closed with, "However, you will hear further from me after I hear from Mrs. Joplin. With every good wish for a great 1945."

No question, growing up black in post–Civil War Alabama had to have been a nightmare. Young Handy was finagled out of the copyright for his first hit tune, "Memphis Blues," and so as not to starve, needed to sell rights to others of his compositions at bargain prices. His accomplishments in both art and business were beyond admirable, and given that in 1945, many American decks were still heavily stacked against blacks, it's easy to understand and sympathize with his anger. But it's unfortunate that that anger, coupled with his intense drive to succeed, rendered him incapable of seeing a world beyond his own nose. Not only did he seem unable to deal reasonably with people as individuals, many of his comments came across as frankly paranoid. It's sad that he could not appreciate the courage and determination of a fifteen-year-old white boy who'd run off to Sedalia in 1899 to learn ragtime piano from a black man he'd never met, and then, half a century later, devoted the remainder of his life and his meager resources to an all-out drive to honor that black man.

As to Handy's comments about Scott Joplin: Joplin was in fact frustrated in the extreme by the way racial prejudice slammed all kinds of doors in his face, but most musicians of the time, Handy included, knew Joplin died not of the effects of bigotry, but of cerebral syphilis, which was then a virtual occupational hazard among entertainers. However, Handy's cryptic remark about who came to be known as "the ragtime king" was right on. He was referring to Irving Berlin, composer of "Alexander's Ragtime Band" and other hugely popular songs about ragtime. Berlin's outrageous assertion that his tunes were responsible for initiating the ragtime craze in the United States rings like a cracked bell. By 1911, when "Alexander's" was published, Americans had been maniacal over ragtime for more than a decade. Eubie Blake made the point that "Alexander's Ragtime Band" was not syncopated and not a ragtime tune, but rather, an excellent piece of popular music, written squarely to the popular taste of the day.

Handy next wrote on January 24 to thank Brun for a copy of *The Record Changer* and some books Brun had sent. "Most of them are running true to form. I have noticed for many years that there is a group that eulogizes the dead Negro, and at the same time, tries to take from the ones who are living that which is properly due." Handy also "noted a vicious attack on me in one of the books," and told Brun he intended to look through all back numbers of *The Record Changer*, "and see what else has been done…. Some people are writing who were not born when I was getting my information first hand in the south, and … it is all to tear down the work that I have built on." Handy stated that he'd need to "get out another book for self-protection," then went on at length to assure Brun that he, Handy, had introduced strains of his composition "Ole Miss" into another piece, "Bugle Blues" (a tune generally attributed to Count Basie) and that he was "fighting for my part of the royalties of [any publication of 'Bugle Blues'] that uses 'Ole Miss.'" Finally, after another page of recapitulation regarding attempted thefts of his money, compositions, and business, Handy assured Brun he really did want to be of help in honoring Joplin.

For a few months, beginning in January, Brun pursued a dicey course toward publication of some of his new musical compositions. Irving Siegel was an accordionist, bandleader, and music publisher with multiple mailing addresses, including one in Miami/Coral Gables, another in Chicago, a third in Marshfield, Wisconsin. In Brun's files was a flyer headlined "Established Music Publishing Firm Wants Representatives," whose content strongly suggests Siegel was years ahead of his time—if he were operating now, he'd likely be King of the Spam Monkeys. At the end of a page of pitch to enlist people to plug songs from their homes was the message, "ATTENTION MAIL ORDER PUBLISHERS, PRINTERS, etc. Publish above copy on one side of your circulars or in your magazine in exchange for which we will honestly and promptly mail all sent to us to the best up-to-date lists in the country."

For the next three months, Brun communicated with Siegel, sending letters on his Scott Joplin Memorial Letterhead. With one exception, Siegel answered on penny postcards. Brun sent the publisher information on songs he'd written, some copyrighted, some whose handwritten lyrics were the only evidence of the compositions to be found among his papers. Siegel praised Brun's tunes: after reviewing "You're Going to Pay on Judgment Day" and "I'm Paying the Way You Said I Would Some Day," the publisher wrote, "I want to congratulate you on your ability to choose commercial subjects and clever titles." Siegel was endlessly optimistic: "I see you have some swell contacts too; we'll cooperate together in every way, and get good results, I'm sure." He continually urged Brun to "plug harder," and requested one small sum of money after another for his own efforts on behalf of Brun's music.

The only concrete evidence of publication, though, was the appearance of "Your Sweet Mama's Headin' for Another Town" in the typewritten, mimeographed *Studio News Magazine*. This cost Brun "$4.20 additional," but probably did not put a nickel into his pocket. Another half-page, apparently torn by Brun from this same publication, contained the lyrics to Irving Siegel's song, "Mem'ries of Mother," a masterpiece of pedestrianism, cliché, and sappiness; on the reverse side of the sheet was a pitch from an operator in Chicago: "I can give you instructions that may start you on the road to many extra $$$$! YOU DON'T HAVE TO BE A WRITER TO WRITE GAGS!" In addition, the gag-teacher noted, "I also critize prose."

Happy Perryman and the Mountaineers was a band sufficiently small-time as to have no entry in the 620-page *Kingsbury Encyclopedia of Country Music*. On March 24, Brun fired off a letter to Siegel: "Was talking with 'Happy' Perryman of the 'Mountaineers' at the Foreman Phillips Barn Dance on the Venice Pier here in Venice last night. He is going to make some recordings soon, and he says he knows you. So I thought it would be a good idea for you to write him.... He impressed me very much.... He likes my new songs, 'Your going to pay on judgment day' and 'I am Paying the way you said I would some Day.'" Brun followed up on April 3, with "Happy Perryman has both manuscripts, he makes recordings in May. I haven't heard from him since I gave him the manuscripts, But I just wrote him this a.m." Then Brun handwrote the lyrics to "I'm Paying the Way You Said I Would Some Day," and noted "the melody is cowboy or Hillbilly swing or whatever you choose for it. Its really a good dance number." Brun added that the tune had been copyrighted in 1945. On a second page, Brun wrote the lyrics for a song, "Let Me Come Back Home." He closed the letter with, "'I'm the singing cowboy' is my next number."

Most likely, Brun did not go to the Venice Pier just to listen to Happy Perryman and his Mountaineers. To advance the cause of ragtime, and probably to put a few coins in his pocket, The Kid played piano during intermissions at venues in Venice and Santa Monica, most notably the Rendevous Ballroom in the latter community. By this time, his financial situation had become perilous, and he seems to have been scratching at every possibility he could think of to raise money. In his files was a contract, handwritten in green ink, and signed by both parties:

Jan 15–45, Venice Cal

This is to certify that Clarence Bell of 70 Venice Blvd is to share 1/2 in all profits with me in My Song "For Your Sweet Mama's Headin' For Another Town" which we are turning over to Irving Siegel Radio and State entertainer for his exploitation from his address 811–1/2 W 40 Ave Miami 34 Florida.

The idea of the old Ragtime Kid trying to compose "cowboy or hillbilly swing," including a tune called, "I'm the Singing Cowboy" might come across as a sad sellout. But consider these liner notes from Jack Rummel's CD, *Brun's Boys*: "A comment from California ragtimer Dick Zimmerman caused me [Rummel] to think there might be a "Western sound" that could be incorporated into ragtime, and what started out to be a solitary composition soon expanded into a trilogy." The third tune in that Rummel trilogy was the lovely "The Cowboy Crooner," which "opens with the musical equivalent of a country yodel and closes with a variation of the song 'Tumbling Tumbleweed.'" Bob Wills' wildly popular 1940s Western Swing music comes directly from the same mold. In addition, many contemporary performers and historians trace the roots of later forms of American popular music such as jazz, stride, swing, R&B, and rock and roll back to ragtime. The often-quoted remark of Max Morath stands as an exclamation point: "Let's stop all this categorization, why don't we? It's all music." So it could be that while Brun likely was trying to put food on his table through his musical compositions, not only was he not selling out, he seems to have been more aware of musical evolutionary history and contemporary tastes and preferences than he's generally been given credit for.

However, nothing ever came of his efforts in that direction. Happy Perryman did record four tunes for Columbia on November 30, 1944, but that seems to have been the extent of his recording career. If he ever recorded other tunes, including any by Brun Campbell, there's no evidence of it.

After some three months, Brun must have wised up; he wrote to Siegel on April 4, offering to sell him four songs "outright…. I would not be interested in any other proposition." The response, three weeks later, was the return of Brun's letters, with "I must have $5 for each song I publish in lead sheet form," or a variation of that demand typed across the top of each page. Apparently, that was the end of the correspondence between the men.

In a letter dated February 4, Roy Carew addressed the moral sensibilities of the times: "Well, we can get along without bringing Mrs. Joplin into the story by an exact date…. Scott had his affairs. That angle won't hurt anything; we can skim along around his love affairs without getting specific or exact … we will have plenty, bringing Scott along through the Sedalia days, and on to St. Louis…. Nobody has to tell us that Joplin was in a class by himself … his music proves it … at each important point in his life in the story there will be musical examples to bring out his ability." Carew told Brun he had begun to write the story, and that he hoped to send some copy in his next letter. He also mentioned that J. Russel Robinson's "word in the right place would be of great value."

Carew probably was responding to mention by Brun of his attempts via J. Russel Robinson and George Waggner to interest Universal Pictures in *Treemonisha*. Robinson had informed Brun that no producers had responded favorably, since "the Negro resents characterization." Robinson added that he'd spent "quite a little time with Walter Lantz, producer of the U's cartoon films, but he produces only seven minute cartoons, but not full length." Brun's reaction to the idea of a cartoon production of *Treemonisha* likely would not have been favorable, but in any event, that particular line of inquiry went nowhere. Robinson closed by telling Brun he'd left "the score at Republic, where I have a very good friend in Harry Engel, former music publisher who is now casting director of that studio…. I'm sure he'll see that *Treemonisha* gets proper consideration at his studio."

Such might have been the case, but the only further communication related to the subject came in a short letter dated February 13 (probably a follow-up to an inquiry from Brun) from someone named Al King, on Robinson's behalf, to report that King had not yet talked to Robinson, but would shortly. So this letter probably represented another dead end in Brun's efforts to have a movie made of Joplin's life. King did enclose "a check for the memorial," and wished Brun "Good luck and success on this worthy venture."

Hal Nichols wrote on February 19 to thank Brun for "the lovely billfold which you sent me for my birthday…. I think it is swell; in fact, it is the niftiest one I have ever had and just suits me to a "T." Was Brun still trying to get around Nichols, or was this another example of the pianist's soft side, a show of sympathy for the ill radio host?

The next letter from Carew, dated March 4, contained several items of interest. The historian apologized for the delay in writing the "Sedalia, Birthplace of Ragtime" article, saying that the beginning of the year, till March 15, was "a very busy time for income tax work, and the rush is very heavy." But he promised to get on the article in time for Brun to have something to present to the Negro Actors Guild, and for the piece to appear in the May issue of *The Record Changer*. He also assured Brun that he would send a donation for the Joplin Memorial, then went on to say, "There is a thought that strikes me in this connection, however; I think it would be a good idea to have a designated depository for the funds while you are building it up to the projected size. I believe that is the customary way such things are done. Also, a committee of big musical names would help." If only Brun could have integrated Carew's common sense and business savvy with his own drive and enthusiasm.

In his previous letter to Carew, Brun had enclosed a copy of one of Handy's letters, probably the rant of January 24. Carew responded: "Your friend Handy's letter is very interesting. However, I don't think he is being harmed to any great extent. I don't believe that there was anything ... in the *Record Changer* to hurt his feelings much, although I wrote in one article that I heard a complete arranged Blues song at least six years before he published the 'Memphis Blues'; it was at a little concert given by a musical friend of mine in New Orleans. What harmed him most, I believe, was that he let BELIEVE-IT-OR-NOT Ripley feature him on a broadcast as the man who ORIGINATED the Blues, Jazz and Stomps. That hurt him, because it stirred up a lot of folks who knew that he didn't originate any of them, and they dug up the truth. Handy has received plenty of credit for all he did, and it made him rich, so I don't see why he should be so hot under the collar. The party he complains of, E. Simms Campbell, is a negro, and he wrote the JAZZMAN article after an interview with Clarence Williams, another negro who knows plenty about Blues and Jazz, so Handy's argument is largely with his own race. This is confidential, between us, of course. You should get some real assistance out of Mr. H. if he really wants to help. However, I rather believe that he is working for Mr. H. (On the cover of my copy of 'St. Louis Blues' it claims to be 'The Most Widely Known Ragtime Composition'; quite a claim)!"

On March 9, Arna Bontemps wrote briefly to Brun to alert him to the fact that "my forthcoming book [*They Seek a City*, later updated and republished as *Anyplace but Here*] is supposed to be published in May.... The book is about Negroes who migrated from the South to the North and West during all of our American history. Two chapters will be about musicians. One will deal with Scott Joplin and the ragtime period."

March 13 brought a long apology from Handy for his inaction, due to his extremely heavy workload, including having to pay attention to offers to make a show or a movie from his book, *Father of the Blues*. On March 15, Brun again had to file his Income and Victory Tax. 1944 hadn't been a good year: $2,484.90 in gross profit shook out to a net income of $1,796.28, plus another $120 contributed by Marjorie May. The nature of her work was not specified. Brun paid

$181 in taxes. Fortunately, rent for the barbershop remained at $180 for that year.

Unfortunately, in 1945, Brun's shop rent increased by fifty percent, to $270. Apparently, this did not go over well with the tenant. On April 30, Brun received a Notice to Quit from R.M. Trezevant, who seems to have been either his landlord or the landlord's attorney, and who, according to notes on the inside covers of Brun's ledger books, lived in Palm Springs, California. Brun had been operating on a month-to-month tenancy, and Trezevant's quit notice specified that he'd need to vacate by May 31. The issue must have been resolved, since Brun did remain at 711 Venice Boulevard for another seven years, enduring a progression of rent increases.

A postscript in longhand on Nichols' February 19 letter had promised a longer letter in a couple of days, but the radio host did not write again until March 29, this time to thank Brun effusively for "the very lovely Easter card … and when I say lovely, I mean lovely…. Last night, I gave the MEMORY ROOM bouquet to you and hope you heard it."

The subjects (all social) and the tone (perfunctory) of Nichols' letters are striking. The radio host's illness could have been weighing on him, but he also might have been tiring of Brun's lobbying.

On April 4, Handy covered three more pages with complaints about the number of people who called upon him for money, and the ingratitude of those he did help. Then he wrote, "It's a funny situation, it is the white man who saw the good in my work in the south and help me; he is the one that featured my music all over the country and many of my race would feature it but they are under contract to the white man, who won't allow them to feature it; some of them can't answer my letters." Contracts that forbade black musicians to communicate with W.C. Handy? The extremes of Handy's accusations make it difficult to take his claim of a conspiracy of suppression at face value.

On April 16, Nichols wrote to say that he thought Brun had "a swell idea for making money for the memorial fund. What I would do … is to have a Master record made and then you can have as many as you want pressed at very little cost…. I believe Bill Locy at Electro Records (in Glendale) priced them to me as 31c or 37c a record in 100 lots."

Though Brun had recorded "Maple Leaf Rag" on April 20, 1944, that appears to have been a limited production, perhaps a one-off, for Nichols' use on his May 12 radio show. Now, Brun's "swell idea" was to make a "Memorial Record" and sell copies to help finance the Joplin statue. Nichols wrote again on May 4 to say, "I will be very happy to loan the record that you made for me of the 'Maple Leaf Rag.' It is a fine recording and I think you are wise in using it…. As soon as you have the records ready for distribution, I will give you a

Label of Brun's Scott Joplin Memorial "Maple Leaf Rag" recording. Brun sold copies of the record for $2, hoping to raise enough capital for a monument over Joplin's grave. Had Brun been less grandiose, his sales of this record probably could have financed a modest headstone (Brun Campbell Archive).

nice plug on the MEMORY ROOM program." This was Nichols' first mention in 1945 of any actual promotional or commercial collaboration.

On May 26, Eccles Disc Recordings sent an invoice for twenty-five dollars, for "1–10" Master and Stamper, EC747, 'Maple Leaf Rag,' done on May 10." This would have been for production of the "Brun Recording Company's" one-sided disc, labeled:

MEMORIAL
THE MAPLE LEAF RAG–1899
by
Scott Joplin (colored)
Played by
Brun Campbell as taught him by
Scott Joplin in 1899–first white pianist
to play it

During a conversation in 2009, Brun's daughter Yvonne Patricia mentioned that her father had paid twenty-five dollars to someone to have recordings made, "and that was a lot of money then!" She clearly implied that such expenditure did not go over well in the household.

Another Eccles invoice for $2.50, for "Dubbing 'Maple Leaf Rag,' 1–12" s/f disc," specified that the disc had been "delivered to Mr. Crosby." Brun sent a postal money order for $27.56, dated June 10, to Chas. Alford at Eccles "for Master Record–Maple Leaf Rag."

In his article, "Brun Campbell," in the January 1971 *Rag Times*, Brun's friend, Floyd Levin, quoted Brun to explain the single-sided recording: "'If they want to hear two tunes, let them buy two records.' Brun could be cantankerous."

Before much longer, copies of the Memorial Record were going out from Venice in fair numbers. In Brun's files was a postal money order remitter receipt, paying Eccles $14.76 for 48 Maple Leaf Rag Records; a second receipt, dated August 19, for $1.60, was to cover shipping and packing recordings to New York. And in a gray medium-sized ledger whose cover bore the handwritten information "Scott Joplin Memorial, Sanford Campbell, Sponser, Jan. 45," Brun maintained a list of buyers of his recording. There were 114 entries at $2 a record between August 1, 1945, and early February 1946. Most of the names were unfamiliar, but some of Brun's correspondents were represented. Both W.C. Handy and Roy Carew bought two copies. Hal Nichols received a complimentary copy as did Lottie Joplin and President Truman.

With his letter of April 23, Handy enclosed four dollars for his two copies of Brun's Memorial "Maple Leaf" record. That was the good news. The composer began the letter by reprising a longstanding complaint about copyright theft of his breakthrough composition, "Memphis Blues," concluding with "Now, I don't feel any bitterness in this." Then, in what I suppose was a response to a heavy-handed remark by Brun, he wrote "I think you should confine your letters to me—to just what you are doing with Joplin and not bring in the race question because I could tell you so much about the master race—it wouldn't sound good…. Colored people have a lot more sense than you think they have, they don't fall for everything … they have a right to suspect and examine anything that a white man starts in their interest because as a rule there is a catch in it." He concluded by saying he knew of a man who "has about 100 Negroes' songs and they are getting just about as much as Joplin did and they will get just about as much for their songs as you can put in your right eye." Perhaps Handy did not know about the contract John Stark signed that provided generous (for the time) royalties on "Maple Leaf Rag," money that largely supported Scott Joplin for the rest of his life.

A May 21 letter from Roy Carew must have made Brun's day and then some. Carew told him that the first part of their "Sedalia, Cradle of Ragtime" article had appeared in the May issue of *The Record Changer*, and that the editor had sent Brun ten copies. Carew went on: "I hope that the story interests Bing—there is enough material in the history of ragtime and Joplin to make a very good picture with very good music. He is very good–Bing, I mean." Putting this together with the fact that Eccles had sent a copy of the "Maple Leaf Rag" recording to "Mr. Crosby," perhaps Brun was trying to interest Crosby in making a Scott Joplin movie. Did Brun and/or Carew imagine the crooner playing John Stark? Carew also let Brun know that the second part of the Sedalia story would appear in the June *Record Changer*, and that "that part of the Sedalia story is more interesting than what appeared in the May issue."

Lottie Joplin wrote on May 23 to tell Brun she had seen W.C. Handy, who said he'd sent Brun a check (probably for the two Memorial Records). Lottie also told Brun she'd received a "messege over the phone" asking whether she had liked the Memorial Record. She told Brun she'd not received it, but very much wanted to have a copy.

On May 31, Nichols wrote that "Mr. Alfred came by Saturday and left your record with me." He also told Brun, "Your manuscript of 'The Ghost of the Maple Leaf Rag' is o.k. now, and I am returning it herewith." But shortly thereafter, Gordon Gullickson, editor of *The Record Changer*, wrote to Brun: "I am afraid this isn't quite up to our standard of writing.... I know it's a true story, very interesting and informative.... Keep up the good work and let me hear from you any time." However, "The Ghost" seems never to have been published.

Arna Bontemps wrote again on June 25 to tell Brun his book was out; he enclosed a promotional letter from the publisher, and apologized that "they did not send me any extra complimentary copies ... perhaps due to the paper shortage." Bontemps hoped Brun would "like the paragraph about you in the chapter called Darktown Strutters."

"Darktown Strutters," Chapter 8, runs from Page 111 to 121 in *Anyplace but Here*, and concentrates most heavily on the life of southern black musicians who had immigrated to St. Louis and Chicago. Bontemps began with recollections by W.C. Handy, then moved on to Scott Joplin. The author introduced the subject by writing, "In a short biography of this 'overlooked genius' ... Roy Carew and Don E. Fowler showed that they could reconstruct a more or less complete story of Joplin's life from evidence revealed on his published sheet music." Then Bontemps followed "Joplin's wanderings" from Texarkana to Sedalia, Missouri in 1899, where he contracted with John Stark to publish "Maple Leaf Rag." The author noted that some time after that agreement, "the publishers stated that they had made a five-year contract with Joplin to write only for our firm." The source of that quote is not specified; the logical candidate would have been Will Stark, John Stark's son and business partner, who lived until 1949. But in any case, no one ever has been able to verify the existence of such a contract. Between 1899 and 1904, Joplin published several ragtime compositions through other houses.

Bontemps briefly described Joplin's moves to St. Louis and New York, and his dedicated efforts toward writing a ragtime opera. His mental deterioration and death were noted, but the cause of the composer's premature decline, central nervous system syphilis, was not mentioned. Bontemps concluded his Joplin section with the remark that above all, this composer "had provided mood music for the great migrations of Negroes from the South."

Near the end of the material, Bontemps tipped his cap to Brun: "Twenty-five years later [after Joplin's death] a white man named S. Bronson Campbell, himself a ragtime pianist, set about to raise a memorial to the near-forgotten 'King of the Ragtime Writers.' As a young man, playing over some popular numbers in the Armstrong Byrd music store in Oklahoma City, Campbell had been handed his first Joplin score by Otis Saunders, friend of the composer. Later he met Joplin personally and learned how the music should be played. The ragtime rhythm never deserted him. To him, it became the music of memory."

On July 3, Bontemps followed up with a brief apology to Brun, saying that due to the paper shortage, he had been unable to even buy copies of his book from the publisher. However, he promised to send Brun a signed copy of *They Seek a City*, and asked for any help Brun could provide in promoting the book.

Editor Gullickson sent Brun a postcard on July 23, saying he'd "look forward to receiving 'Ragtime Trail.'" But no such title was ever published, nor was there a copy in Brun's files. Perhaps The Kid's writing still was not up to *Record Changer* standards, or Brun might finally have submitted the piece under a different heading.

Sad as it was, Handy's letter of September 26 reads as a classic in black humor. He rails against double-duty "stabbing in the back" in articles about him in *Esquire* by Clarence Williams and E. Simms Campbell, claiming they denigrated Handy and his "St. Louis Blues," and asserted that Handy "must have gotten [the tune] from some other composer who should be getting the money." Handy felt further insulted by an August 9 article in the *New York World-Telegram*, stating that a musical comedy was in preparation "around the 'late' W.C. Handy." "Get the word 'late.' I am dead! Another stab in the back!" In an accompanying copy of a letter to an unidentified recipient, Handy warned that "anyone presuming to dramatize my 'late' life will be haunted to the full extent of the law." And Brun likely did not miss the point when Handy wrote he had paid for a gravesite and a headstone in Woodlawn Cemetery "as a guarantee that nobody will have to take collections to memorialize me when I am gone."

Another letter dated September 26 came from the office of St. Louis Mayor Kaufmann, and brought more discouragement. An assistant wrote Brun to "acknowledge receipt" of his letter about "Scott Joplin, a Negro composer ... whom you allege to be the creator of a new music." The letter-writer went on to scold Brun, reminding him that "every public-spirited citizen in .... St. Louis is vigorously pressing the measures of war and ... until the completion of the war and matters that must be done for the preservation of America, the Mayor feels that recognition of the great of other days must wait." Given that victory in Europe had been declared on May 8, 1945, and in Japan on August 14, the letter comes across as a fine example of political disingenuousness, and reminds us how prevalent racial prejudice still was in ragtime's most prominent city.

Brun must have objected to Handy's vitriol in that September 26 letter; the composer wrote again on October 4 (enclosing a circular for *Father of the Blues*, which contained a highlighted reproduction of an apology by the *World-Telegram* for their unfortunate reference to the late Mr. Handy) to say that Brun had misunderstood, that the intended target of Handy's anger was not Brun, but Williams, E.S. Campbell, and Jelly Roll Morton, all of whom had stabbed him in the back by saying that he had been reaping unjustified rewards from "St. Louis Blues." The composer added, "I don't want to be included in the book with dead Negroes and in the same book with Jelly Roll Morton. As long as you are working for Joplin, I am with you, but I don't want to have to work with the other people."

Which book was Handy was referring to? Could Brun have mentioned the idea for what eventually became his memoir, *When Ragtime Was Young*? Were he and Carew considering writing a book on early black music? More likely, Handy was anticipating the upcoming 1947 *Esquire's Jazz Book* which consisted in part of reprinted articles from *Esquire* during the 1930s. Two of these pieces were written by E. Simms Campbell, a great jazz enthusiast and a first-rate cartoonist of the time. His single-panel drawings, *Cuties*, was syndicated by King Features for more than a quarter-century; he was also the *Esquire* art editor and the designer of Esky, the sly faced, white-mustached logo of the magazine.

One of these two E.S. Campbell *Esquire* articles, "Blues Are the Negroes' Lament," was largely an interview with pianist/singer/composer/publisher Clarence Williams. In fact, this piece was first published in *Jazzman* in 1939, and is the article Carew referred to in his March 4 letter to Brun. In the other article, "Jam in the 'Nineties," Campbell had referred to "the great Handy," and listed seven of Handy's major compositions, and in "Blues Are the Negroes' Lament" had expressed anger similar to Handy's about the endless difficulties encountered by black musicians and composers. But he must have crossed the Handy Line in that article by writing "Clarence Williams ... who has written hundreds of Blues and who I think, as do many of America's finest musicians, is the greatest living Blues writer."

Between October 10 and November 8, Brun carried on a rapid-fire mail exchange with Zoe Norwood and W.C. Boswell, staff writer and editor respectively of *Platter Chatter* magazine. In an October 13 letter, Ms. Norwood thanked Brun for his communication of three days earlier, parts of which she said she would publish in *Platter Chatter*. She also encouraged Brun to submit articles, asked what his "rate of compensation" would be, and enclosed two dollars for a copy of his "Maple Leaf Rag" Memorial Record. Finally, she told Brun she'd "happened to pick up a hand-played piano roll of 'Maple Leaf Rag' in a junk store," and offered to send it to him.

Ms. Norwood followed up on October 17 with a handwritten letter to tell Brun she'd be sending the piano roll that Saturday, then asked him whether he liked any musical form other than ragtime, and specified her own preferences in then-current jazz. She also hoped Brun might be able to send her addresses for W.C. Handy and Richard M. Jones, and asked him to "explain to me the purpose and activities of the Scott Joplin Memorial," so she might be able to get something about the work into *Platter Chatter*. Finally, Ms. Norwood encouraged Brun to write "a story ... of some personal experience in the old days—something with a human interest slant."

Brun must have responded promptly to Ms. Norwood's October 13 letter, because she wrote again on October 18, thanking him for his "letter and article on Ragtime," calling the piece "a very interesting story." She did not specify a title for the work, but took pains to let him know that the magazine was "willing to pay for the stories we print," and if he really did "wish to write without compensation," as he stated in his letter, would he please "confirm this for our records." As intensely as Brun was chasing the long green at that time, his apparent offer to "write without compensation" seems odd. Perhaps he thought the proposal might have increased his chances of getting published, in turn giving him increased credibility for his solicitations.

Five days later, Ms. Norwood wrote to tell Brun she was sending him an edited copy of his article, that his first letter definitely would appear in either the December or the January issue, and that she had not yet received the Memorial Record. But on November 5, Brun received an enthusiastic endorsement of his record from Ms. Norwood. She referred to the work as being "not only authentic but very pleasing in a musical way," and asked Brun "Who and how first got the idea of ragging a piece of music? Did the idea come from the jazz players? Or did jazz come from ragtime?" Ms. Norwood said she'd read the manuscript he'd recently sent, thought it was fine, and that she believed "the editors intend to take it." However, she added that she was no longer working in the office, and that Brun would have to communicate with the editor, W.C. Boswell. A letter from Mr. Boswell dated November 8 ignored Ms. Norwood's prior remarks and questions regarding compensation; the editor asked Brun to specify payment for "the story," and said that if the request was "within reason, we will print it in our December issue."

Brun must have written to tell Ms. Norwood that the piano roll had arrived safely and that he believed Joplin had in fact played it, because Ms. Norwood wrote, "I'm glad the ... piano roll was in good condition. I always thought it was played by Scott Joplin, as I had read somewhere of such a roll being made by him. I am glad to hear my guess confirmed."

Maybe it was, but more likely, it wasn't. Joplin made seven piano rolls during spring 1916, when he was already suffering from the cerebral syphilis which killed him less than a year later. Edward Berlin refers to one of these rolls as follows: "The Uni-Record roll was probably made with the direct punching method and might, therefore, reflect Joplin's actual performance. It is not an impressive performance as the rhythmic coordination is irregular; that may be how Joplin, in failing health, sounded in 1916, though some roll aficionados doubt it was a live performance."

In point of fact, there were two "Maple Leaf Rag" piano rolls among Brun's possessions. Both were manufactured by the Standard Music Roll Company of Orange, New Jersey, and both bear the serial number 8440. One is the company's "Art-O-Roll," packaged in a box bearing pictures of great classical composers and classical scenes; the other is in the usual plain paper-covered cardboard roll box. The Art-O-roll, wound firmly, is 5 inches in circumference; the plain roll is 4 inches. The smaller roll probably is the one Ms. Norwood sent to Brun, since its leader label carries the words "Hand Played," while that of the Art-O-Roll does not.

Piano roll collector and researcher Robert Perry wrote, "The two rolls ... are not hand played by Joplin—both are manufactured by Standard ... they are both serial number #8440, which means both rolls should be musically identical. Standard used a number of sub-brands, of which 'Hand-Played' was one. You'll note no artist is listed on the label, just Joplin's name as composer. I suspect that ... both rolls will be found to be drafting board arrangements, rather than handplayed, unfortunately—just one more example of the countless 'Maple Leaf Rag' arrangements put out by various roll companies ... but they should sound good anyway–Standard had a good product."

Mr. Perry was also kind enough to alert me to the existence of Perfection piano roll Number 8440, and wrote, "Standard used the 'Perfection' and 'Hand-Played' labels for different markets for their smaller cheaper roll, so it'll be the exact same product as Brun's 'Hand-Played' copy." Which indeed it is.

But two piano rolls with the same identification number—why was one shorter than the other? According to David Reffkin, "It sounds like the shorter one is a direct excerpt of the longer one. The short roll ... excludes the B strain (the second musical theme of the piece) and its repeat, the last repeat of the A (first) strain, and the repeat of the D (fourth) strain." Player piano historian and restorer Daniel Grinstead confirmed those observations and extended them, stating that the longer roll reproduced the sheet music for "Maple Leaf Rag" note for note, beginning in the key of A-flat, then moving to D-flat for the trio (the third theme), and returning to A-flat for the fourth theme. Grin-

Brun pumped a player piano to record this rendition of "Maple Leaf Rag" on a piano roll he believed had been hand-played by Scott Joplin. Present-day experts are unanimous in the opinion that the roll was not hand-played, but created mechanically (Bryan S. Wright Collection).

stead further observed that the music on the roll is so even in its playing, he had to assume it was not handplayed. His opinion was strengthened by how the repeats of the strains were rendered identically, making it difficult to imagine anyone having played the music by hand. Grinstead felt certain that "the rolls had been perforated by machine from the sheet music, and that they are quite faithful to the original. Although the musical results may sound unexpressive, even mechanical, to the modern ear, Joplin might well have been pleased with this roll. It is known that he disapproved of any tampering with his ragtime—improvising, faking, or playing too fast. Few ragtime musicians, past or present, obeyed these instructions."

Gordon Gullickson wrote again on October 29, "The news-item you mention is truly the discovery of the year." This must have been in reference to the Joplin piano roll. Gullickson opined: "I should say you could turn a nice piece of change for the Memorial if you could make a recording of the piano roll and have it pressed up. But it is rather difficult to find a player piano these days, let alone one in a recording studio…. A lot of us would certainly like to hear the way Scott Joplin played."

On the inside back cover of the gray ledger that contained the names of buyers of his Memorial Record, Brun wrote in pencil, "Made master of Roll Thur night Dec-9–48." In addition, among Brun's papers was an undated flyer from the now-defunct Clock Publishing Company in Santa Monica. The organization produced mostly country-western records of the day on the High Time Records label, but on a "Specials" Page of the flyer was a Collector's Corner ad for "'Brun' Label–Piano Solo, 'Maple Leaf Rag.' Recorded from a hand played piano roll by Scott Joplin."

Surviving examples of the recording are exceedingly rare, but apparently, we can all hear an approximation of the performance. The penultimate track of the *Joplin's Disciple* CD consists of Paul Affeldt introducing the piece and specifying that Brun had pumped the piano to play the Joplin roll. Then the CD concludes with the music. However, there's another mystery here. The CD rendition of "Maple Leaf Rag" is identical to the longer piano roll from Brun's collection—the one that does not carry the "hand-played" designation. Perhaps Brun found this roll after he'd received the shorter roll from Zoe Norwood, recognized it as a full version of the composition, and used it for his recording.

On October 20, Handy sent Brun a copy of a letter he'd written to Lottie Joplin, expressing interest in publishing *Treemonisha*, and saying that he would call her to try to arrange to "get together." But on November 12, among a description of the "many handicaps" he was "working under," the publisher told Brun he had "heard no more from Mrs. Joplin." This is very odd. Lottie Joplin might have tried to strike a better deal than Handy would have been willing to accept, but for her to have simply ignored an overture from the famous composer-publisher does not ring true. There's a big piece missing in this puzzle.

E. Simms Campbell, Handy's nemesis, wrote Brun on November 3, thanking him for his "very interesting and informative letters," requested a copy of the "Maple Leaf Rag" Memorial Record, and said he'd read the Sedalia article in *The Record Changer* "with much interest." The illustrator apologized for the delay in "writing about Scott Joplin and all of you giants of the Ragtime era." E.S. Campbell promised to get to the job soon, told Brun the article would include illustrations, said he'd send Brun "a rough draft of the article so that you can check and double check ... as to authenticity—of course I will get in touch with Mrs. Joplin also." Mr. Campbell put his money where his pen was: he enclosed twenty dollars for the Joplin Memorial Fund.

Brun continued to pursue avenues for publicity for his memorial project. He sent biographical material to Ted Yerxa, who hosted a radio show, owned a small recording company that specialized in jazz, and wrote a daily nightlife column in the *Los Angeles Daily News*. All his ventures—as well as Yerxa himself—went by the name "The Lamplighter." In his letter to Brun, Yerxa said he found the material "extremely interesting," and in a follow-up letter dated November 26, promised to use it and let Brun know when it would appear. He added that he had not yet received "the record."

Along with a letter dated November 29, Carew returned Brun's manuscript, "Otis Saunders and the Maple Leaf Rag," which Carew thought "makes a very interesting story." He hoped Brun could "make a sale of it," and "If not, I imagine Gullickson [the editor of *The Record Changer*] can use it." It was not stated to whom Brun might have been hoping to sell the piece; perhaps that was another embryonic movie venture.

Carew wrote further, "I thought that you would have something to say relative to the RAGTIME article. There are always people who knew or know about someone who was greater than the great, and they try to push themselves into the limelight with their misinformation." This reference was to the article, "Ragtime, History and Analysis," in the October 1945 *Record Changer*, by Dr. Bartlett D. Simms and Ernest Borneman, a German polymath who included jazz among his many interests and enthusiams. The authors claimed—erroneously, as had E. Simms Campbell in "Blues Are the Negroes' Lament"—that Tom Turpin's name had originally been Tom Turner, and flat-out accused Scott Joplin both of plagiarism and being "a rather mediocre pianist." Then in a chronology of ragtime, blues, and pop tunes, Borneman listed Otis Saunders as the composer of "Maple Leaf Rag." That was too much for Brun, who in two unpublished articles, "The Maple Leaf Rag" and "Otis Saunders and the Maple Leaf Rag," took Borneman severely to task:

I do not know [Borneman's] source for this information, but I do know that it is not correct. As it happens, "The Maple Leaf Rag" was Scott Joplin's "Baby" from the very beginning.... Joplin in a talkitive mood one day when he was teaching me how to play ... was telling Scott Hayden & Otis Saunders & myself, that he was playing a version of Maple Leaf Rag back in 1889 up to the trio when he was 21 years old.

The two articles are reproduced in full in the "Short Pieces" section of this book.

Editor W.C. Boswell wrote Brun on December 18 to say he'd "been under the weather due to an automobile accident," and would write again soon.

Brun's final communication for 1945 was a signed Christmas card from Lottie Joplin. There was no message.

1946–1947: The Pen Is Mightier Than the Pest

By early 1946 the war was over, but the Joplin memorial statue existed only as a watercolor painting. It must have been obvious that trying to fuel that particular promotional campaign through mailed solicitations wasn't going to cut it. Brun needed to find a different, more effective, source of fuel for his machine.

The correspondence in the Campbell files dropped dramatically in 1946. It's possible Brun decided to be more selective as regards saving letters, but given that he continued to file away meticulous business records till the time of his death, it's more likely that he did decide to change his approach toward actualizing the Joplin memorial. Not to say there was any lessening of his fervor. The futility of trying to raise funds to erect a mammoth statue over an unmarked grave, more than 3000 miles away, of a largely forgotten composer of a largely forgotten musical genre must have sunk in, and what with the encouragement he'd been getting from Roy Carew and *Platter Chatter*, Brun might have begun to wonder whether he'd reach more wallets and purses by getting press media to disseminate information about his project. From 1946 until his death in 1952, he concentrated his efforts on writing long and short histories of ragtime, and trying to get a Scott Joplin film biography or biopic produced. In addition, he moved more heavily into making phonograph recordings.

Hal Nichols wrote on January 12 to tell his friend he was "preparing a program in which I will use your recording of the 'Maple Leaf Rag' and will give a plug for the records." Nichols also said he'd "received the book you sent containing your story and picture which is very fine publicity." (This would have been in reference to Arna Bontemps' *They Seek a City*.) Nichols said he hoped Brun would shortly see success in his project, adding, "You deserve a lot of credit for the work you have done on it. Most fellows would have given up long ago." Nichols closed with a melancholy comment regarding how many of the "old boys have passed away now."

The only other 1946 mailing from Nichols came a couple of weeks later, and consisted solely of Brun's "Memory Room" Listener membership card. At least some of the radio host's reticence could be attributed to the serious illness that reportedly troubled the last decade of his life, but it's possible Brun had simply pumped that particular well dry.

A short letter from Lottie Joplin, written February 27, stands as a sad account of Brun's likely situation at the time. Quoted in full, it reads:

Dear Mr. Campbell,

I am sorry you have to give the people their money back. But I am sick and have no way to help you any more than I have. I will thank you for the hundred dollars. Just mail it in a letter.

Thanking you in advance.

Yours Sincerely,
Mrs. Scott Joplin

It's uncertain just how much money Brun had to return, or to how many people, and for what reason, but it's likely that contributors to his poorly organized money-making ventures had run out of patience. Though Brun kept a ledger in which he listed sales of his 78 rpm recordings (and it appears he did deliver goods for payment) his files contained no records of outright contributions toward the Joplin monument. If he'd had been willing to settle for an ordinary headstone for Joplin's grave, he likely would have raised sufficient capital to carry off the project. But in the mind of The Ragtime Kid, that surely would not have been nearly grand enough to honor the King of Ragtime Composers.

During the last years of his life, Brun told several interviewers that he'd sent money to Lottie Joplin to help her through her omnipresent, nonspecific illnesses. One of those payments was the hundred dollars Mrs. Joplin acknowledged in her letter; it came from *Esquire* magazine. On April 10, associate editor W.A. Richards wrote, "Dear Mr. Campbell: Thanks for sending us your article, THE ORIGINAL HOT MEN OF THE 90'S. We're planning to use this in *Esquire* and in the 1947 Jazz Book, and have sent a check for $100 to Mrs. Scott Joplin, as requested in your letter of March 15…Will you please send us a paragraph of biographical information and a photograph…. We will let you know when the piece is scheduled for publication."

Talk about a watershed moment. Monetary considerations aside, publication of an article in *Esquire*, followed by inclusion in the upcoming *Esquire's Jazz Book* would have done wonders for Brun's visibility and credibility. It might even have served as a catalyst to transform the Joplin Memorial from a work of imagination to one of reality. But like the article promised by E. Simms Campbell, Brun's article never appeared, not in the magazine, not in the book.

It's astounding that Brun assigned his hundred-dollar earnings to Mrs. Joplin. In 1946, one hundred dollars was a considerable sum, even more so considering Brun's tax return in February for calendar year 1945, which specified his gross income as $2,434.26, and his net as $1,993.67. One hundred dollars represented more than two weeks' work. For this man, living with his family in a tiny five-plex housing unit, and under pressure to refund money likely brought in by two years of work and the sale of his personal possessions, to have turned over a hundred dollars to Lottie Joplin represented a staggering act of generosity. But Brun would have wanted to keep her aboard his bandwagon, and considering her endless complaining about her health, his gifts might have been prompted at least in part by perceived self-interest.

Even more amazing, the hundred dollars did not represent by half Brun's benevolence. On an envelope bearing his Scott Joplin Memorial return address, Brun wrote an undated note in pencil: "Monies sent, $100, $100 Esquire, 17, $217 Total Mrs. Joplin."

These payments were not Brun's only significant money drain in 1946. The expenditures to support his recording ventures might seem paltry to us today, but the $169.55 in postal money orders that he sent to Eccles in 1946 for dubbing, pressing, and shipping records represented eight percent of his income that year. The major financial hit, $75.63, came in August, for dubbing and pressing 100 copies of Brun's own composition "Essay in Ragtime" (EC858), and pressing an additional 100 copies of "Maple Leaf Rag."

In a letter dated May 6, Mr. Richards, the *Esquire* associate editor, wrote that he could not yet specify a publication date for Brun's article, but that after it appeared and had been copyrighted, *Esquire* would release motion-picture rights back to the author. Richards also promised him a copy of the article as soon as it appeared, and thanked him "for the additional material to be inserted."

That last line puzzled me, but Roy Carew's letter of May 5 cleared the uncertainty. Carew wrote, "I am returning to you herewith the article THE ORIGINAL HOT MEN OF THE 90'S ... which you sent me to look over. I also enclose the article (in duplicate) as I revised it. You will notice that the principal changes are contained in pages 1 and 2, and actually are not changes, but a sort of an introduction to the subject. I think you will find that beginning with page 3, the article is practically as you wrote it. It is your article, from your angle, so keep it that way, it's all right with me. I thought that a look back to the state of popular music when ragtime made its appearance would sort of smooth the beginning. I will make a few comments to you, however."

Carew went on to say he did not think Von Tilzer had published Tom Turpin's "Harlem Rag," that mention of Jelly Roll Morton's "King Porter Stomp" being a follow-up to "Maple Leaf Rag" might have been based on a misunderstanding by a "young fellow in England writing about Joplin," and that he did not think Scott Hayden had written "Sunflower Rag" alone. [The correct title of the tune is "Sunflower Slow Drag," and yes, Hayden did in fact write it in collaboration with Joplin].

In "The Original Hot Men of the 1890s," Brun had written:

All the original 'Rag' men of the 90's died poor, except Tom Turpin of St. Louis, Missouri, and from an unimpeachable source I am informed that there is a quite a bit of money piling up for Jelly Roll Morton with no heirs to claim it. This same source has written me wanting to know if I happen to know if any of Jelly Roll Morton's heirs are now alive and to contact him in case I do.

Then, in pencil, Brun added: *Mrs. Morton is alive, and I met her in Hollywood after I wrote this.*

Brun's comments prompted this reaction from Carew: "I left what you said about Jelly Roll's money just as you wrote it. If his heirs begin to write you you can turn them over to Mr. H., and if they get buzzing hard enough around him, he will get hotter than he ever was in the 90's." Did this bit of snark directed at W.C. Handy and his music publishing company imply that Handy was collecting income, possibly in an improper manner, from Morton's compositions? Carew was a great friend and admirer of Morton; he founded and operated the Tempo-Music Publishing Company exclusively as an outlet for Morton's work.

In Brun's files among his unpublished short pieces were two identical manuscripts of "The Original Hot Men of the 90's, A Condensed History of Early Day Ragtime." One of these had been mildly edited in Brun's hand. In another envelope, dated March 21, 1950, from Warner Bros., there was a second version of the article and a rejection with the usual boilerplate thanks-but-no-thanks. This copy featured an entirely new first part, had been rewritten in a more educated manner, and on the last page, "47 years later" had been changed to "51 years later." So Brun must have written the piece, Carew edited it for him, and after the *Esquire* publishing agreement finally fell through, Brun tried to get the work into print elsewhere or used as the basis of a film. He never succeeded.

On June 13, then again on July 24, Brun heard from Charley Jones, who represented both *Downtown Wichita* and *Jayhawk Press*. In the first letter, Mr.

Jones thanked Brun for sending a copy of the Memorial Record, and said that he'd played the recording for the people in the record shop across the street, and that they were greatly impressed by both the performance and the story Mr. Jones had "carried in *Downtown Wichita* and had already written you for a dozen of the platters." Unfortunately, Mr. Jones probably made the barber's teeth ache by saying he'd turned the record over to his "jitterbug daughter."

In the second letter, Mr. Jones congratulated Brun on the possibility that Victor might put out his records, a prospect that likely represented no more than hopeful thinking on Brun's part. Mr. Jones also said he'd consider Brun's offer to have *Jayhawk Press* put out his "booklet entitled 'Sedalia, Missouri, The Cradle of Ragtime,'" but Jones was concerned because paper was still very difficult to come by. As part of his sales pitch, Brun must have mentioned he'd had an aunt who'd worked at the George Innes store in downtown Wichita: Mr. Jones referred to the aunt and the location, wrote that the current occupant of that building was going to carry phonograph records, and advised Brun to get in touch with him.

Carew wrote on July 26 to tell Brun that the tune, "Pretty Little Dinah Jones," written in 1902 by J.B. Mullen, was still under copyright, so that if Brun wanted to use "DINAH herself" in a movie plot, he'd need to get permission from the copyright holder. It's difficult to imagine how Brun might have intended to use "Dinah" in a film about Scott Joplin—the lyrics tell a very short story of a "little maid" and her "honey boy" who lived "near the Everglades ... in a cabin built for two, little pickaninny rolling on the floor ... the same sweet moon ... shining bright as it did in days of yore." But the melody is strongly representative of early twentieth century popular ballads, so perhaps Brun was considering using it as background music in his film.

Carew also told Brun that "the little article about *Treemonisha* ... will come out in the September *Record Changer*," and promised to send copies to Brun and Lottie Joplin. (Brun used his mentor's article as a chapter in some versions of *When Ragtime Was Young.*) In that essay, Carew wrote that he'd been searching—unsuccessfully—for a copy of *Treemonisha* since 1916. His long quest had come to an end when his mail carrier unexpectedly delivered a copy to him, one signed by Lottie Joplin, and sent at Brun's recommendation. The historian was highly impressed with the opera, stating that it stood as clear evidence of Joplin's genius as a composer and showed him to be a wise interpreter of the problems facing blacks at that time.

The next letter in Brun's files was dated January 27, 1947; it came from Lu Watters. Watters, a musician and bandleader based in the East Bay, outside San Francisco, specialized in early jazz, and was a primary figure in the early 1940s ragtime revival. He also operated nightclubs, and was the owner of

West Coast Recordings, which put out the *Ragtime 3* album that consisted of six 78 rpm records, one side of each disc featuring Brun Campbell at the piano, with music of Watters' Yerba Buena Jazz Band on the reverse sides. The inside front cover of the album bore a photo of the young Brun, and a history written by The Kid on early ragtime and Scott Joplin. In his letter, Watters told Brun, "the national distribution of West Coast Records is being set up now, and in two months should be functioning well. We are also corresponding with England and other countries to get the records over there. (I think your album will go good over in England)."

That must have been welcome news. Judging by Brun's tax return of March 1947, 1946 had been a tough year. The barber's gross and net incomes remained about level, at $2,635 and $1,943.49 respectively, but his rent, which had gone up by fifty percent the previous year, now increased another thirty dollars to three hundred a year. He paid $141 in taxes.

The *Sedalia Democrat* of June 29, 1947, carried an article, "Did You Know Ragtime Music Was Born in Sedalia?" Even allowing for the hyperbole, not many Sedalians did. But E.V. Durling, a columnist for the *Chicago Herald American*, had written a piece that included the line, "ragtime music originated in Sedalia, Mo., first written by a man named Scott Joplin." When the *Democrat*'s editor wired Mr. Durling to obtain more information, the columnist referred him to one "S. Brunson Campbell, 711 Venice Boulevard, Venice, Calif.," and it was Katy Bar the Door.

Brun provided material for a lengthy article which was spread over several pages of the newspaper. His stories of Joplin's life and art, centered primarily in Sedalia, culminated with a preprint of his biography of Joplin, "Rags to Ragtime and Riches," which surfaced again more than two years later in *Jazz Journal*'s July 1949 issue.

The Kid really let 'er rip in that *Democrat* article, unleashing an impressive collection of engaging anecdotes, many of them unsupported and unsupportable. He wrote that "ragtime ... was born in Sedalia, Mo., written and played by Scott Joplin, a Negro, in the year 1891, and copyrighted records will bear me out." He mentioned the widely circulated but unsubstantiated story that Joplin and John Stark had signed an exclusive five-year contract in 1899. Brun also claimed that Joplin had admired a musical composition, "Maple Leaf Waltz," by Sedalia resident Florence Johnson, so much that he titled his breakthrough tune "Maple Leaf Rag." The Kid told the *Democrat*'s readers he owned "some" of Joplin's "hand-played piano rolls," and stated that he had "made a piano recording of his Maple Leaf Rag, just as [Joplin] had taught me to play it. It has been acclaimed the finest specimen of early ragtime in existence." He repeated the almost-certainly apocryphal claim that Joplin's "own race was so proud of him in Sedalia that they formed a club in his honor and named it the 'Maple Leaf Club,'" and gave the June 18, 1910, date for Joplin's marriage to Lottie Stokes. Otis Saunders received recognition for his influence on Joplin's progress as a composer.

Inaccuracies notwithstanding, the article stands as the first indication that, to paraphrase another Joplin rag title, Something really had been Doing in Sedalia a half-century earlier, something of which the town could be justly proud. In retrospect, it stands as a landmark piece, the first extensive report of ragtime history in a general-audience publication.

July 19 brought an important letter, five handwritten pages from Tom Ireland, written to his "Old Friend Bruno." In 1947, Ireland was eighty-two, a prominent and highly regarded citizen of Sedalia since the late 1800s. He'd worked as a journalist on several Sedalia newspapers and, most importantly, had been a major figure in the heyday of black music in Sedalia, playing clarinet in the Queen City Concert Band. Brun had written to him in June, requesting his recollections about the old ragtime days in Sedalia, and Ireland came through with clearly recounted memories of important people and places in Sedalia's ragtime world at the turn of the century. Ireland lived until 1963. Sadly, his house, which should have been declared a National Monument, was torn down after his death.

Brun deserves a ton of credit for pursuing and obtaining historical material that might have been lost to us for all time upon Ireland's death. Perhaps fueled by the growing recognition he was receiving as Someone Who Was There When It Happened, the Barber of Venice seems to have developed to some degree as a serious ragtime historian. Not that the storytelling and embellishing diminished, but the regard in which Carew and others held him seems to have validated his already whopping self-esteem, and spurred him to greater efforts.

On November 30, a curious telegram came to Brun's shop: "RECORDS ON MARKET NOW SHIPPING ALBUMS GO YOU LETTER FOLLOWING= HAMBONE KELLY." There was no person named Hambone Kelly—Hambone Kelly's was the name of Lu Watters' postwar nightclub on San Pablo Avenue in El Cerrito, California, located in the building that had been Sally Rand's swinging Hollywood Club during the Second World War. Watters must have been letting Brun know his *Ragtime Volume 3* albums were finally on the market.

Watters' next letter came on December 9. The bandleader promised "ads on the album in the January issues of several jazz magazines," and specified that Brun would receive fifteen copies "immediately," and that records would be sent to Lottie Joplin, if Brun would please furnish Watters with her address again; he'd misplaced Brun's earlier request. Finally, Watters promised to send

Brun "the balance of your royalties for 1947 as soon as the final figures are in for this December."

1948: The Kid at the Crossroads

Brun jumped directly into 1948. On January 2, he wrote to *Esquire* to say he hoped his article, "The Original Hot Men of the 90s" would appear in print before too much longer. Not an unreasonable request, given that a hundred-dollar payment had been sent to Lottie Joplin in April of 1946; the work also was to be included in *Esquire's Jazz Book of 1947*. But by 1948, The Hot Men still had not seen print.

On January 6, *Esquire's* managing editor, Frederic Birmingham, thanked Brun for his "gracious letter," then wrote, "We should like to cooperate in every way in order to help you with your forthcoming book, but I know you will appreciate that your article is one which demands a particular treatment, and we do not anticipate planning anything of this sort for some time." Then, Birmingham offered to release the manuscript to Brun, so that he might sell it to another publication, to "realize additional funds for Mrs. Joplin and ... further your book."

What happened? For once, it doesn't appear that Brun's characteristic impatience and tactlessness had anything to do with the negative outcome. There might have been a change in personnel and/or publishing criteria at *Esquire*, and an article that had triggered enthusiasm in a previous editor could have had no such effect upon his successor. Another possibility is that if E. Simms Campbell had had any involvement in the original acceptance, there might have been a shakeout at the magazine involving him, and Brun suffered the consequences. Whatever the cause, it was beyond unfortunate. With publication of his article in *Esquire's* magazine and Jazz Book (and some editorial assistance), Brun might well have succeeded in getting *When Ragtime Was Young*, his major piece of writing, into print.

Ironically, at about this time, recognition began to spread among serious students of ragtime and jazz that Brun was a genuine ragtime pioneer, a guy who'd been present at the feast and was still setting a good table. W.C. Handy forwarded him a letter written on January 2 by Sidney Martin, who "was working on a book about American music, to be published here in Paris next year." Martin was looking for information about Scott Joplin and Tom Turpin. On March 20, R. Erskine Kerr, of Lake Charles, Louisiana, wrote to ask Brun for a consultation. In the book, *Songs of America*, published the year before by Ziff-Davis, author David Ewen had specified New Orleans as the birthplace of ragtime, and neither Scott Joplin nor Sedalia had been mentioned. Referring to

Brun as "certainly an authority on rag-time music," Kerr asked him to please write to the author and set the matter straight, so that "if a revised edition is put out, no doubt he will be happy to make the necessary corrections."

Handy wrote his own letter to Brun on January 19, using the upcoming Negro History Week (February 8–15) as an excuse for a three-page letter which trumpeted the accomplishments of the Handy Brothers Music Company, Inc. Handy took pains to point out that among the "one hundred and seventeen million books in American libraries ... may be found.... BLUES, An Anthology; UNSUNG AMERICANS SUNG; FATHER OF THE BLUES; and NEGRO AUTHORS AND COMPOSERS OF THE UNITED STATES." In addition, the composer wrote that he was "firmly entrenched in the Blues, Jazz, and Negro Music section of the 1931 Encyclopedia Brittanica." At the end of three pages of shameless self-promotion, Handy closed by writing, "...the weather has had us all hemmed in, so we are lucky to even come to the office. I mean by this, that I haven't had time to talk with Mrs. Joplin or do anything you requested in your last letter."

Lottie Joplin wrote to Brun on February 24, to let him know "I sent those copies to Mr. Russell and I am sorry I could not send you the picture. I saw it but it was in music but I will still try to get one." "Mr. Russell" (whose birth name was Russell William Wagner) was William Russell, dean of New Orleans jazz history and a major record dealer, and Brun might have persuaded Mrs. Joplin to send him a copy of *Treemonisha*, as he'd convinced her to send a copy to Roy Carew. Perhaps Brun was hoping that Russell, with his extensive connections in the field, might facilitate production of a *Treemonisha* film. As to Mrs. Joplin's mention of "the picture ... in music," she probably was referring to the photo of Joplin that appeared on the cover of one of his tunes, such as "Swipesey Cake Walk," "The Cascades," or "Euphonic Sounds."

Brun's only other 1948 correspondence from Joplin's widow was a Thanksgiving card. Given his financial generosity and his five-years' struggle on behalf of her husband, the card comes across as more than a casual holiday greeting.

The good news on Brun's IRS return for 1947 was that he paid only $73 in taxes, but that was because of the bad news: his gross income had dropped that year to $2,188.90, and his net to $1,546.61. No postwar boom in the Campbell household economy.

On February 2, Arna Bontemps wrote to Brun: "Thank you for your most interesting letter. It arrived during my absence in New York, so you will have to wait a few days for me to pass the information along to Mr. Van Vechten. But I hasten to assure you that we are tremendously interested in the accumulation of material you have gathered relating to Scott Joplin and his life. We want by all means to have it preserved here in the Fisk University Library."

Bontemps went on to offer placement of the Joplin material in either the Library's Gershwin Music Collection or the Collection of Negroana.

So shortly before this letter, Brun must have contacted Bontemps to offer his Scott Joplin collection. Fisk University in Nashville was, and had long been, a major center for performance and history of black-related music; the library boasts outstanding special collections of music and memorabilia of such luminaries as Thomas Andrew Dorsey, the Fisk Jubilee Singers, George Gershwin, James Weldon Johnson, and Jimmie Lunceford. Once it became clear that Brun was never going to collect enough money to construct a monument over Joplin's grave, he might have been directed toward Fisk by the reference in Handy's letter of November 27, 1944. In addition, Roy Carew and other friends might have encouraged this approach.

Whatever did cause Brun to pull the Fisk trigger in February 1948, The Kid was not about to quietly dump his holdings and walk off into the California twilight. From that point, he increasingly focused his attention and energies on writing ragtime histories, and once his Joplin collection was established at Fisk, he used it as a lever to pry at doors to various publishing and moving-picture organizations that might have restored Joplin to the throne of the King of Ragtime, and established Brun as the most loyal noble in his court.

Between February 26 and April 15, Brun received seven letters from Arna Bontemps and other officials at Fisk University, as well as related correspondence from Handy and Carl Van Vechten. Bontemps' first communication began by assuring Brun that the order for one of his albums by the Comptroller was "bona fide," then proceeded to write, "You may be sure that I will write a nice letter to Mrs. Scott Joplin to tell her about the collection when it is received. The Joplin music will go either into a bound volume or a folio. We'll be happy to do that." Bontemps also promised Brun that there would be a proper news release about the collection and that the Fisk public relations director would be certain to send him copies. The librarian closed by saying, "It would be good if we could receive the collection in time to exhibit items from it ... during the Spring Festival of Music and Art in April."

On March 5, Brun wrote to Bontemps:

Dear Mr. Bontemps:

Here is a complete list of Joplin's musicial acheivements which should be typed and put with his collection.

S.B.C.

What followed was a handwritten tabulation of Joplin's music by year of composition: his rags, two operas, two ragtime waltzes, rags written in collab-

Ca. March 5, 1948

Dear Mr. Bontemps: Here is a complete list of Joplin's musical achievements which should be typed and put with his collection.

S.B.C.

#2

1906 - Ragtime Dance
1907 - The Nonpareil
1907 - Gladiolus Rag
1907 - Searchlight Rag
1907 - Rose Leaf Rag
1908 - Fig Leaf Rag
1908 - School of Ragtime
1908 - Pineapple Rag
1908 - Sugar Cane Rag
1909 - Paragon Rag
1909 - Wall St Rag
1909 - Country Club
1909 - Solace (a mexican serenade)
1909 - Euphonic Sounds
1906 - ~~Ragtime Dance~~
1910 - Stop Time Rag
1912 - Scott Joplin new Rag
1914 - Magnetic Rag
1917 - Reflection Rag (Joplin's last Rag)

Opera's
1903 - "A Guest of ~~Honor~~ Honor"
1911 - "Treemonisha" - opera in 3 acts

1899 - Original Rags
1899 - Maple Leaf Rag
1901 - Peacherine Rag
1901 - Easy Winners
1902 - A Breeze from Alabama
1902 - Elite Syncopations
1902 - Strenuous Life.
1902 - The Entertainer
1902 - The Ragtime Dance Song (words & music by Joplin)
1903 - Weeping Willow Rag
1903 - Palm Leaf Rag
1904 - The Favorite
1904 - The Chrysanthemum
1904 - The Sycamore
1904 - The Cascades
1905 - Eugenia

3.   Ragtime Waltzes
1905 - Bethena - (a concert waltz)
1909 - Pleasant Moments

Songs written to Joplin Rags
1903 - Maple Leaf Rag (words by Sydney Brown)
1910 - Pineapple Rag (words by Joe Snyder)

Joplin Rags written in Collaboration
1900 - Swipesy Cake Walk. (Arthur Marshall)
1901 - Sun Flower Slow Drag. (Scott Hayden)
1903 - Something Doing. (Scott Hayden)
1907 - Heliotrope Bouquet (Louis Chauvin)
1907 - Lily Queen (Arthur Marshall)
1911 - Felicity Rag (Scott Hayden)
1913 - Kismet Rag - (Scott Hayden)

Miscellaneous
1895 - "A Picture of Her Face" (a waltz song)
1895 - Please say you will (a waltz song)
1896 - Combination March
1896 - The Crush Collision March
1896 - Harmony Club (Waltz)
1901 - Augustan Club. (Waltz)
1902 - March Majestic (6/8 march)

#4
1902 - Cleopha (Two Step)
1905 - Rose Bud March (6/8 march)
1905 - Binks Waltz
1906 - Antoinette (6/8 march)

Music written by Joplin for songs by others:
1901 - I'm thinking of my Pickanniny Days.
(words by Henry Jackson)
1903 - Little Black Baby (words by Louise Armstrong Bristol.)
1904 - Sarah Dear Ragtime Song (words by Henry Jackson)
1907 - When your Hair is like the Snow (words by Owen Spendthrift)

Arrangements by Joplin
1907 - Snoring Sampson Ragtime Song by Harry La Mertha
1908 - Sensation Rag. by Joseph Lamb
1905 - Leola - Two Step. (unverified)

Brun's handwritten account of Scott Joplin's compositions, sent to Arna Bontemps at Fisk University. For the time, it was a remarkably complete and accurate list. Since 1948, details regarding multiple composers for different compositions have surfaced, as have a small number of Joplin-only originals. One of these, "Silver Swan Rag," was only discovered when Albert Huerta, a piano roll collector, found a roll of that title among his holdings. The roll was unattributed as to the composer, but Richard Zimmerman and other ragtime scholars agreed that the piece was characteristic of Joplin's work, and that it would be extremely unlikely that any other composer would have created it. Later, a second piano roll of the same tune, produced by a different company, was found; this one included credit for Joplin as composer (Brun Campbell Archive).

oration, "miscellaneous" compositions, music written by Joplin for songs by others, songs written to Joplin rags and arrangements of music by other composers.

A week later, Bontemps replied: "I HAVE THE HONOR TO ACKNOWL-EDGE THE RECEIPT OF THE GIFT MENTIONED BELOW AND I BEG YOU TO ACCEPT OUR SINCERE THANKS. FAITHFULLY YOURS, Arna Bontemps, Librarian."

A list of Brun's specific contributions was included with the letter:

Record Changer Magazine	Sugar Cane
Scott Joplin's pictures	Euphonic Sounds
Picture of his piano	Fig Leaf Rag
Picture of the building that housed the Maple Leaf Club	Gladiolus Rag
	Scott Joplin's New Rag
Picture of Smith's School of Music	Paragon Rag
Picture of the Negro Queen City Band	The Chrysanthemum
Letter from Tom Ireland	Sunflower Slow Drag
Joplin's Biography	The Entertainer
Picture of Mr. Campbell and Kid Ory	The Easy Winners
Music	Searchlight Rag
The Ragtime Dance	The Favorite
Treemonisha—a three-act opera in rag-time	Maple Leaf Rag
	Reflection Rag
Original Rags	March Majestic
Nonparel	Palm Leaf Rag
School of Ragtime	Weeping Willow
Eugenia	Magnetic Rag
Elite Syncopations	Wall Street Rag
Pine Apple Rag	Joplin's World Famous Jazz Classics
Country Club	Rose Leaf Rag
Antoniette	Pleasant Moments Waltz
Swipsy	Heliotrope Bouquet
Kismet Rag	Cascade Rag
The Sycamore	

Some of these items raise interesting questions.

The piano referred to was the partial subject of an article by Chris Ware, in *The Ragtime Ephemeralist*, Volume 1, 1998. The photo was probably sent to Brun, at his request, by Lottie Joplin, but it is uncertain whether this particular "Joplin's piano" was located in New York or Chicago. In any case, scholars have considered that the pages of music on its rack were likely written by Joplin; one, a short fragment, was recorded by Reginald R. Robinson (*Euphonic Sounds*, Delmark DE-718), who had taken notice of the music, then analyzed it.

Lottie Joplin had sent Brun a brief biographical sketch of her husband for

The Kid to use to create interest in producing a motion picture based upon Joplin's life. (That account is reproduced in "Not The Best-Case Scenario–Scott Joplin and His Maple Leaf Rag," in the "Short Pieces" part of this book.) However, the Joplin biography in the Fisk Library collection is considerably more literate and very different in content, and probably was written by Brun and edited by Roy Carew, or written by Carew. A striking aspect of this version of the composer's life and death is that it ends by labeling as an "unusual legend" the claim that Joplin's funeral was highlighted by a procession of vehicles, each bearing the title of one of his tunes. Brun has taken a good deal of heat for passing this story along to interviewers as gospel.

The picture of the two Kids–Campbell and Ory—smiling and shaking hands, with Ory's trombone tucked under his right arm, appeared on the cover of the April 1950, *Jazz Journal*—two years after the donation of the collection to Fisk. During the mid–1940s, Brun played intermissions during concerts by Ory's band at the Rendevous Ballroom in Santa Monica, so the photo might well have been taken at one of those gigs.

A search for "Joplin's World-Famous Jazz Classics" yielded a surprising result: in the Francis P. Squibb Papers at the University of Chicago Library, the work is described as "Scott Joplin's World's Famous Jazz Classics for Piano," an undated publication. (The latter version is the correct title.) Since the composer never would have used the word "jazz" to describe his music, and John Stark hated jazz with a passion, refusing at one point to honor an invitation by Paul Whiteman to attend a Whiteman orchestra concert in St. Louis, it's unlikely the work would have come out before Stark's death in October 1927.

David Reffkin, who has had a copy of the rare folio in his collection for years, confirmed this thought. On the front cover is printed, "Published by Stark Music Co. St. Louis, U.S.A." and "Sole selling agents Dixon-Lane, Inc. 812 Pine St. St. Louis, U.S.A." A copyright date of 1928 by Stark Music Company appears inside the cover. Stark himself might have prepared the material in the folio, but with Joplin and ragtime having faded from popular view and the Jazz Age at its peak, it's likely that his successors included "jazz" in the title as a marketing ploy.

The first piece in the collection is "Maple Leaf Rag," and at the bottom of the page is printed, "Copyright 1926 by Mrs. Lottie Joplin. Copyright Assigned to Stark Music Co." The notice is for "Maple Leaf Rag." Since that tune was first published and copyrighted in 1899, the date in the folio is consistent with the then-standard 28-year copyright renewal interval to prevent the work from falling into the public domain.

According to the special collections librarian at Fisk, the copy of *Treemonisha* is softbound and "sheet music." Perhaps it's the copy Lottie sent to J. Russel

Robinson, who returned it to Brun after he struck out with it at Universal. The special collections librarian also verified that the various Joplin compositions in the collection are pieces of commercial sheet music, not original manuscripts.

On March 16, Bontemps wrote again to acknowledge receipt of Brun's Joplin collection, and promised that appropriate announcements and a letter from him to Lottie Joplin would be forthcoming shortly. Another letter, two days later, explained to Brun that "unfortunately, neither the Fisk Library nor Fisk University issue the kind of certificate you mention. The Librarian is authorized only to acknowledge gifts of library materials on behalf of the trustees. Even the form of the acknowledgment, which you received, had to be approved.... You will, of course, be widely acknowledged when our Public Relations Office sends out its news release to 120 newspapers and magazines throughout the Unites States."

That letter to Mrs. Joplin went out on March 24, telling her how pleased Fisk was to receive "a most attractive collection of materials related to Scott Joplin ... for its special collection of Negroana." (Brun's contribution might have initially been part of the Negroana Collection, but at this time it is an independent collection.) Bontemps assured Joplin's widow that the material would keep "the memory of Scott Joplin fresh," and that it would be preserved "with the fond care which it deserves." The librarian also made clear how grateful he and the university were for Brun's decision to donate the collection to Fisk.

Brun seemed to miss no opportunity to promote his project. On March 25, Ted Hallock, Assistant Editor of *DownBeat*, wrote to thank him for having sent information about his gift to Fisk, and reported that they were "hoping to use the story in either our issue of April 7 or April 21."

Tuesday, April 6, was a red-letter evening for The Ragtime Kid. On *Song Story Night*, his old pal, Hal Nichols, told the tale of Brun's quest to build a monument "of granite or bronze" over Scott Joplin's grave, but that instead, had done something "more useful and lasting, more alive and vital," and that "Scott Joplin will be accorded a place of honor in the Library of Fisk University of Nashville, Tennessee, alongside of George Gershwin and other notable men of music." Nichols made a few errors along the way, such as claiming that Joplin wrote "the first real ragtime number," and that his "ragtime opera *Treemonisha* is so difficult that musicians are still unable to play it." But the radio host must have delighted Brun by concluding, "I'm going to play a recording of 'Maple Leaf Rag,' Joplin's most famous, played by Mr. S. Brunson Campbell in the way Scott Joplin taught him to play it in the true ragtime style."

On April 8, Marsha Hursey, the Fisk press representative, wrote to tell Brun that "in a few weeks you will receive copies of the news stories that I will send out concerning your contribution to the Library," and that "our office is very enthusiastic about this material and want to have it publicized as soon as possible."

Compliments poured through Brun's mail slot. On April 13, W.C. Handy wrote, "I think you have done wisely in respect to the Scott Joplin Memorial.... I found your list so interesting and complete that I shall attach your letter to his TREEMONISCHA which is in my library at home and this will be for posterity." Then, after a couple of paragraphs of complaint about his health and the fact that "they keep me on the go day and night," Handy signed off with best wishes and thanks.

On April 18, Carl Van Vechten wrote, "I was very happy to hear from Fisk that you had decided to deposit your wonderful Scott Joplin Collection there.... I think you have made a wise choice."

Whether Brun's memoir *When Ragtime Was Young* was press-ready at this time (in Brun's or anyone else's estimation), he queried Gordon Gullickson, who, in a letter dated April 28, referred him to Bill Grauer, editor of *The Record Changer*. Gullickson had heard that Grauer was "going to publish a number of small books on jazz and ragtime." But there's no evidence of that line of inquiry's having gone further.

By June, news of Brun's contribution to Fisk had reached St. Louis. A headline in the June 4 *St. Louis Argus* read "Once Ragtime King of Market St. Immortalized in Fisk Library." The article quoted Arna Bontemps to the effect that a wide variety of materials having to do with the music of "Scott Joplin, pioneer ragtime composer," and including musical scores and photographs, had been donated to Fisk by "Mr. S. Brunson Campbell of Venice, Cal., a former pupil of the great musician."

There was a surprise in Roy Carew's letter of July 3: "Just a line to answer yours of a few days ago.... I see you have made a donation to STANFORD UNIVERSITY–manuscripts, it states. Whose manuscripts did you have?" An inquiry to the head of the Department of Special Collections at the Stanford University Libraries brought the information that their sole Brun Campbell representative was a copy of the "Maple Leaf Rag" Memorial Record. Carew also told Brun that he'd sent the Fisk press releases to a friend in London and asked the friend to use them for publicity in Brun's interest.

In the same letter, Carew warned Brun confidentially that he'd checked the Library of Congress copyright index, and had found that neither Brun nor Lu Watters had copyrighted Brun's compositions, "Essay in Ragtime" and "Chestnut Street in the 90s." The historian strongly advised Brun to correct the oversight, while implying between the lines that The Kid would be wise to not place a whole lot of trust in Watters' business dealings.

The next letter in the files, postmarked July 14, was from Watters. Along with an apology for the delay in payment, there was an accounting and a check for Brun's royalties from West Coast Recordings between April and December 1947, and between January and June 1948. Royalties on "Harlem Rag" and "Maple Leaf Rag" were at two cents per record; those on "Chestnut Street in the 90s" and "Essay in Ragtime" were at four cents. The total came to $114.80.

On September 5, Bill Russell wrote a long letter to Brun. Russell, eighteen years Roy Carew's junior, was a protégé of the older historian, and began his magisterial 720-page "scrapbook" on Jelly Roll Morton, *Oh Mr. Jelly*, with the tribute, "This is the book Roy Carew should have written." At the time he wrote to Brun, who then was putting together photographs for *When Ragtime Was Young*, Russell was living in Canton, Missouri, his birthplace. He told Brun he'd be driving to St. Louis the following week, and would try to get The Kid a picture of the building that once had been Babe Connor's famous Castle Club bordello. Brun had referred to that establishment in "A Hop Heads Dream of Paradise," a two-page chapter from the first version of his ragtime history titled *The Original Ragtime Kid of the 1890s*:

> at St. Louis Mo., one of the most colorful Negro Madame's, Babe Conners' reigned supreme. It was in her place in 1894 that the song "Ta-Ra-Ra-Boom-Dee-A" was written and introduced. Some of Scott Joplin's and Tom Turpins first rags were played in Babe Conner's place. It was in such places as these that ragtime music was first heard before it was put down on paper by Scott Joplin and Tom Turpin, two of ragtimes first Negro composers of the 90's. Those "Dusky Damsels" in Babe Conner's house were the most beautiful to be had and the elegance of the St. Louis' dusky fancy girls was startling indeed.

Authorship of the 1890s hit "Ta-Ra-Ra-Boom-De-Ay" has been credited to Henry J. Sayers, but Sayers said he'd picked up the song during the 1880s from Mama Lou, a black performer at Babe Connor's place. Brun also wrote, in Chapter 5 of the fourth version of *When Ragtime Was Young*, that Babe had claimed authorship of the tune for herself.

Russell said he'd try to get other pictures from St. Louis and New Orleans, but considering the difficulty of dealing with the owners of the photos and the expense of having photographs copied, he wasn't optimistic. He wrote, "It still looks like a tough and probably expensive job to get the photo of L. Chauvin at the Republican Club on Market Street." (This was the former site of Tom Turpin's Rosebud Club.) But Russell came through. In an undated envelope in Brun's files was an old snapshot of the legendary ragtime pianist, co-composer with Joplin, of "Heliotrope Bouquet." The picture was clumsily mounted on a cardboard backing, which appears to have been torn out of a scrapbook or off a papered wall. This is the picture that appeared in Blesh and Janis' *They All Played Ragtime*, and which has been reproduced in several publications since. Perhaps we have Brun's persistence and Russell's cleverness to thank for this bit of history.

Gladys Schwarcz, an editor at Doubleday and Company in New York, wrote on September 16 in answer to a query from Brun on September 7. She explained that discussion of royalties on any book published by Doubleday would be discussed only when the book had been accepted for publication, then added, "If you … would rather send us the manuscript after the pictures have been compiled, we will be happy to see it at that time."

Unfortunately, Brun's lack of patience and inattentiveness to detail torpedoed his ship. On September 24, he sent Ms. Schwarcz this three-page, handwritten letter:

Sept. 24–48
Gladys Schwarcz
New York. NY.

Dear Madame:

Enclosed is a copy of the book script. I am sorry to have to send it in such condition, but the typists I am able to get, don't seem to know their business. The originial is very much cleaner. While this manuscript may seem rather short the meat of the subject is all there, and remember, under each picture I have (all mentioned in the script) 30 have a short story about each picture under them, with courtesy lines. Here are the pictures: My "Kid" picture at the age of 16, the two first "Rags" published. Pisco Johns Saloon at San Francisco Barbary Coast before and after the quake and Fire. "Emperor Norton," Lulu White's Mansion at New Orleans on Basin Street. Frank Earlys old Cafe at New Orleans. (Quite a story about this place will be under the picture) Big Club 25, New Orleans. Tom Turpin's (he wrote Harlem Rag 1897) original Hunting and Shooting Club at 2220–2 Market St St Louis Mo. Chestnut St looking west from 22nd. This street was the breeding place for ragtime. Queen City negro Band of Sedalia Mo taken in 1896. This was the first band in America to play Ragtime. W.C. Handy father of the blues. 12th Street in Kansas City MO. That is the street 12th Street Rag was named after. The notorious "Everleigh Club" of Chicago. Simpson Auditorium and its history. This is where the Ragtime piano playing Contest for the World's Championship took place in 1907 between Eddie Barnes and England's Champion Phil Stebbins. Jubilee Hall, Fisk University, Nashville Tenn, Fisk Library where I established the Scott Joplin Music Memorial. Louis Chauvin the greatest Negro ragtime pianist in the World in the 90's and early 1900s.

It is the only picture of him known in the World. If the script and pictures do not interest you, Please return the Script as soon as you can. Enclosed find postage for its return.

Sincerly,

S. Brunson Campbell

Not exactly a model professional cover letter—sloppily handwritten, rambling, studded with errors, complaints about typists used to excuse a slipshod presentation, and ending with a "Hurry up or else" ultimatum. Brun could not have done more to guarantee himself a rejection. There are no further letters from Gladys Schwarcz in the files.

Still, Brun seems to have remained hopeful on the possibility of publishing *When Ragtime Was Young*. On page nine of his Scott Joplin Memorial Ledger is a list dated November 5, 1948, of 24 advance subscribers who had put up three bucks apiece for copies of his book-to-be. Some of the names were of his music-related correspondents; most, such as "Levi, City Hall," were less than specific, and probably represented neighboring friends and workers. But Subscriber Number 16 was of particular interest: Ray Bradbury. In 1948, the future sci-fi superstar lived in Venice, and was a customer at Brun's barber shop. He used Brun as a model for Cal the barber in *Death Is a Lonely Business*, his 1985 homage to Venice. The portrayal is far from flattering, setting up the old barber as not only a liar but a phony who claimed to have been a pupil of Scott Joplin's, but who never actually did go to Sedalia.

Some of the names on the list, Bradbury's included, were crossed out in pencil; others were marked "Delivered." Did Brun give unpublished manuscripts of *When Ragtime Was Young* to some subscribers? Did he refund their payments, in line with Lottie Joplin's earlier sympathetic comment about his needing to give people back their money?

Brun also seems to have been sanguine about the possibility of making money from phonograph records. On September 30, Eccles billed him $57.17 for dubbing his performance of "Twelfth Street Rag" and pressing 100 copies. In addition, among Brun's effects was a recording on the Echoes label, distributed by Record Roundup, a shop specializing in jazz recordings, and the property of Brun's friend Ray Avery, a noted jazz buff and photographer. It would appear that Brun's record represented Avery's first commercial recording venture on the Echoes label: Side 1-A was labeled "'12th Street Rag,' played by Brun Campbell and his ragtime piano," while Side 1-B supposedly played "Grandpa Stomps." However, Brun had written in ink, "Weeping Willow Rag, Composed by Brun Campbell" on Side 1-A, and "12th Street Rag" on Side 1-B. (Brun had renamed "Grandpa Stomps" to "Weeping Willow Rag," in honor

Razor strop, stored with Brun's personal effects, presumably from Brun's establishment. Although the dark stains have not been DNA-tested, they doubtlessly represent bloodstains (Brun Campbell Archive).

of Scott Joplin, though Brun's "Weeping Willow" bears not the slightest resemblance to Joplin's haunting, lyrical composition.) The inked identifications were in fact the proper ones, so the labels had been reversed.

The final item in Brun's saved correspondence from 1948 was a letter from Roy Carew, dated November 22. Carew complimented The Kid on his performance of "Twelfth Street Rag," but suggested he might "do as well with numbers on which you don't have to pay a royalty," the publisher-held copyright for "Twelfth Street Rag," still having been in effect. Carew then wished Brun "Good luck on any 'bites' you get," in reference to *When Ragtime Was Young*, and enclosed corrections keyed by page numbers and lines to the "Ragtime" chapter from Versions 1, 2, and 4 of *When Ragtime Was Young*.

By the time the 1948 holiday season came around, Handy's books had been published (if by his own firm), and now, Bontemps' new book was out. Maybe Brun's turn was coming up. Don't major events happen in series of three? The Kid did have his superstitions. In Chapter 5 ("Ragtime") of *When Ragtime Was Young*, Version 4, he wrote, "It ['Maple Leaf Rag'] was first published with a cover of black-bordered white paper with the words, 'Maple Leaf Rag' printed in black letters. Those two colors are the symbol of death. I am superstitious enough to think that that first cover on his masterpiece, 'The Maple Leaf Rag' put the 'Jinx' on Joplin and caused him to die an untimely death." Brun would have done better with a little less superstition and a bit more sense, both common and business. But then, he wouldn't have been Brun Campbell.

1949–1952: Last Act: Spotlight on The Kid

As Brun's days dwindled down, so did his income. His 1948 tax form showed a gross of $2,065.87, which netted him $1,263.16, and his rent skyrocketed 63 percent to $490. Providentially, he paid no taxes for the year. But the old man's activities on behalf of ragtime, Scott Joplin, and Brun Campbell didn't lessen in the slightest.

People with any interest in ragtime had come to know, or at least know of, the old Ragtime Kid, Scott Joplin's first white pupil, the first white man to play "Maple Leaf Rag." On February 17, 1949, a young pianist from Portland, Oregon, Jerry Heermans, wrote, "I saw in *Playback* [an international jazz magazine] about your book 'When Ragtime Was Young.'" Heermans enclosed three dollars, and requested an autographed copy, "when it is ready." He also mentioned Brun's phonograph recordings, adding that he had not seen any available for sale.

This letter set off a lively exchange between the older man and the young ragtime/jazz performer. Much of the back-and-forth had to do with searches for sheet music and copyright information regarding particular early rags, but Brun also took on the role of mentor, making suggestions to Heermans regarding the way ragtime should properly be played. A good deal of information and opinion about Rudi Blesh and Harriet Janis, authors of *They All Played Ragtime*, also came across in the letters.

Brun replied to Heermans on February 21, to explain that due to high costs, it would be a while before his book would be published, and for the three dollars Heermans had sent, Brun offered a copy of his 78 rpm recording of "12th Street Rag," along with "my recording of 'Maple Leaf Rag,' taken from a piano roll played by the composer and my teacher, Scott Joplin. Joplin made this roll at the turn of the century." Brun further informed the young pianist that he could get a copy of the *Ragtime Volume 3* album from Lu Watters, that Brun would send him a copy of his "Cavalcade of Jazz" flyer in exchange for Heermans' copy of *Playback* which contained the announcement of Brun's upcoming book, and that Heermans should watch *Jazz Journal* for a series of four articles on ragtime written by Brun.

Brun advised Heermans frequently and at length regarding how to succeed in piano entertainment. On July 11, he instructed the young man to play Joplin and Turpin "as written," but that "Turpin's style of ragtime was a little faster than Joplin's. You play a very fine style of Ragtime. Don't try to imitate anyone's style, stay with what you feel in your playing." He praised Heermans for taking a course in marine refrigeration, because "Every young man should learn a trade … for in later years, if you have to you can fall back on it…. I am glad I had one to use in my declining years." Brun closed this letter with, "Don't forget to practize your piano at every chance, for that's important."

The July 15 letter from Brun contained some very interesting comments. He told Heermans "I may be able to furnish them [Blesh and Janis] with Joplin's and Chauvin pictures for their album, also I would be willing to co-operate with them on the album by letting them have my master and stampers to Joplin Hand played piano roll of 'Maple Leaf Rag.' Yes!"

There's no evidence that Brun followed through on this idea. The mother and stamper discs among his effects do not carry recordings of that piano roll. Brun closed the letter by reminding Heermans that "to be better than the other guy, you must practize more than he does."

In his letter of July 26, Brun praised Sadie Koninsky's "Eli Green's Cake-walk," and said he had played it on clarinet in 1901; in a later letter to Heermans, he wrote, "Most of those old songs, I played on the clarinet." Brun finished the July 26 letter by opining that playing with a band would be good experience for Heermans, but "practize is what makes you perfect. Be better than that other fellow. Stay with Ragtime." Finally, Brun offered a pithy opinion of what he considered his teacher's most difficult piece: "'Euphonic Sounds' was Joplin's toughest."

On August 25, Brun wrote that he was waiting for "word from London in regards to my book," and that he believed "they [*Jazz Journal*] intend to pub-lish it." Meanwhile, he kept busy: "I am working with Rudi Blesh, on his book, and the Ragtime album. He's on his vacation now." He encouraged Heermans to tune in, if he could, to KFOX at 10:30 pm on the next two Saturday evenings, that Brun had "worked out a Whole Ragtime program for them." At that late hour, the shows would not have been Hal Nichols' *Memory Room*, but since Nichols owned the station, he'd have to have given his blessing to the venture.

In a November 7 letter, Brun went ballistic over Rudi Blesh, expressing classic Brun sentiments in classic Brun language. Apparently, Heermans had told Brun he'd received a visit from Blesh and Janis. Here's Brun's reaction:

Just received your long-awaited letter & I thought you handled the situ-ation fine. And I know Blesh and Mrs. Janis are doing a fine job of getting fine material for the book. Now if he stays to the copyrighted facts instead of listening to a lot of nonsense, no doubt he will have a fine book. In your conversation with him I notice he says: We've gotten some data from him (me) which is O.K. Only other people have given us data on the same peo-ple and compositions which differ from what he has given us, now, I'll have to ask him what he means by that when he writes me. To many chickens spoil the broth. Carew is a case in point, like this, I wrote him to look up when Carbolic acid Rag was Copyrighted, I told him I played it in 1901. He wrote me back, that Clarence Wiley was the composer and it was copy-righted he thought in 1904. But he finally went to the copyright Dept, and found out I was right [few illegible words] in 1901. I have his letter. He also wrote me to send him my original copy of Black and White Rag Copy-righted in 1908. He said this Rag did not show up in the records as copyrighted in that year, but in 1923. Botsford the composer, copyrighted it then, with a few changes. So you see Jerry, the copyright records lie sometimes. Now understand Mr. Carew is one of my best friends as is Bill Russel, both are fine men and both are doing their bit, in helping to preserve the history of Ragtime, but Carew has given some stuff to Rudi that I gave him, so you can see how in a small way I get shove around. I always try to stay to the facts but I can make a mistake too. Now if Rudi had of told me that he was going to make the trip he did I could of put him in touch with negros in St. Louis and Sedalia & Hanniable MO, that would have been of great help to him, negros that I am sure Carew or Bill Russel knows nothing about. I have been doing some research on Joplin when he was in Hanniable Mo in 1895–96, from people who had a music store there in those years, and helped Joplin on some of his first compositions. I've got it in black and white. That's the kind of evidence I try to dig up, from things I heard Joplin tell about, but was unable to locate them, until I got your letter about Ray Walker at Olympia Wash. So you see how things work out some time.... Well Jerry I was very glad to hear from you, so you do what you think is right in regards to Rudi. Between you and me, I am some what peeved. Rudi found out from Carew, that I was going to write a book on Ragtime, and jumped in and stole my thunder, a friend of mine put me wise to it, so when I heard it, I quit assembling my material, so here's hoping Rudi does a good job. What will be, will be.... Always play the game square whatever it is. It pays.... I let you know when Rudi writes me.... I wrote him a pretty nasty letter....

Unfortunately, the majority of Brun's letters to Heermans are undated, so it's not possible to place his angry remarks about Blesh and Janis into chronological order. In context, though, they all seem to antedate the November 7 letter. Here are some examples:

In regards to your enclosed letter from Circle Records from Mrs. Harriet Janis, Don't give her anything or information, unless you find out for certain just how She and Blesh are going to treat me about the book on Ragtime. As you know they wrote me about sending my book Manuscript and Pictures to them which I did. Since then I can't hear a word from them, Mrs. Janis is editing the book and is plenty smart. She has the money in Circle Records and is Blesh's partner. If she asks you for copies of any old Rags, and pictures of any of the composers on the title page, nix it. Unless as I say that you find out from her just where I stand about the book. I only asked them for 25 books for the use of my Manuscript & pictures and 15 percent of the motion Picture rights & I think I made them a very generous offer.

Now Jerry let me know just as soon as you hear from Blesh, I been hearing quite a lot about him, and it ain't good.... Keep your nose clean & practice every time you get a chance....

I heard some more about Blesh (was good) but if he shows up remember, be a good listener.

Don't send Blesh anything until you hear from me. He is trying to outsmart me on the manuscript & pictures. I can't hear from him, but mums the word.... Look out for Joplin's "Cascades Rag" 1904, the copy had his picture on it, wearing a crown, when he was Crowned King of Ragtime.

In fact, the "Cascades" cover does feature a photo of Joplin in the middle of the page, enclosed within a decorative oval at the top of which is clearly a crown. No, Joplin isn't exactly wearing it, but the implication of his standing in the lineage of ragtime composers is made clear.

You're letter and all that goes between us is very confidential sacred, you may rest assured on that. Hope you get to the point where you can practic more, you have a good style for ragtime, please develope it more. For practize makes for perfect. Blesh probably wants to check on "Swipesy" ... for in my manuscript I say Joplin imeditaly put his first 4 rags down on paper, "Swipesy," "Sunflower Slow Drag," & The Favorite 1902. Of course, Swipesy was written by Joplin & Aurthur Marshall and Sun Flower Slow Drag was written by Scott Hayden and Joplin. I did not learn them from Joplin that year. I learned Maple Leaf Rag and Original Rags. But the way I worded it, sounded as though I learn them the same year, so I suppose that what he wants to check. Yes. I heard from Ray Walker and I have gotten some information about Joplin when he was in Hanniable Mo in 1895–6 which I think will stand up as authentic. Am waiting for some more. As far as you doing the right thing, go by what your heart dictates and I believe you will always be right, but always think things out (sleep on it) before you make a decicion.... Got a letter from Rudi, every thing is OK. Wants to check with me. So cheer up Jerry. I'm a fast worker if I have to be.

Brun went on to mention that his interview with Kay C. Thompson would appear in *The Record Changer* in about a month. In fact, the piece was published in *Jazz Journal* in April 1950, so this undated letter from Brun probably was written in late 1949, and he likely was referring to the only letter from Blesh in his files, which was postmarked November 7, 1949. Blesh wrote, "We just got back after three weeks in the middle West and found your card awaiting us ... as for the arrangements with you, we confirm that we will supply you free of charge 25 of the ragtime books and also that we will give you 15 percent of our share of any motion picture rights that may be sold as a result of your arranging same directly through your personal contacts. This is in accordance with our previous letter to you, in this connection."

Blesh also asked whether Brun could supply information "on Joplin's stay in Hannibal during 1895–1896," then added, "We will be writing you shortly too, about some further details on various matters that we need to fill in, as well as some facts we have found at variance with those mentioned in your manuscript, and which we would like to check again with you."

Finally, Blesh requested that Brun keep their "arrangements completely confidential, to the point even of not acknowledging that they exist." Blesh explained that if other interviewees were to request similar arrangements, "it might cost us hundreds of dollars which we cannot afford to expend."

So what really did go on between Brun and the historians? It's doubtful that Blesh and Janis did anything underhanded. Rather, Brun probably recognized during his interviews with Blesh that he'd be badly outclassed in a ragtime history-writing contest, and decided to try to give himself a boost by joining forces with the famous writer and critic. Though Brun castigated Blesh for "taking his manuscript," such that he would never be able to get it published, in reality he had no cause for complaint. His name appears on nine of the 270 pages of *They All Played Ragtime*; most of that material was extracted from *When Ragtime Was Young*, and told of Brun's 1898 encounter in Oklahoma City with Otis Saunders and the "Maple Leaf Rag," the boy's runaway to Sedalia to learn from Scott Joplin how to play ragtime, his years as an itinerant pianist, the lucky half-dollar story, and the donation to Fisk University. Moreover, all the passages were couched in strongly favorable, admiring tones. Brun's decision to give his material to Blesh was the best choice he could have made: considering both his poor writing skills and his unfamiliarity with professional publishing, *When Ragtime Was Young* was a very long shot to make it into print. In retrospect, The Kid's portrayal in *They All Played Ragtime* probably represented the single most valuable recognition of his credentials as a ragtime pioneer.

Existing extracts from Blesh's interviews with Brun contain further information that did not make it into *They All Played Ragtime* because the material could not be verified. These comments include:

"Says, Aug 13.49: Chauvin composed Turpin's Ragtime Nightmare."

"Aug 29, 1949: You are right about 'Chestnut St in the 90s' [Brun's composition, a tribute to the geographic center of ragtime in St. Louis during those years]. It is Shouvan's barrel house style which I think he originated. You will notice it carries some ragtime blue style in it. Play my record over of Frankie and Johnnie and listen to the way I used both hands and you will also detect Shauvan's style. He learned me to play it that way."

"You will notice Jop used Barrel House piano in a few strains of his first rag, Original Rags. Further claims that Jop learned this style from Shouvan (inaccurate)."

"My first hand experience with Joplin and Saunders was the two of them were very good teachers. Joplin was stern with me, while Saunders was just the opposite. Saunders almost white, and Joplin coal black in color, both about the same size."

"Nov. 9, 1949: Joplin in Hannibal in 1895–96. There was a music store there run by Mr and Mrs. Morton Walker; in those years the wife, Marie Walker was a very talented musician, she helped Jop with some of his early compositions, in 1895–96, but I am unable to supply you with the information at this time which ones there were, as Marie is dead, but husband Morton is alive and I presume in his 80's. I have contacted his nephew Ray Walker, who is now trying to get in touch with uncle. Marie Walker's daughter is alive and remembers her mother helping Joplin. Now if I do not get any more info. what I have sums up this way as I see it: Marie no doubt helped Joplin on those early songs: 'Please Say You Will,' 1895, 'Picture of her Face'–1895, 'Harmony Club Waltz,' 1896, 'Combination Waltz,' 1896, 'Great Crush Collision,' 1896. There also was a woman in Mo had a hand in Maple Leaf, this probably is the woman. I think the dope correct but you can take it at its face value."

On October 13, 1949, Brun signed a contract with Ray Boarman, proprietor of the Yerba Buena Music Shop in Oakland, for $21. The Kid sold Boarman "the masters or mothers or both, and the exclusive rights for the issuance of … 'Ginger Snap Rag,' 'Twelfth Street Rag,' 'Frankie and Johnnie Rag,' and 'Salome Slow Drag.'" In return, Brun was to receive royalties of two cents per record sold, and assurance that Boarman would pay all production expenses, that "adequate advertising and promotion" would be done, and that the records would bear the label of the Yerba Buena Music Shop. Brun had the option of cancelling the contract after six months if he felt Boarman had "not done a satisfactory job of distribution and publicity." It's not clear how this arrangement might have affected Brun's collaboration with Ray Avery at Record Roundup as regards distribution of "12th Street Rag" on the Echoes label. In addition, it's worth noting that Brun's recording of his composition "Salome Slow Drag" was advertised along with the record of the "Maple Leaf Rag" piano roll in the Clock Publishing Company flyer. This arrangement could have either antedated or followed Brun's agreement with Ray Boarman and Yerba Buena—or, Brun being Brun, the associations might even have been concurrent.

On New Year's Day, 1950, J.T.H. Mize wrote to Brun. Aside from being chief of the Music Section of the Special Services School for officers of the Army, Marines, and Air Corps, Mize was the editor of *Who Is Who in Music*. He wrote that his staff was preparing a biography on Brun for the upcoming edition of *Who Is Who*, and requested a photo since "we are using photos for about 2/3rds of the 'big wheels' in all fields of music.... Even a good photo taken in one of those automatic 25c places would be all right."

Mize asked whether Brun had "done anything further with your proposed book on Joplin. I continue to be very interested in that, but most surely do not wish to detour or delay you from any other publishing possibility. But if you haven't done anything definite by May 1 (when the WHO will be out and completed) I most certainly wish to go into the possibility of our publishing that."

May 1 came and went, but there seem to have been no further communications between Brun and Mize. However, the 1951 edition of *Who Is Who in Music*, published in Chicago, did carry a biographical sketch of Brun, though with no photographic accompaniment. Brun was defined as an "American Ragtime Pianist, Author, and Authority on Ragtime." He was described as having "blue eyes, graying brown hair, weighs 150, and is 5'8" in height." The piece contained a number of errors or fabrications, including the claim that Brun was Joplin's only white pupil, that he was working on a biography of Scott Joplin "tentatively titled *The Original Ragtime Kid of the 1890s*," and that his parents' names were Arthur Ensign and Mary Bourquiri Campbell. It's interesting that Brun's father, Luther Ensign Campbell, wrote most of his doggerel pieces under the name Art Ensign; why Brun would have given Editor Mize this name is unclear. How or why Lulu became Mary is also puzzling.

The remark about a Joplin biography clarifies a different uncertainty. The specification in Brun's sketch that the work in question was to be titled *The Original Ragtime Kid of the 1890s* suggests that Brun, likely frustrated by having given his *When Ragtime Was Young* material to Blesh and Janis, decided to quickly set up another book. That would explain the genesis of *The Original Ragtime Kid of the 1890s*, which was no more, really, than a reworking of his first project. And though Joplin's presence was significant in both manuscripts, neither one could in any way be considered a biography of Scott Joplin.

On March 6, New Orleans jazz pianist Armand Hug wrote to thank Brun "for the nice letter," saying, "I feel honored to have a man like yourself pay me such a nice compliment." Hug told Brun he'd played in New Orleans all his life, knew "most of the jazz men around here," and that discographer and historian Orin Blackstone "told me he was very familiar with your work both as a pianist and writer." Hug hoped Brun might give him some publicity via writeups, offered to provide him further information, and requested that Brun send a signed record to him in exchange for an autographed copy of one of his own records. Among Brun's effects, I found a copy of Capitol 863, with "Huggin' the Keys" on one side, and "Dixie Rag" on the other. Both labels are signed "To Brun Campbell, a great pianist. Sincerely, Armand Hug."

Hug added a short P.S. to his letter: "I am white." Brun likely had assumed that this lifelong jazz piano player from New Orleans had to have been black, and addressed him in some way that indicated the misperception.

On September 30, 1950, Lu Watters, c/o Hambone Kelly's, wrote to tell Brun it had been a rough year: "sickness that forced me to lay off the trumpet for a year, trouble with the band, and a general mess of worry running a nightclub." Lu told Brun that royalties from West Coast Recording would soon be available, but "because of the legal difficulties that arose from the Dawn Club [Lu's prior nightclub], this will cut the royalties pretty low." He asked Brun to "make copies of the original agreements and forward them to me so I can show them to the powers that be" [in reference to the soon-to-be new owners of West Coast]. He added, "If they don't agree to paying the royalties in the future I will try to stop them from issuing any of the sides there were agreements on."

The next letter from Armand Hug came more than a year after the first, July 20, 1951. Hug told Brun he'd received a copy of *Jazz Journal* recently, and had read Brun's ragtime article in it. He told Brun "it was very fine and I want to thank you for the nice compliment you gave me." Hug also told Brun he'd seen "a copy of *The Record Changer*" the day before "and saw your picture. It was a very good picture and I enjoyed seeing all the Scott Joplin music." Hug closed by telling Brun to "keep up that old ragtime spirit as only you can do."

The article in *Jazz Journal* was from the May 1951 issue, and was titled, "More on Ragtime." Brun had indeed been kind to Hug, writing, "Amongst present-day exponents of ragtime, I consider Armand Hug, of New Orleans, one of the greatest of this generation." *The Record Changer* reference was to an unattributed two-page spread in the July-August 1951 issue, which contained a short write-up and several photos of the pioneers of the genre—one of whom was "S. Brun Campbell, ardent champion of ragtime during its years of neglect, with his collection of Scott Joplin mementos." Most of the individual items in the photo are commercial sheet music copies, not original manuscripts, but at the center of the display is a copy of "Treemonisha, Opera, Scott Joplin," which was published by the composer's Scott Joplin Publishing Company. (All Joplin's efforts to have this work published and performed by anyone other than himself failed.) Unfortunately, the writer of the article referred twice to "Tom [rather than John] Stark, the music publisher who almost singlehandedly brought ragtime to the attention of the public…"

Meanwhile, the press was taking increasing notice of Brun, interest being fueled by a ceremony on April 17, 1951, at Hubbard School, the black high school in Sedalia, to honor Scott Joplin. Brun did not come out for the festivities, but from his home in Venice tried to persuade his friend, pianist Dink Johnson, to play at the ceremony, and lobbied to have the proceedings carried by radio to

New York, where he hoped to arrange for Louis Armstrong to present a scroll to Lottie Joplin. The broadcast never took place, and the event proceeded with exclusively local performers. Musical selections by Sedalia's Men's Choral Club included "Stout Hearted Men," "The Lost Chord," "Nola," "Battle Hymn of the Republic," and "Maple Leaf Rag." Mayor Herb Studer delivered a talk centered on the history of ragtime, Joplin's accomplishments in the field, and Sedalia's role in the furthering of the new musical genre. Z. Lyle Brown, president of the Men's Choral Club, presented a bronze plaque to J.B. Hylick, principal of Hubbard School, and Hylick replied with appreciation.

All in all, it was a historic event, and the Sedalians provided unequivocal evidence of the high regard in which they held Brun. Charles W. Hanna sent the Kid a cordial page-long letter and enclosed a photo of the Men's Choral Club with conductor Abe Rosenthal and accompanist Lillian Fox standing smartly in front. Hanna told Brun, "This club is made up of Business and Professional men who are banded together by the love for singing; to promote good fellowship and to advance the interest in and promote good music." After requesting that Brun get recognition for the Club "in any publications," Hanna wrote, "Remember, the Chamber gave us the run around and this move is taken by the Sedalia Men's Choral Club alone." Which should not be surprising, since in 1951, schools, restaurants, and just about every other public facility in Sedalia were still segregated, and it wasn't all that long since the Ku Klux Klan had been holding open meetings in Liberty Park.

Though Brun was confined to his California home and barber shop by age, increasing infirmity, and lack of money, he was not to be denied at least an auxiliary role. The April 15 *Sedalia Democrat* contained an article, "Concert as a Tribute to Scott Joplin: Men's Choral Club To Present Plaque Tuesday Night," which quoted Tom Ireland as remembering "Joplin as a serious man with respect to both music and life." Then the writer turned his attention to Brun: "Today's leading authority on Joplin and his music is Brunson Campbell of Kenice, Calif., who ran away from his Manhattan, Kas., home early in life to study under Joplin. Campbell is regarded as the number one 'rag-time' pianist still living, and second only to Joplin among the many who have played this music. He now devotes much time to seeking wider recognition for his teacher."

The day before the Sedalia celebration, the *Kansas City Star* carried an article by music editor Clyde B. Neibarger, "Ragtime Pioneers in Sedalia, Mo. Gave That Music a Big Boost Toward Fame." Neibarger described the upcoming ceremony, referred to Blesh and Janis' *They All Played Ragtime*, and accorded Brun considerable copy and latitude: "S. Brunson Campbell, nicknamed 'The Ragtime Kid,' says Kansas City, too, can claim much credit for the ragtime fad. Campbell took lessons from Scott Joplin in Sedalia in 1898. Currently, his activity and articles about ragtime have boosted interest in ragtime. He is striving now to promote the making of a Hollywood movie about Scott Joplin and ragtime."

Brun hit Page 1 of the May 21 issue of the *Los Angeles Examiner*, where columnist E.V. Durling wrote, "Passing By: S. Brun Campbell, veteran pianist, once known at 'The Ragtime Kid,' Campbell was taught to play ragtime by Scott Joplin, composer of the 'Maple Leaf Rag.'"

A long article on the first page of the December 8, 1951, issue of the *Venice Evening Vanguard*, though highly complimentary to Brun, was full of errors and inaccuracies. The reporter, Lester L. Robinson, referred to Brun as "the 'Original Ragtime Kid' of Sedalia, Mo.," and as "co-author of the book on jazz, *They All Played Ragtime*." Considering the time and effort Brun put in to persuade the public that ragtime was different from jazz and was to be preferred over jazz, he could not have been happy to read that. Later in the article, the reporter compounded his felony by writing, "Campbell furnished much of the material that went into the book, *They All Played Jazz*." Robinson referred to The Kid as a "writer of many articles in modern jazz and music magazines … known all over the world…. It has been through Campbell's many efforts that ragtime is now becoming popular again," and called Brun the "dean of ragtime historians … the last of the original ragtime pianists of the 1890s and 1900s." He quoted the old man at length regarding the origins and subsequent history of ragtime, going back to the 1890s when "ragtime was socially and musically in the dog house, or to be more specific in the 'Bawdy house.'"

The reference to Brun as co-author of *They All Played Ragtime* could have been due to either a misunderstanding by the reporter, or a conscious misrepresentation by The Kid. If the latter was in fact the case, it wasn't terribly smart. When Brun began his campaign to resurrect ragtime and Scott Joplin's reputation, there weren't many people who could have challenged him if he'd happened to stray a bit here and there from strict truth. But by 1951, that situation had changed. Brun would have done better to have claimed responsibility for much of the material in the book, "much" being a word with reasonably elastic properties.

A quote from the *Vanguard* article sheds light on a prior uncertainty in Brun's life. Robinson wrote that Brun had lived in Venice "for 25 years, having operated the one-man City Hall Barber Shop at 711 Venice Blvd. since he came here in 1926." This helps in locating Brun during those shadow years between 1918 and 1930, and corresponds both with his daughter Patricia's statement that the family left Tulsa at least in part for her health (she had been born in Tulsa on July 12, 1925), and with the fact that Brun and his wife, Marjorie May, were listed in the 1925 Tulsa City Directory, but not after that year. Apparently, if the Campbells did spend any time in another location, it was not for long.

I

The only white pianist personally coached by Scott Joplin . . .

● The only white pianist to be personally coached by Scott Joplin was the "Ragtime Kid" of the 1890s," S. Brun Campbell. Retired from music for many years, Campbell is now a barber in Venice, Calif., but recently cut several records for the Jazz Man label. In his words: "I was born March 26, 1884, in Washington, Kan. I met Scott Joplin in the late part of 1898, when I was almost 15. It came about through his pal, Otis Saunders, whom I met in Oklahoma City in the summer of 1898. Otis had a pen and ink manuscript of *Maple Leaf Rag*, and I played it for him

II

"I studied with Joplin and Saunders about three weeks.

at his request. I became so infatuated with that new music, ragtime, that when I returned to my home at Arkansas City, Kan., I ran away and headed for Sedalia, Mo., where I met Joplin. He was so impressed by my playing that he took me in hand and taught me all the intricacies of *Maple Leaf Rag* and some of his other early rags. I studied with Joplin and Saunders for about three weeks. Being a sight reader, I didn't need very much coaching. It was Joplin who gave me the moniker of the "Ragtime Kid," as I became a professional ragtime pianist at the early age of 16, and pioneered the playing of almost all of Joplin's early rags

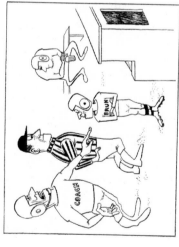

III

"I played barrel houses, minstrel and old medicine shows . . ."

through the midwest and some southern states. I played the red light district, barrel houses, minstrel and old medicine shows, steam boats, theaters, and about every place a pianist could play in the early days. I knew almost all of the pianists and composers of early ragtime from 1898 until 1908, when I married and gave up the piano. I can tell you that Joplin was very proud of me and the work I was doing, spreading the gospel of ragtime to the white people. And I am happy to know that I did my bit in those early days." (From a letter by S. Brun Campbell.)

"Evolution of Jazz," three-panel cartoon from *DownBeat*, depicting Scott Joplin as Brun's ragtime football coach. The artist quotes Brun as saying he studied with Joplin for approximately three weeks (courtesy *DownBeat* Archives).

Brun was quoted as saying that he'd been trying to "get hold of some of his early day recordings of ragtime tunes. But they are collectors' items and he has had no ... success in finding them." In fact, Brun made no recordings before the 1940s. Either the reporter misunderstood or misquoted his subject, or this was another of Brun's embellishments.

A second front-page piece appeared in the *Vanguard* on January 7, 1952: "Famous Ragtime Personalities Flood S. Brun Campbell, 'Ragtime Kid,' Now Living in Venice, With Yule Cards." After a short recapitulation of Brun's prominence in the ragtime revival of the time, and mention of his having been Joplin's pupil, the anonymous journalist mentioned a number of the "holiday cards and greetings" Brun had received from famous songwriters and ragtime personalities throughout the nation. Included in the list were prominent Sedalian Charles R. Hanna, J. Lee Anderson, who'd drawn a cartoon strip in *DownBeat* that portrayed Joplin as Brun's football coach, ragtime/jazz writer Kay C. Thompson, E. Simms Campbell, W.C. Handy, Roy Carew, and Erskine Kerr. Dr. Edmond Souchon, past president of the New Orleans Jazz Club and leader of the marvelous 6–7/8 String Band, had also sent holiday greetings, as had Ray Avery, Armand Hug, and Hal Nichols, though in an impressive display of journalistic carelessness, they were referred to as Roy Avery, Arnold Hug, and Al Nickols respectively.

Aside from obituaries, the last newspaper mention of Brun seems to have been in E.V. Durling's column of March 4, 1952, in the *Los Angeles Examiner*. A reader had inquired of Durling as to whether Irving Berlin had ever been known as "The Ragtime Kid." Durling replied in the negative, stating that the original Ragtime Kid had been S. Brun Campbell, "an accomplished cafe pianist specializing in ragtime." Maybe "cafe" was not exactly the right word for Brun's venues, but all right. Ironically, the sobriquet Berlin had tried to pin on himself, "The King of Ragtime," was the nickname that previously and properly had been bestowed on Brun's teacher and idol, Scott Joplin.

In Brun's files were two inspection sheets from the California State Board of Barber Examiners, the first dated May 2, the second, September 11. The examiners graded Brun's shop on twenty-four points, and despite the stories told by his customers about his defiencies as a barber, the shop did well in the May inspection, scoring Good to Fair on all counts, no Poors, and in the September reckoning, a number of the Fairs had improved to Goods.

Brun's handwritten records of income and expenses for the barber shop continued uninterrupted until very close to the end of his life. His last entered income was for the week of November 10, 1952; his last expenses were noted for the week of November 17.

There was only one more letter in Brun's correspondence files—sent by

W.C. Handy on November 10, 1952, just two weeks before The Kid's death. The letter was addressed to "Dear Sir," and after a brief recollection of Handy's recent accomplishments and accolades, the composer took a page and a half to glory in his recent success in helping to elect Eisenhower and Nixon, largely through composing and playing a tune called "Hike with Ike."

Brun died November 23, 1952, from arteriosclerosis and congestive heart failure, and was buried in Valhalla Cemetery in North Hollywood. His grave marker reads, "In Loving Memory, Sanford Brunson Campbell, 1884–1952." His obituary in the *Santa Monica Evening Outlook* identified him as "The dean of ragtime historians and the last great ragtime artist of the Gaslight Era ... the first White pupil ever accepted by the originator of ragtime, the fabulous Scott Joplin, of Sedalia, Mo.," the composer of "famous recordings of numbers he authored," and "an authority of jazz music." The article closed with a tribute to his "clever fingers."

III

Short Pieces

Unpublished historical narratives, rhymes, and pipe dreams, with contemporary comments by Larry Karp, David Reffkin, and Richard Egan

In addition to his multiple variations on *When Ragtime Was Young* and *The Original Ragtime Kid of the 1890s*, Brun wrote a number of shorter works during the 1940s. Some were histories of early ragtime music and its composers and performers; others were exhortations directed at the composers and musicians of the day with the goal of persuading them to abandon the jazz idiom and return to ragtime performance. Some of Brun's shorter essays were originally parts of one or another version of *When Ragtime Was Young* or *The Original Ragtime Kid*, and some were extracted for publication in magazines, primarily *The Record Changer* and *Jazz Journal*.

The works in this section of the book are transcribed from Brun's manuscripts, and have not been published elsewhere, at least not in the original form in which their author cast them.

To allow the reader to get a good sense of Brun's writing and in some cases compare unedited pieces to those reworked by Roy Carew, I have presented the works as I found them, complete with errors of spelling and grammar, unfortunate sentence structure, and typographical missteps.

Otis Saunders and "The Maple Leaf Rag"

by S. Brun Campbell, The Original Ragtime Kid of the 1890s

When I first met Otis Saunders in Oklahoma City, Oklahoma, in the latter part of 1898, I was going on 15 years of age. Otis was a handsome, light-colored young Negro, about 25 years old. Standing 5 feet, 7 inches tall, straight hair, and weighing 150 pounds, he bore himself straight and proud, walking at a fairly rapid gait. Moreover, he was a neat, clean dresser, wearing his high roller Stetson hat at what was then called an "ace deuce angle," [one side of the hat tilted lower than the other] and invariably, his eyes revealed a definite expression of gaiety. At the time, everything looked rosy to Otis, for he was a fine pianist and one of the early great Negro pioneers of that new music, Ragtime. It was no wonder that things looked bright to Otis, for he had two good jobs. At the Armstrong-Byrd Music Co. of Oklahoma City, he worked behind the counter as a salesman and player of popular sheet music. This job occupied him from 1 p.m. to 6:30 p.m. daily, while at night, he played on West Second Street in the red-light district for a white madam by the name of Scare Face Mary. At the time, Otis had a pen-and-ink manuscript of "Maple Leaf Rag," the cover of which read, "Maple Leaf Rag by Scott Joplin and Otis Saunders, Sedalia, Missouri."

It was Otis who gave me my first lessons in playing "Maple Leaf Rag," following which I met Scott Joplin and Saunders at Sedalia Mo, a short while afterward. Joplin subsequently took me in hand, teaching me all the intricacies of "Maple Leaf Rag." Needless to say, he was a splendid teacher, and I might add, a good deal more strict with me than Saunders had been. They both played about the same style of Ragtime. That is, they played at a fairly slow tempo, and they both played well in a Ragtime manner that was known in those days as Scott Joplin's Sedalia Style, or sometimes, just plain Sedalia style, meaning the style played by the early Negro pianists of that section in the 1890s.

On several occasions, it hs been suggested, mostly on the basis of rumor, that Scott Joplin was not the true composer of "Maple Leaf Rag." For example, in an article appearing in the Record Changer of October 1945, entitled, "Ragtime–History & Analysis," by Dr. Bartlett D. Sims and Ernest Bornemann, Mr. Bornemann presented on page 31 a "Selective Chronology of Ragtime, Blues, & Pop Tunes" that influenced Jazz history. In the list referred to, he named Otis Saunders as the composer of "Maple Leaf Rag." I do not know his source for this information, but I do know that it is not correct. As it happens, "Maple Leaf Rag" was Scott Joplin's baby from the very beginning, and as I pointed out in an interview appearing in the London Jazz Journal of April 1950, Joplin was playing an early version of "Maple Leaf Rag" in the 1880s, prior to his Sedalia period. It is, of course, true that Otis Saunders arranged "Maple Leaf Rag" in its present day form, re-writing the last half of the trio. However, his contribution ended there, in connection with which, I also know that Joplin and Otis had a falling out over "Maple Leaf Rag," for Otis thought that his name should appear on the covers of the published sheet music along with Joplin's as composer. Joplin, on the other hand, took the position that he had paid Saunders for whatever work that he had done on the tune, and that "Maple Leaf Rag" was his exclusive property, and under the circumstances, I entirely agree with Joplin.

Ultimately, Saunders' failing was Wine, Women, and Song. Neverthe-less, he had a splendid Baritone singing voice that he used to charm the ladies, and it goes without saying, when he turned on his charm, he usually got his woman. Otis, when I knew him, was a real sporting-house pianist, and in my mind, there is no question that he sold some of his Rags to Joplin, Turpin, James Scott, and others that were later published under their names. Of course, this is only my opinion and belief; the procedure was perfectly legitimate, and I do know that Otis would sometimes do so in order to obtain a fast dollar, especially if he were bent on impressing some gal whom he was trying to make. Moreover, there is no question that Otis was a great help to Joplin in his early Sedalia days, among other things, helping him arrange his first published, "Original Rags." This num-ber was essentially a medley of Rag strains, which Joplin sold to Charles Daniels (Neil Moret), who was then with Hoffman Music Publishers of Kansas City as a silent partner. Daniels re-arranged Joplin's medley to suit himself, having it copyrighted by Carl Hoffman, Music Publishers in 1899. Later, when Daniels left Hoffman and joined Remick Music of Detroit, Michigan, in 1904, "Original Rags" was transferred to the latter concern. Today, it is owned by the Music Holding Corp. of New York.

After Joplin and Saunders had their falling-out over "Maple Leaf Rag," they became friendly once more, and were together in St. Louis at the time of the St. Louis World's Fair Exposition in 1904. It was about this time that Joplin wrote "The Cascades," a Rag named after one of the main fea-tures of the Fair, called the "Cascades of Lights." During its run, the St. Louis Exposition attracted the greatest army of Ragtime pianists, both Negro and White, that was ever assembled, for there were plenty of jobs in sporting-houses, saloons, parks, theatres, tent shows, and the like. In fact, Market Street, 18th Street, and Chestnut Street in the Negro district were alive with Ragtime pianists, such as Scott Joplin, Otis Saunders, Tom Turpin, Louis Chauvin, Sam Patterson, Owen Marshall, Scott Hayden, Arthur Marshall, Joe Jordan, and the White pianist, Eddie Barnes, and many others, and every train brought more, for that was the year that the Negroes held the World's Fair Ragtime Piano Playing Contest. Many of the greatest Negro Ragtime pianists participated in that contest, the winner being a Negro then from Indianapolis, Ind., by the name of Alfred Wilson, originally from New Orleans.

Naturally, this widely publicized contest did much to acquaint visitors to the Fair with the new Ragtime music, which was just beginning to take popular root, and after the Fair, Ragtime pianists commenced to migrate all over the world, spreading their musical gospel. In Europe, it was played before the Crown Heads. John Phillip Sousa, America's foremost concert band leader, adopted it, as did Arthur Pryor, and many others. Minstrel bands strutted up the Main Streets of America as they played a snappy Rag, and even the old Medicine Shows featured it. Thus, Ragtime soon became the greatest musical craze the world has ever known. Born in the gay 90s at Sedalia, Missouri, in an era referred to today as the "Good Old Days," this remarkable revolution owes its origin to "Maple Leaf Rag," which was first published in 1899 by John Stark & Sons, Music Publishers at Sedalia Mo. Its composer, Scott Joplin, died in 1917 at the age of 49, his final resting place being a New York City cemetery. Presumably, Otis Saunders, the man who helped him arrange it, is also dead, for all trace of him is lost. At any rate, he vanished, no one knows where. However, Scott Joplin and Otis Saunders will always be remembered by me as the Ace and King of Ragtime, and I say, "Here's to them both!" Understandably, I cannot help wishing they were with us today to be in on the Ragtime revival that is now taking place, for I know they would get a great kick out of what is happening. Meanwhile, though they have both passed on, it is consoling to think that "Maple Leaf Rag" still lives, a fitting monument to their musical greatness!

The Maple Leaf Rag

by S. Brunson Campbell
[handwritten]

   In the Record Changer Magazine of Oct–1945 there is a musicial chart under the title of "A Selective Chronology of Ragtime Blues and Pop tunes that influenced Jazz History"–by Ernest Borneman. The claim he made as to the composer of Maple Leaf Rag is all wrong. He gave the name of Otis Saunders as its Composer. The true facts are, Otis Saunders was a Mulatto, & Scott Joplin's Pal.–Otis Saunders re-arranged the Maple Leaf rag into the present day Copy (1899) and wrote the last half of the trio. The Maple Leaf Rag was Scott Joplin's "Baby" at the beginning. Joplin in a talkitive mood one day when he was teaching me how to play it at Sedalia MO, (in late 1898) was telling Scott Hayden & Otis Saunders & myself, that he was playing a version of Maple Leaf Rag back in 1889 up to the trio when he was 21 years old. He never was able to complete it, to his satisfaction, although he had many pianists helped him work on it. One fine musician & pianist who helped Joplin on his first Rag compositions in 1889 (among them was Maple Leaf Rag) was a white woman by the name of Marie Walker who with her husband Morton Walker ran a Music Store in Missouri in the late 1880s. Joplin as I remember never told what town in Missouri, the Walkers had their music store, but I pressume it was a town close to Sedalia or St. Louis, as Joplin first landed in St. Louis in 1885. So by 1889 he must of made many music Connections, for when Ragtime Burst upon the Public in the 1890s Joplin was prepared with plenty of Ragtime Material. The part Marie Walker played with Joplin in 1888–1889 is pacially verified by her nephew Ray N. Walker who owns a Music Service Store (Everything for the Musician) out here on the West Coast. Ray is up in years & plays some good Ragtime yet. The original Trio that Joplin had originally to the Maple Leaf Rag was of the Stomping Ragtime Variety. I can play his original version of the Trio, which Saunders omited in the published version. Who wrote the first half of the trio, I do not know, probaly it was Marie Walker. At any rate it was not all peaches and cream with Joplin and the Maple Leaf Rag, but he certainly knew what he wanted put into that great Rag, and eventually got it. Which is more proof of his greatness. Having heard Joplin tell the story about the Maple Leaf Rag proves to me that many roving Negro pianists like Joplin, was playing Ragtime in the 1880s. But why Negro piano Ragtime music, was not put down on paper until the 1890s & published, is one of the mysteries that goes with the history of Ragtime music.

Ragtime historians, composers, and performers Richard Egan and David Reffkin here offer thoughts on Brun's statements regarding the composition of "Maple Leaf Rag," particularly regarding Otis Saunders' possible role.

Richard Egan:

"Ragtime was a pool of many men's ideas, and the one who could put it down on paper was considered the rightful composer, even if he did not originate the tune..."

-Brun Campbell: The Ragtime Kid (An Autobiography)

"The Maple Leaf Rag" may indeed be the pool of many men's (possibly women's) ideas, and it is possible that Joplin was already playing parts of it in the late 1880s. It is also possible that Otis Saunders (or others) contributed significantly to the trio, and that they contributed other musical ideas throughout. But Joplin was the serious student, the serious musician who had been encouraged by Saunders to attend the George Smith College, and while Saunders (with others) was off amusing himself with wine, women and song, Joplin was putting the music down on paper and working with the form and structure of the piece. Had Joplin not done so, and if it really is a collaborative effort, would Saunders (or others) have ever seen the piece to publication? Had Saunders published it as his composition, would it have approached Joplin's high quality? Would it have been in the classic AABBACCDD structure? To all of these questions, I emphatically say "No!"

Perhaps, as Campbell asserts, Joplin played the trio in a "Stomping Ragtime Variety." We may assume that Campbell's recordings of "Maple Leaf Rag" approach Campbell's perspective/perception of Joplin's stomping style. And perhaps Saunders did indeed contribute the second half of the trio. This is interesting, because this means that the most technically difficult and awkward section of the rag is Saunders' contribution, not Joplin's.

The 13th measure of the trio features a syncopated left hand phrase followed abruptly by a lower A flat octave at the beginning of the 14th measure. The difficulty of this passage has challenged pianists (most definitely myself), and when I judge other pianists' abilities, I always listen to how they handle C13–14. Campbell avoided the syncopated left hand entirely, but instead played four solid ascending eighth notes. My assumption had always been that Campbell avoided the difficult passage because he couldn't handle it as written. After reading these articles, I now consider it possible that he played the version taught to him by Scott Joplin. This could be either Joplin's "Stomping Ragtime Variety" or a simplification from Joplin who recognized young Campbell as a green ragtime neophyte.

I can imagine that the "Maple Leaf Rag" was long in developing, and that it was a decade-long pool of the ideas of many pianists (which, incidentally, would contradict Campbell's story of the 1897 silver dollar commemorating the year Joplin wrote his first rag), but the true tour de force of the rag is the D section, which pulls the entire piece together with creative genius. This section, in its refinement and voicing, most closely resembles other early Joplin rags. While Joplin may have borrowed ideas from others to compose the first three strains, I believe that this section is 100 percent Joplin, and that once he completed the four-section piece, he was satisfied to have the rag published.

David Reffkin:

After reviewing comments in *King of Ragtime* (first edition), by Edward Berlin; articles in *The Rag Times*; Addison Reed's PhD thesis, *The Life and Works of Scott Joplin*; and tapes of seminars from the early years of the Scott Joplin Ragtime Festival in Sedalia, Missouri (attended by Rudi Blesh and others, including myself), there is no way to confirm even a fraction of the truth about Saunders. We are left with hearsay and innuendo. But we are also left with more good questions that can be preserved in this history for later research.

Saunders and others advised Joplin to attend the George R. Smith College for music study. The speculation (noted in Reed) is that he learned how to write syncopated rhythms. If this technical knowledge eluded other musically uneducated blacks in the region, Saunders himself may not have had the expertise to write anything in "Maple Leaf Rag." Playing it is another matter. Ragtime compositions were not always written down, rather created and refined at the keyboard in practice and on the job. Setting the notes on paper to be published and distributed was a key attribute of the music of Joplin and some of the composers that followed him.

In Berlin's book, Saunders is described as having claimed co-authorship of Tom Turpin's "St. Louis Rag." But this was never proved, and he may have been predisposed to these claims. His dispute reflects the same issue concerning another Joplin rag, "The Favorite," again with no musicological evidence at all. Also, there is no supporting evidence that Marie Walker in Hannibal helped Joplin.

The tricky term in his description is "arrangement," because composers, musicians and publishers define the term more specifically and distinctly than most people outside the music business. Composition and arrangement, to say nothing of orchestration and adaptation, sometimes border a rather thin line, and the terms cause understandable confusion, especially when used beyond even their customary definitions. Note the printed credits for "Sensation Rag": "Composed by Joseph F. Lamb," and "Arranged by Scott Joplin." This attribution, historians have determined, implies that Joplin's name recognition helped get the piece published. It is not an indication of his hand in its composition or editing.

The Joplin/Saunders/Campbell relationships will remain mostly undefined, subjected to historical and present-day speculation supported by mere whiffs of evidence.

The First Ragtime Circuit

Originally Chapter 9 of The Original Ragtime Kid of the 1890s

The three most important cities at the beginning of ragtime in the 90's was Sedalia, Mo., St. Louis and Kansas City, Mo., which formed a sort of nucleus for the beginning of a Ragtime Circuit, which the early ragtime pianist was to travel and sell their wares.

They played in questionable places in these three cities. These early Negro composers and pianists made the rounds, back and forth from one city to the other, playing and exchanging ideas.

On the north side in the colored district of Sedalia once could hear such great Negro composers and pianists beating out the rhthms of the Scott Joplin's Sedalia, Mo. style of ragtime such as Otis Saunders, Aurthur Marshall and Scott Hayden and the great Scott Joplin himself. At Kansas City, Mo., between Second and Fourth Streets on North Main and west on Sec-

ond and Fourth in the 'Tenderloin' District, in houses like Madame Anderson's, the echo's of the ragtime pianists rhythm could be heard way into
the dead of the night. Over at St. Louis in the 'district' in places like "Babe
Connor's" around Chestnut and Market Streets, west of Eighteenth you
could hear such Negro ragtime pianists as Louis Chauvin, Sam Patterson
and the Dean of the St. Louis style of ragtime, "The Great" Tom Turpin
himself. The three cities mentioned formed the first ragtime circuit and by
accident it expanded. When Otis Saunders, a pal of Scott Joplin over at
Sedalia, Mo. had a lovers quarrel with his girl (also a pianist) who left Saunders and went to Wichita, Kansas, where she got a job playing piano in the
redlight district there from Madam Inez Miller, a notorious character of the
district. Saunders followed her there and he likewise got a job playing
piano for Bessie Osborne, another 'madame' of the "District." The two of
them were the two first ragtime pianists to rock the district with genuine
Negro ragtime. Saunders tried to get his girl to make up and return to
Sedalia, but instead she left Wichita and landed at Arkansas City, Kansas,
and played piano for a Madam 'Georgie,' not liking a small town she went
south to Oklahoma City where Saunders caught up with her again. He
found her playing piano in the district there for "Scar Face Mary." He also
got a job as pianist right across the street for Madame Lee. Eventually
they made up and returned to Sedalia, but on the way back, they went
back by another route. From Oklahoma City they went west to El Reno,
Okla., where they played for the notorious Frank Swaggart who ran a large
dance hall in the 'District,' from there they went north to Kingfisher, Okla.,
where they played for a few weeks and then returned to Sedalia, but on
that trip they made good money in all the places they stopped and passed
the word around to other negro pianists what good towns they were, and
those towns were included in the circuit.

From then on the ragtime circuit expanded, and in a few years the circuit covered all of America and Alaska. Those early Negro pianists who first
spread the gospel of ragtime never realized that they were making ragtime's history as they traveled that early ragtime circuit. Even Saunders
himself never realized when he took Joplin's ragtime to New Orleans in
late 1899, that some day New Orleans would be the most important city in
America on the early Ragtime Circuit. Where the Lulu Whites of the "District" would furnish jobs for the ever increasing ragtime pianists. The 'district' who all had there Frankie and Johnnies,' and Stack O'Lees, gamblers,
pimps, macks, and hop heads. But it was at first the "Music of the Devil" so
the ministers preached and it attracted his disciples. But it grew up eventually and became a respectful music.

To-day, the circuit of the jazz pianist and jazz musician is in the cocktail bars and notorious night spots the world over. Now I am asking you–Is their circuit any more respectable than the circuit the early ragtime pianist traveled? I hardly think so! Just more glamourous that's all.

The Original Hot Men of the 90s: A Condensed History of Early Day Ragtime

by S. Brunson Campbell

As discussed in "1946–1947: The Pen is Mightier Than The Pest," the confusion over finding two similar but not identical manuscripts of "The Original Hot Men of the 90s" was cleared by comments in a letter to Brun from Roy Carew. After Brun submitted the piece to *Esquire* and received encouragement regarding its publication, he asked Carew to look over the work with an eye toward joint authorship. Carew did some editing, including writing the introduction, but claimed that his contribution was minimal, that the article had been written from Brun's point of view, and that he should proceed as sole author.

Carew's assessment of his editorial contributions was far too modest. If Brun had been able to work on his longer manuscripts with an editor as skilled as Roy Carew, he might well have succeeded in getting *When Ragtime Was Young* published.

Let's start with Brun's copy.

The original Negro Hot men of the 90's were most all composers and pianists and all except one had musicial training, his name was Louis Chauvin, a great natural pianist and one of the best rag men of his time. I will list the others in this order: Tom Turpin of St. Louis, Mo., who wrote the first so called 'Rag' which was named 'The Harlem Rag' and was published in 1897. He also wrote the 'Bowery Buck' in 1899, 'The Ragtime Nightmare' in 1900, the 'St. Louis Rag' in 1903, and 'The Buffalo' in 1904. Tom Turpin was not only the greatest fast ragtime pianist but he was also a politician and owner of a couple of saloons and a few sporting houses, he also had a theater. In all these places he had good jobs for the top negro pianists and he was in a position to get fine rag material from them.

But the King of Ragtime and its perfector was a young negro pianist and composer whose name was Scott Joplin, born in Texarkana, Texas, in 1868, November 24. He had traveled all through the middle west and was playing his original ragtime as far back as 1891, six years before any published 'rag' appeared in written form. He finally landed in Sedalia, Mo., and got a job playing piano for a negro who owned a saloon whose name was Tony Williams. A short while after he was in Sedalia, Mo., he entered the Smiths School of Music there, and it was just what he had been looking forward to for so many years. This gave him his chance to work out his revolutionary ideas in music, so he put in manuscript form his first rag titled 'The Original Rags!' In 1897 he sold it to the Carl Hoffman music publishers of Kansas City, Mo., who published in 1899. Then in 1898 he put in manuscript form his famous 'Maple Leaf Rag.' He rearranged it with his pal Otis Saunders, who collaborated with Joplin on the last half of the Trio. Before Scott Joplin died in 1917 he had over forty 'Rag' hits to his credit, and was known throughout the Ragtime Era as the King of all ragtime writers. He also wrote a complete ragtime operetta in three acts and also published it in 1911. It was only produced once, and that was at his home in New York. Bud Scott of Kid Ory's Dixieland Band played with Joplin when he produced his operetta Treemonisha. I think Scott Joplin was the greatest ragtime pianist of them all for the reason his rags were the hardest to play and had to be played slow, as Joplin always suggested, to get all out of them that he put in them. The original Sedalia style of ragtime was Joplin's, which I have said was slow.

With Scott Joplin in Sedalia were other fine ragtime negro pianists and early composers who were from Scott Joplin's Sedalia School of Ragtime. They were Aurthur Marshall, Scott Hayden, James Scott, Louis Chauvin, Tony Williams, Melford Alexandra, Otis Saunders and Ida Hastings, negress pianist. Tom Turpin and other St. Louis negro pianists would visit Joplin occasionally. They would have their ragtime piano playing contests at Sedalia and St. Louis, Mo., like the jazz session of to-day. Sedalia was a wide open town in those early days of ragtime and good ragtime pianists always could find a job. The Smiths School of music there attracted the most progressive of the Negro musicians as there was an endowed department for them. [At this point, as Page 2 ends, there is a handwritten addition with #3 at the top left, apparently a message from Brun to Carew]: under the supervision of the blind Negro Prof. W.G. Smith who got a great deal of his education at a School for the blind in St. Louis. He taught instrumental music. Scott Joplin and other negro pianists of the early Ragtime days took courses from him there at Sedalia, one of his famous puplis was the blind negro pianist John William Boone "Blind Boone," who created quit a sensation all through the Middle West, on his tour. He had a manager (You have blind Boone distription and history which I sent you). Work in the history of the Harlem Rag. Robt DeYoung St. Louis 1897. Harry Von Tilzer publisher–1897. Stern in N.Y. 1899. Wm Tyres arrangement. [Manuscript resumes, top of Page 3]:

Louis Chauvin was the greatest natural negro pianist I ever heard. But all of them were good and some were better than others, and it was a treat to listen to any one of them play the piano, for they were the original hot men of the 90's and how they could play ragtime.

Ragtime is a kind of music characterized by a strongly Syncopated Melody superimposed upon a regularly accented accompaniment. The influence of these early negro hot men of the 90's is still being felt in Boogie-Woogie, the Blues, Swing, Cowboy, Hillbilly and Jazz music and other types of hot music. But all through the Ragtime Era the name of Scott Joplin stands out as the most progressive of the entire lot of the Early Negro Composers.

We early ragtime pianists played on old and battered uprights and square pianos; some were inlaid with Mother of Pearl. These were seldom in tune. Then there were the newer uprights, some with Mandolin attachments, and when they got out of tune they were very 'tin panish.' The present day Boogie-Woogie dates back to the early ragtime pianist who was called a 'Faker.' He had a good right hand, but did not make much difference what he did with the left hand (bass), just so he kept his rhythm. Then other smarter piano players got the idea of Walking and Rocking the bass, out of this grew the Boogie-Woogie style with its fast rolling bass with an undercurrent of great power.

There was an original style of dress with the ragtime pianist and male characters of the underworld. No one seems to know just where the style originated. One of the styles which seemed popular was the High Roller Stetson hat. Box back coats, generally of blue serge were worn with button cloth top shoes, tooth pick or bull dogged toes. The shirt was of loud patterns, some with stiff bosoms and detatchable cuffs worn with high white or colored collars. The cuff buttons were made of two-and-a-half and five dollar gold pieces. The shirt stud was a similar gold piece or a diamond stud was used. A Tiffany or Belcher mounted diamond ring was also worn. The vest was of the loudest patterns of silk or linen material, double or single breasted. Then there was the loud sheppard plaids and stripped suits. The coat collar was made of velvet and the coat lapels were silk faced. When the suit happened to be made of black broadcloth it would be dressed up with big white pearl buttons, big as a silver dollar, the vest would be double or single breasted with a watch chain worn across the front. The tie would be a flowing bow with loud patterns or a four-in-hand or cravat. Occasionally you would see some dude pianist wearing a bowler hat (derby to you). It was a ragtime age and we were dressing in a ragtime style.

When Scott Joplin signed a five year contract with Stark and Son music publishers to write rags for them at Sedalia, Mo., he made his one first lucky step [A five-year exclusive contract between Joplin and Stark has been mentioned often in ragtime histories, but there's no evidence that such an extended agreement ever really existed]. Shortly after Stark and Son moved their outfit to St. Louis, Mo., and Joplin soon followed. Then things really commenced to happen in the ragtime field. Otis Saunders, Joplin's pal, and Louis Chauvin were the first negro pianists to take Joplin rags to New Orleans and introduce them to the New Orleans negro pianists.

This is where Jelly Roll Morton puts in his appearance on the early ragtime horizion. It was not long after Saunders and Chauvin landed in New Orleans that Joplin 'Rags' were echoing from negro saloons, pool halls, dance halls and the redlight district. It was the New Orleans negro pianists who then migrated North through the Gulf and Southern and Middle-Western states that spread ragtime North to St. Louis, Missouri. By 1903 St. Louis had more ragtime pianists than they knew what to do with, so they migrated in every direction out of St. Louis. Some went to Chicago, some to New York and the West coast. But the largest number stayed in the middle West, as all cities and towns of any size were wide open and they all found ready work.

The list of original Hot Men I have mentioned would not be complete unless my good friend W.C. Handy, Tony Jackson and Jelly Roll Morton were included for they too were hot men of the 90's. The original 'Rag' men of the 90's were Scott Joplin, Tom Turpin, Louis Chauvin, James Scott, Scott Hayden, Otis Saundes, Aurthur Marshall, Melford Alexandra, Tony Williams, Tony Jackson, Jelly Roll Morton and W.C. Handy.

Of the white ragtime pianists of the 90's was Ben Harney a pianist and singer from Louisville, Ky, who claimed to be the originator of ragtime and the first white to transcribe ragtime for the piano. He was a little man with a big voice. He was an accompanist to a negro banjo player. He toured the Middle-West long before he went east to start the 'coon song craze.' Of historicial importance are his songs: "Mr. Johnson, Turn Me Loose," "You've Been A Good Old Wagon But You Done Broke Down," and "A Cake Walk in the Sky." In 1897 or 1898 he had a book printed by Witmarks which he titled 'How to Play Ragtime on the Piano,' although his instructions were interesting, they were anything but complete. My opinion is Ben Harney was the originator of the Coon Songs of the 90's and not the originator of ragtime. When Ben Harney was touring the Middle-West in 1908, I met him and we had quite a visit. At the time he was billed as the originator of ragtime. He played mechanically with heavy hands as he spread the gospel of ragtime. In 1899 the first rag written and arranged and played by a white pianist was "Rags to Burn" published in the same year by the Jenkins

Music Publishers of Kansas City, Mo. The pianists name was Frank X. McFadden.

Now it is time for me to get into the picture it was in the late 1898's when I was in my early teens. I was playing over some popular numbers in the Armstrong Byrd Music store in Oklahoma City, Okla., and among the crowd that had gathered to hear me play was a highly educated mullato pianist. He came over to the piano and asked me if I would play a piece of music he had. It was a pen and ink manuscript of a number titled the "Maple Leaf Rag." It was very hard to play, with unusual rythm. I asked this mullato; who was about twenty-five years old, a neat dresser and a fine pianist whose name was Otis Saunders, who wrote that kind of music and he told me a young negro pianist and composer by the name of Scott Joplin of Sedalia, Missouri. I asked Otis Saunders if he would coach me on playing the "Maple Leaf Rag" and he did. When it was time for him to return to Sedalia and join his pal Scott Joplin, I asked him if I came to Sedalia would he and Joplin teach me to play ragtime. He said he would if I got my parents consent, which of course they would not give, but in the summer of 1899 I found my way to Sedalia and met up with Otis Saunders, Scott Joplin, James Scott, Scott Hayden, Louis Chauvin, Aurthur Marshall and Tony Williams and other negro pianists. They gave me ragtime music to take home with me and Joplin and Saunders taught me to play the "Maple Leaf Rag" and Joplin's "Sun Flower Slow Drag" [This piece actually was co-written by Joplin and Scott Hayden]. Being a young white boy it was not so very long that the white people of Sedalia were wondering who I was and why I was always hanging around those negro pianists. They commenced asking questions, so Otis Saunders advised me to go home and when I arrived home my Dad invited me to the wood shed for a little 'conference.' But I was determined I was going to be a great ragtime pianist, so in 1900 I landed in St. Louis where I again met Joplin and Saunders. I also met Tom Turpin and some older negro pianists. From then on I was the first white pianist to introduce Scott Joplins rags through the Middle-West and the first white pianist to play Joplin's "Maple Leaf Rag." It was Joplin who gave me the name 'The Ragtime Kid.' Up to 1908 I could hold my own playing ragtime piano with the early negro hot men of the 90's. I gave up the piano in 1908 as a professional ragtime pianist, I met a very charming young lady who insisted that I give up my musicial career. But in those early years of ragtime I had many odd experiences and profited by them. I am happy I had a part of pioneering the playing of ragtime music with those early negro giants of ragtime, to me they were all geniuses and much credit should be given them.

No one seems to know just how great Otis Saunders was. His failing was women and I have known of him writing a complete rag for ten dollars and let some other negro pianist transcribe it under their name. He sold several rags to a negro pianist in St. Louis who had one of them transcribed in his own name. Saunders wanted fast money and he generally got it that way. It has always seemed strange to me that he never had a rag published in his own name.

So now after forty-seven years I can still beat out the "Maple Leaf Rag" in good old Scott Joplin's Sedalia, Missouri style. When Jelly Roll Morton died a few years ago he was the last of the original Hot Men of the 90's, so that just about leaves me as the last of the Hot Pianists of the 90's. I understand, however, that Shelton Brooks, Sr., who wrote "The Dark Town Strutters Ball" is well and alive out here in Calif. All of the original 'Rag' men of the 90's died poor, except Tom Turpin of St. Louis, Missouri, and from an unimpeachable source I am informed that there is quite a bit of money piling up for Jelly Roll Morton with no heirs to claim it. This same source has written me wanting to know if I happen to know if any of Jelly Roll Morton's heirs are now alive and to contact him in case I do. Mrs. Morton is alive and I meet her in Hollywood after I wrote this.

Scott Joplin when he wrote the "Entertainer Rag" in 1902 dedicated it to James Brown and his Mandolin Club. Joplin had some connection with "King Porter Stomp," in 1906, with Jelly Roll Morton, but I can not get the facts at this late date. Joplin told me he wrote the first cakewalk titled "The Black 400 Ball," but he never had it published as far as I know. Mrs. Joplin is residing at 212 West 138th St., New York, but as this is being written she is very ill.

W.C. Handy, 'The Father of the Blues' also resides in New York.

Scott Joplin's Ragtime compositions published under his name are as follows:

Though not a bad effort for the time, Brun's list of compositions by Joplin and other composers contains numerous omissions and errors, and should not be used as a definitive source.

Original Rags—1898 Written in 1896 and rewritten in 1897	A Breeze from Alabama—1902
Maple Leaf Rag—1899	Entertainer Rag—1902
Sunflower Slow Drag—1899	Ragtime Dance Song—1902
Swipsey Cakewalk—899	The Favorite—1902 or 1904
Strenuous Life—1900	Palm Leaf—1903
Elite Syncopations—1901	Sycamore—1903
Peacherine Rag—1901	Eugenia—1903
Easy Winners—1901	Weeping Willow—1903
	Something Doing—1903

Guest of Homar-Opera—1903 never
  published to public
Cascades—1904
Chrysanthemum—1904
Leola—1905
The Nonpariel—1907
Gladiolus—1907
Searchlight Rag—1907
Rose Leaf Rag—1907
Lily Queen—1907
Fig Leaf Rag—1908
Pineapple—1908
Sugar Cane—1908
Scott Joplin's School of Ragtime (rag-
  time instructions)—1908
Antionette—1908
Paragon Rag—1909
Wall St. Rag—1909
Country Club—1909
Solace Rag—1909
Pleasant Moments—1909 (ragtime waltz)
Euphonic Sounds—1909
Pineapple Rag (song)—1910
Stoptime Rag—1910
Felicity Rag—1911
Treemonisha—1911-a complete ragtime
  operetta, published by Scott Joplin in
  New York City.
Scott Joplin's New Rag—1912
Kismet—1913
Magnetic Rag—1914
Reflections—1917 Joplin's last rag

Tom Turpin's ragtime compositions which bear his name.

The Harlem Rag—1897

Bowery Buck—1899
Ragtime Nightmare—1900
St. Louis Rag—1903
Buffalo—1904

Aurthur Marshall's ragtime compositions published under his name
are:

Peach Rag—1909
Pepper Rag—1909
Kinklets—1909
Ham and—1910
Scott Hayden's ragtime composition
  bearing his name is "Sun Flower
  Rag"—1903

James Scott's ragtime compositions bering his name are:

Frog Legs—1906
Grace and Beauty—1909
Hilarity Rag—1910
Climax Rag—1914
Broadway Rag—1922 James Scott's last
  rag

Negro collaborators with Joplin
are:

The Maple Leaf Rag, 1899—Otis Saun-
  ders, who wrote the last half of the
  trio
Sunflower Slow Drag—Scott Hayden
Swipsey Cakewalk—Aurthur Marshall
Heliotrope Bouquet—Louis Chauvin
Lily Queen—Aurthur Marshall
Felicity Rag—Scott Hayden

Joplin arranged "The Sensation Rag" for Joseph F. Lamb.

Multiple historical accounts indicate that Joplin facilitated the publication by Stark of Joseph Francis Lamb's first rag, "Sensation," but I know of nothing to suggest Joplin did any actual work on the piece. David Reffkin adds that since the orchestration of "Sensation" lists Joseph F. Lamb and Scott Joplin without the "arranged by" notation, the mystery is extended. The credit for orchestration, incidentally, states "arr. by Rocco Venuto."

Now who do you think was the hottest of the Original Hot Men of the 90's? I am sure the original Hot Men of the 90's would agree with me in saying to the musicians of the world-"play ragtime and help preserve it, but play it as it is written."

Following is the version edited by Roy Carew, beginning with Carew's introduction.

The Original Hot Men of the 90s:
A Condensed History of Early Day Ragtime

by S. Brunson Campbell

During the 1890's great changes came over American popular music, both vocal and instrumental. On the vocal side there appeared a new and livelier style of coon song, pioneered and introduced by such writers and entertainers as Irving Jones, Williams and Walker, Syd Perrin, Ernest Hogan, Cole and Johnson and many others. In instrumental music there was developed the cakewalk, music for the dance of the same name which swept the country around the years 1895 to 1900. The cakewalk dance was introduced earlier, but the distinctive music for it seems to have appeared in print about the latter part of 1895. By distinctive cakewalk music is meant that form which carried a sustained amount of syncopation; the cakewalk could be danced to any good two-step or march, but when the composition carried the name "cakewalk," there was syncopation, rather thin, but sustained through most of the number. A cakewalk also was pretty sure to have a minor part in it. While the cakewalk was having its vogue, another musical revolution was in the making, this time a real breaking away from the old forms; in the midwest, in tavern back rooms and other questionable surroundings, less well known Negro musicians and piano players were working into genuine Negro ragtime.

It seems certain that the World's Columbian Exposition in Chicago gave impetus to matters other than dusty science. Although the country in 1893 was experiencing a depression, or perhaps because of it, all conditions and colors of folks flocked to Chicago. Entertainers came from all sections of the country looking for the opportunity to make their talents support them. Negro piano players were not missing, we may be sure, each striving to outdo the competition. For many months there was a mingling of talents from all sections, and the most alert and competent among the players picked up many ideas, crude perhaps, but tangible, and when the Exposition was over they drifted away, some back to the home towns, some to fresher fields. Among these itinerant players were many from midwest towns which, at that time, were growing at a great rate. From the evidence at hand it seems that St. Louis always had a considerable number of such gentry; a river port and rail center, itinerant players, singers and entertainers passed back and forth through the town, and it is in St. Louis that there appeared the first evidence in print of Negro ragtime. It was in the latter part of 1897 that Tom Turpin, whose real name was Thomas Million Turner, succeeded in having his Harlem Rag published by Robt. DeYong & Co., of St. Louis. Apparently Turpin was unable to put his number on paper, for the number is noted as being arranged by D.S. DeLisle. Evidence that the ragtime form had not become fixed at the time is found in the fact that another arrangement by DeLisle was published a little later by Stern in New York, who also published a third arrangement by Wm. S. Tyres still later. White composers had rushed into print ahead of Turpin in 1897, but with a couple of exceptions their compositions lacked real ragtime merit, apparently being written largely to capitalize on the ragtime craze by using the name.

The claim that Tom Turpin's name had originally been Turner is not correct. Turpin's father was "Honest John" Turpin. Neither is the information about arrangements factual: the practice of the time was to try to boost sales by listing the name of an established composer/musician as arranger for a tune by a new composer, especially if that greenhorn was black.

The original Negro "hot men" of the 90's were nearly all piano playing composers with a certain amount of musical training. One notable exception to the rule was Louis Chauvin, a great natural pianist and one of the best rag men of his time. Chauvin, an itinerant like most of his contemporaries, is credited with being top man at the piano during his sojourns in St. Louis. Tom Turpin was known for his very clean cut, fat ragtime playing. Besides being a pianist Turpin was also a politician and owner of a couple of saloons, gambling and sporting houses, and also a theatre. In all these places he had good jobs for the best Negro pianists and was in a position to get fine rag material from them. Following his "Harlem Rag," Turpin had other rags publish—"Bowery Buck" in 1899, "Ragtime Nightmare" in 1900, "St. Louis Rag" in 1903 and "Buffalo Rag" in 1904, all good rags.

Along with St. Louis, another Missouri town was making ragtime history. The town of Sedalia, which although not a large town, was a bustling rail center of considerable importance in the west central part of the state. In those days Sedalia was a wide open town, with the usual attraction, and good players had no trouble in getting regular work there. To Sedalia there came, probably in 1897, a young Negro pianist and composer by the name of Scott Joplin who was destined to become the "King of the Ragtime

Composers." Born in Texarkana, Texas, on November 24, 1868, Joplin was gifted with exceptional natural ability, and for several years had been traveling over a considerable part of the country. Doubtless Joplin had been in Chicago in the Exposition days, and probably was playing the predecessor of his brand of ragtime in those days. Arriving in Sedalia he got a job playing piano for one Tony Williams who operated a saloon with a gambling joint upstairs. A little later, acting on friendly advice, he entered the Smith School of Music in Sedalia, under the supervision of the blind Negro Professor W.G. Smith, who taught instrumental music. Prof. Smith was a graduate of a School for the Blind in St. Louis, one of his fellow students there being John William Boone, "Blind Boone," who became quite a sensation over much of the country and Canada with his concerts at which he demonstrated his mastery of the piano, playing difficult classical selections and responding to audience requests for operatic and popular numbers as well. Blind Boone's manager was John Lange, Jr., who directed his concerts for thirty-five consecutive seasons.

At the Smith School of Music Scott Joplin got what he had wanted for years—a good musical foundation on which to develop his unique musical ideas. With the knowledge gained in school, Joplin began to put his original ideas on paper, and about 1898 put into manuscript form his first rag entitled Original Rags, which he placed with Carl Hoffman, a Kansas City music publisher who published it in 1899. About this same time, Joplin was working on the composition which later made him famous, "The Maple Leaf Rag." In going over the manuscript, his pal, Otis Saunders, made some suggestions and collaborated on the last half of the Trio. Taking the perfected manuscript of "The Maple Leaf Rag," along with one or two other numbers, Joplin called on John Stark and Son of Sedalia, and succeeded in selling the compositions to them. After a slow start "Maple Leaf" edged its way into popularity, and became the most famous rag of all, holding its preeminence up to the present day. Before Scott Joplin died in 1917 he had over forty 'Rag' hits to his credit, and clinched for all time his title "The King of the Ragtime Writers." He also wrote a complete ragtime opera in three acts which he published in 1911. The opera was presented only once and that was at Joplin's home in Harlem. Bud Scott of Kid Ory's Dixieland Band played with Joplin when he gave the only presentation of his opera Treemonisha. I think Scott Joplin was the greatest ragtime pianist of them all for the reason that his rags were the hardest to play and had to be played slow as he suggested, to get all out of them that he put in them. The original Sedalia style of ragtime was Joplin's, which as I stated was slow.

With Scott Joplin in Sedalia were other fine Negro ragtime pianists and composers who may be classed as being of the "Joplin Sedalia School of Ragtime." They were Arthur Marshall, Scott Hayden, James Scott, Louis Chavin, Tony Williams, Melford Alexandra, Otis Saunders and Ida Hastings, a negress. Tom Turpin and other St. Louis Negro Pianists would visit Sedalia to see Joplin occasionally. In those days they would have ragtime piano playing contests at Sedalia and St. Louis, somewhat like the Jazz sessions of today. Sedalia offered double inducement for good ragtime pianists—it was a wide-open town at that time, and good players could always find jobs, and the Smith School of Music offered good instruction in music for Negroes by teachers of their own race, like Professor Smith. Louis Chauvin was the greatest natural Negro pianist I ever heard. But all of them were good and some were better than others, and it was a treat to listen to any one of them play the piano, for they were the original hot men of the 90's and how they could play ragtime.

Ragtime is a kind of music characterized by a strong Syncopated Melody superimposed upon a regularly accented accompaniment. All through the Ragtime Era the name of Scott Joplin stands out as talented in this style of composition and the most progressive of the entrie lost of early Negro composers. The influence of ragtime and of those early Negro hot men of the 90's is still being felt in the Blues, Boogie Woogie, Swing, Cowboy, Hill-billy and Jazz music and other types of hot music.

We early ragtime pianists played on old and battered uprights and square pianos; these were seldom in tune. Then there were the newer uprights, some with mandolin attachments, and when they got out of tune they were very 'tin panish.' The present day Boogie-Woogie dates back to the early ragtime pianist who was called a 'Faker.' He had a good right hand, but it did not make much difference what he did with the left hand (bass), just so he kept his rhythm. Then other smarter piano players got the idea of walking and rocking the bass; out of this grew the Boogie Woo-gie style with its fast rolling bass with an undercurrent of great power.

There was an original style of dress with the ragtime pianist and male characters of the underworld. No one seems to know just where the style originated. One of the styles which seemed popular was the High Roller Stetson hat. Box back coats, generally of blue serge were worn with stylish trousers; shoes were button cloth top models with either tooth pick or bull dogged toes. The shirt was of loud patterns, some with stiff bosoms and detatchable cuffs worn with high white or colored collars. The cuff buttons were made of two-and-a-half and five dollar gold pieces. The shirt stud was a similar gold piece or a diamond stud was used. A Tiffany or Belcher mounted diamond ring was also worn. The vest was of the loudest pat-terns of silk or linen material, double or single breasted. Then there was the loud shepherd plaids and striped suits. The coat collar was made of velvet and the coat lapels were silk faced. When the suit happened to be made of black broadcloth it would be dressed up with big white pearl buttons, big as a silver dollar, the vest would be double or single breasted with a watch chain worn across the front. The tie would be a flowing bow with loud patterns, a four-in-hand or cravat. Occasionally you would see some dude pianist wearing a bowler hat (derby to you). It was a ragtime age and we were dressing in a ragtime style.

When Scott Joplin signed his five year contract with Stark and Son music publishers to write rags for them at Sedalia, Missouri, he made his one first lucky step. Shortly after that Stark and Son moved their outfit to St. Louis, Mo., and Joplin soon followed. Then things really commenced to happen in the ragtime field. Otis Saunders, Joplin's pal, and Louis Chauvin were the first negro pianists to take Joplin rags to New Orleans and introduce them to the New Orleans negro pianists. This is where Jelly Roll Morton puts in his appearance on the early ragtime horizion. It was not long after Saunders and Chauvin landed in New Orleans that Joplin 'Rags' were echoing from negro saloons, pool halls, dance halls and the redlight district. It was the New Orleans Negro pianists who then migrated North through the Gulf and Southern and Middle-Western states that spread ragtime North to St. Louis, Missouri. By 1903 St. Louis had more ragtime pianists than they knew what to do with, so they migrated in every direction out of St. Louis. Some went to Chicago, some to New York and the West coast. But the largest number stayed in the middle West, as all cities and towns of any size were wide open and they all found ready work.

The list of original Hot Men I have mentioned would not be complete unless my good friend W.C. Handy, Tony Jackson and Jelly Roll Morton were included, for they too were hot men of the 90's. The original 'Rag' men of the 90's were Scott Joplin, Tom Turpin, Louis Chauvin, James Scott, Scott Hayden, Otis Saunders, Arthur Marshall, Melford Alexandra, Tony Williams, Tony Jackson, Jelly Roll Morton and W.C. Handy.

Of the white ragtime pianists of the 90's was Ben Harney a pianist and singer from Louisville, Ky, who claimed to be the originator of ragtime and the first white to transcribe ragtime for the piano. He was a little man with a big voice, and was an accompanist to a Negro banjo player. He toured the Middle-West long before he went east to start the 'coon song Craze.' Of historical importance are his songs: "Mr. Johnson, Turn Me Loose," "You've Been A Good Old Wagon But You Done Broke Down," and "A Cake Walk in the Sky." In 1897 or 1898 he had a book printed by Witmarks which he titled 'How to Play Ragtime on the Piano,' although his instructions were interesting, they were anything but complete. My opinion is Ben Harney was the originator of the Coon Songs of the 90's and not the originator of ragtime. When Ben Harney was touring the Middle-West in 1908, I met him and we had quite a visit. At the time he was billed as the originator of ragtime. He played mechanically with heavy hands as he spread the gospel of ragtime. In 1899 one of the first rags written and arranged and played by a white pianist was "Rags to Burn" published in the same year by the Jenkins Music Publishers of Kansas City, Mo, and the pianist's name was Frank X. McFadden.

Now it is time for me to get into the picture it was in the late 1898's when I was in my early teens. I was playing over some popular numbers in the Armstrong Byrd Music store in Oklahoma City, Okla., and among the crowd that had gathered to hear me play was a highly educated mulatto pianist. He came over to the piano and asked me if I would play a piece of music he had. It was a pen and ink manuscript of a number titled the "Maple Leaf Rag." It was very hard to play, with unusual rhythm. I asked this mulatto; who was about twenty-five years old, a neat dresser and a fine pianist whose name was Otis Saunders, who wrote that kind of music and he told me a young Negro pianist and composer by the name of Scott Joplin of Sedalia, Missouri. I asked Otis Saunders if he would coach me on playing the "Maple Leaf Rag" and he did. When it was time for him to return to Sedalia and join his pal Scott Joplin, I asked him if I came to Sedalia would he and Joplin teach me to play ragtime. He said he would if I got my parents consent, which of course they would not give, but in the summer of 1899 I found my way to Sedalia and met up with Otis Saunders, Scott Joplin, James Scott, Scott Hayden, Louis Chauvin, Arthur Marshall and Tony Williams and other negro pianists. They gave me ragtime music to take home with me and Joplin and Saunders taught me to play the "Maple Leaf Rag" and Joplin's "Sun Flower Slow Drag." Being a young white boy it was not so very long that the white people of Sedalia were wondering who I was and why I was always hanging around those negro pianists. They commenced asking questions, so Otis Saunders advised me to go home and when I arrived home my Dad invited me to the wood shed for a little 'conference.' But I was determined I was going to be a great ragtime pianist, so in 1900 I landed in St. Louis where I again met Joplin and Saunders. I also met Tom Turpin and some older Negro pianists. From then on I was the first white pianist to introduce Scott Joplin's rags through the Middle-West and the first white pianist to play Joplin's "Maple Leaf Rag." It was Joplin who gave me the name 'The Ragtime Kid.' Up to 1908 I could hold my own playing ragtime piano with the early negro hot men of the 90's. I gave up the piano in 1908 as a professional ragtime pianist; I met a very charming young lady who insisted that I give up my musical career.

But in those early years of ragtime I had many odd experiences and profited by them. I am happy I had a part of pioneering the playing of ragtime music with those early Negro giants of ragtime; to me they were all geniuses and much credit should be given them.

No one seems to know just how great Otis Saunders was. His failing was women and I have known of him writing a complete rag for ten dollars and let some other Negro pianist transcribe it under their name. He sold several rags to a negro pianist in St. Louis who had one of them transcribed in his own name. Saunders wanted fast money and he generally got it that way. It has always seemed strange to me that he never had a rag published in his own name.

So now after forty-seven [handwritten change to 51] years I can still beat out the "Maple Leaf Rag" in good old Scott Joplin's Sedalia, Missouri style. When Jelly Roll Morton died a few years ago he was the last of the original Hot Men of the 90's, so that just about leaves me as the last of the Hot Pianists of the 90's.

This is where the edited manuscript ends. The edge looks like a clean line, scissored off. Carew might have advised Brun not to open himself to a possible legal mess involving Jelly Roll Morton's heirs and W.C. Handy, and to omit the error-filled list of ragtime compositions. Or perhaps the historian saw no reason to pay further postage to return a portion of Brun's piece that would stay basically the same, and sent only the work he'd revised.

The handwritten change of forty-seven to fifty-one years can be explained by Brun's having submitted the (edited) manuscript to Warner Bros. some four years after *Esquire* had returned it to him. The date on the return envelope from WB is March 21, 1950.

Ragtime in the Red Light Districts

This piece originated as Chapter 4 in Version 3 of *When Ragtime Was Young*; it terminated with the story of Brun's adventures with Madame Lillian, which was included in the composite *When Ragtime Was Young* section of this book. Though an article titled "Looking Backwards–Round the 'Houses' with Brun Campbell" appeared in *Jazz Journal* in June 1949, it contained only scattered, edited material from "Ragtime in the Red Light Districts" and nothing whatever about his adventure with Lillian.

In addition, the manuscript of "Ragtime in the Red Light Districts" reads as if the hand of a writer more accomplished than Brun had touched it, particularly where Brun writes about the Everleigh Sisters of Chicago and other notable madams of the day. I can think of two possibilities, not mutually exclusive: Roy Carew might have edited the essay, or Brun might have appropriated the work of other writers. He gives no source for either general information or quoted lines. Much has been written on the Everleigh Sisters, most of it similar from source to source.

In those days almost every city in America of over 5,000 population was wide open, with its redlight districts, saloons and gambling houses. Saloons served free lunches and in some of these places, such as Miller's at Ninth and Main Streets in Kansas City, one could get a good meal with a five cent glass of beer. The breweries generally furnished the food for those free lunches if the saloon keepers handled their brand of beer.

During the late 1890's in almost every redlight district in America at night one could hear the shots ring out from some jealous "Frankie's" gun whose "Johnnie" had done her wrong. One could hear the chants of the crawfish, catfish, chitterlings, and hot tamale men as they called out their specialty in eats. The district would be jumping to the rhythm of the ragtime pianists, and barrel houses sold rot-gut whiskey at five cents per glass. Some of the old barrel houses had pianos and the pianists who played on these battered relics, whether white or black, usually were good. But they were whiskey heads and could not hold a good job.

Chinese laundries in the districts were only fronts for hop joints; in the back rooms of these places were bunks for the customer to lie and "cook up" and smoke. Most all of the proprietors sold lottery tickets.

Gambling houses flourished in the tenderloin districts, and pawn shops did a thriving business.

Thieves, cut-throats, confidence men, "macks," pimps, [A "mack" is a pimp, particularly one who is violent with his girls; why Brun included both words in this passage is unclear], hop-heads, coke fiends, gamblers and all kinds of hangers-on made up the floating population of these districts. The madames in the bawdy houses smoked high priced cigars while their girls used Sweet Caporal cigarettes. Every sporting-house of any class had an upright piano, some with mandolin attachments. Many were out of tune and sounded very tin-pannish. Almost all the coon-shouters in these places were women.

When men went on a bender, "something on the naughty side and on the other side of the tracks," they wanted lively music, and ragtime filled the bill. In the sporting houses on the "line" they could dance the ragtime dances with the fancy girls in the houses. Even if the pianos were out of tune it made little difference to the dances, for they were having a good time; and the ragtime "piano-playing fool" hardly ever stopped banging the keys as long as the houses had spending customers who bought beer at a dollar a bottle. The colored maids served drinks in the rooms and parlors, and if business was rushing the madames themselves would serve thirsty customers.

These districts were dotted with lunch rooms, lunch wagons, and those always popular eating places made from old abandoned street cars, where one could buy steamed pig tails, fried catfish, roast pork, steamed crawfish, baked beans, steaks and chops, real chili-con-carne—and fried chicken that was out of this world. Many of the great swing artists of today have at one time or another played in these sporting houses or in the districts.

The piano players in these places usually received a dollar a night, plus board and room and plenty of liquor. Many of the early ragtime pianists became drunkards, coke fiends and hop-heads; the strain on them was too great for the hours they played. So they took dope as a bracer.

Among the notorious madames of these districts was Minna Everleigh, formerly co-owner of Chicago's Everleigh Club, a brothel that flourished around the turn of the centruy. Minna and her sister, Ada, known as the "Scarlet Sisters Everleigh," retired with more than a million dollars after the club at 2131–33 South Dearborn Street was closed by order of Mayor Carter Harrison in 1911.

The Everleigh Sisters served a brief apprenticeship in the wide open red-light district of Omaha, Nebraska. On February 1st, 1900, Minna and her sister went to Chicago with some $50,000 and an up-to-date idea for a new kind of "Millionaire's Club." The idea clicked, and within a few months the Everleigh sisters were operating an establishment famed for it's demure and ladylike hostesses, its ragtime pianists, and its string orchestra and floor shows.

The Everleigh club became known as the most elegant (and expensive) sporting house west of Paris, France, and was a mecca for thousands of playboys, merchant princes, politicians, and wealthy cattlemen. The girls in this palace of sin were from 18 to 22 years of age, and Miss Everleigh used to tell these "beautiful, fashionable gowned girls who entertained guests in the perfumed air" that "It's a recommendation to say you work here." There was even a gold piano and a thousand-volume library for guests who wished to pass a quiet evening.

When the Everleigh sisters moved to New York they took up a west side residence and buried their past behind a mask of gentility, and only a few intimates knew their identity in recent years. They brought along such souvenirs of the old Chicago days as many fine oil paintings, their gold piano, brass and mahogany beds, marble statues, and diamonds estimated at being worth several hundreds of thousands of dollars. Their chief diversions were going to the theater and writing poetry. They attended church regularly and rode in fine carriages, and invariably left a large contribution for the church. Minna died on Thursday, September 16, 1948, in the Park West Hospital in New York, at the age of 70; but her sister, Ada, still survives.

In San Francisco, Tessie Wall was a most notorious madame. Josie Arlington, at 225 Basin Street, ran the most costly and elegant sporting house in New Orleans. Other madames who ran their houses close to the Everleigh standard were Babe Conner (who ran an all-negro resort in St. Louis), Rose Bailey of New York, Anna Chambers of Kansas City, Minnie Stevens of Boston, Belle Stewart of Pittsburgh, and Vina Fields (colored), Carrie Watson and Effie Hankins of Chicago.

On San Francisco's Barbary Coast, in such dance halls as the Thalia, the Midway, The Diana, and Purcell's Negro Dance hall and Saloon, were originated such dances as the Grizzly Bear, Bunny Hug, Pony Prance, Turkey Trot, Texas Tommy, and other close-semi-acrobatic dances which swept the country during the ragtime craze. Pacific Street was a real ragtime street during that period, and it saw some ragtime piano playing fools.

How About You?

by S. Brunson Campbell

A Short Secular Sermon

During his last ten years, Brun never stopped preaching the gospel according to Campbell, but usually he was savvy enough to try to captivate his audience by duding up the musical evangelism in colorful historical garments. However, there were times when he couldn't quite keep from donning preacher's robes and really having at it. "How About You?" was the result of one of these moments, with the reference to the Fisk donation establishing the year of composition as 1948.

I do have to question whether Brun actually did raise nearly enough money to erect a great monument over Joplin's grave, and whether Lottie Joplin's illness in fact played anything like a determining role in Brun's giving up on his original dream.

And between 1908 and 1943, did Brun truly think "very seldom" about his old ragtime days and never touch a piano? Over and over, his written testimony contradicts that claim.

From 1908 until 1943 I never even touched a piano, and very seldom thought about the old ragtime days of my youth. I have sat on the sidelines all those years and I watched the changes that took place in early American music, and the one thing I had noticed was especially about jazz—that the one pianist and pioneer composer of ragtime, Scott Joplin, who was my piano teacher in the late 1890s, was hardly ever mentioned. Isaac Goldberg in his book "Tin Pan Alley" is the only writer up to 1930 who ever mentioned Joplin. So I decided in 1943 after thinking what a raw deal Joplin had been given by writers, and knowing others were claiming credit for what Joplin had done, I took it on myself to try and right this great wrong that had been done to my old friend and teacher, Scott Joplin.

So I bought a piano, and to my surprise I found after a short while that I still had that old ragtime rhythm. After some practice, I made a memorial record of Scott Joplin's "Maple Leaf Rag" just as he had taught me at Sedalia, Mo. in late 1898. (I was the first white pianist to play it). Then I started a movement to rise money to erect a memorial tombstone over his grave in New York (which just has a small marker) for what he did for American music. By accepting contributions and selling the memorial record of the "Maple Leaf Rag" I was able to raise enough money to erect a suitable tombstone over his grave. But right at the time, Mrs. Joplin was confined to her bed with an illness of long standing. She wrote me that she could give me no physical help in attending to the erecting of the tombstone, and as she was in need of money for her illness, it was decided to send the money to her.

I next wrote some short stories about Joplin and ragtime for Platter Chatter Magazine and Jazz Record. In the "Jazz Record" I suggested a ragtime revival of Joplin rags. Roy J. Carew and myself also wrote a story for the Record Changer in May and June of 1945 titled "Sedalia, Missouri, the Cradle of Ragtime." And I also wrote a story for the Record Changer titled "Ragtime Begins." Some months ago I wrote a story for the Sedalia, Mo. Democrat where Joplin spent the most important part of his life. And in April of this year I gave the Fisk University at Nashville, Tenn. the finest collection of Scott Joplin's musical works in the world, thanks to Roy J. Carew and Bill Russell for their contributions to the collection. I am very happy to know that I have made Mrs. Scott Joplin very appreciative of all my efforts in behalf of her husband, Scott Joplin.

Now, you musicians who read this—in my opinion you must go back to ragtime. Jazz music has been jazzed up so bad that there isn't any jazz left. In these troubled times, when people are worried, you should give them a more lively music than you have been. Ragtime fills the bill. So let's have a ragtime revival. I've done my part to bring it about. How about you?

Cavalcade of Jazz, or "The Two-Four Beat"

by S. Brunson Campbell

Doggerel Days

Brun's mother, Lulu Bourquin Campbell, did not figure prominently in *When Ragtime Was Young*. Brun told us she had some musical abilities and worked as a seamstress, and (according to Hal Nichols) she burned Brun's collection of Scott Joplin's musical creations, perhaps accidentally. Aside from a few basic genealogical data, that's about it.

On the other hand, Lute Campbell seems to have had a strong influence on his son. He was front and center through a considerable part of *When Ragtime Was Young*, ready to dispense praise, punishment or advice as he saw fit. Lute was a multifaceted man, a barber and a salesman; his musical abilities extended to the performance of both vocal and instrumental works. He also was an inventor, particularly of farm-related equipment. According to U.S. Patent Office records, he laid claim in 1894 to the invention of a toe-weight, and in 1898, registered a patent for an overshoe. (Toe-weights can be added to or incorporated into horseshoes to influence the stride characteristics of a horse; an overshoe is a flexible cover that may enclose an insole, to fit on a horse's foot over the metal shoe so as to lessen the impact of a rough or an uneven road.) But whichever ladder of success Lute might have been climbing at any time, he seems never to have reached the top rung. Other ladders always seemed to lead to more interesting places.

Brun saved a good deal of material having to do with his father. Along with a postcard photo and a maudlin poem titled "The Great Round-Up" was a certificate dated March 31, 1927, which attested that Lute E. Campbell had "successfully completed the Class in Real Estate Instruction given by the Harry H. Culver and Company." With these items was a slip of fragile, yellowed paper on which was penciled "Highclass speculation Stock offering soon. Guaranteed by First Mortgage 6 percent Bonds on 186,000 Acre abundantly watered and timbered Ranch. Particulars: Golconda, Albuquerque New Mexico." Apparently Get-Rich-Quick in Real Estate proclivities ran heavily in Brun's father, as they had in his grandfather.

Lute also had literary aspirations, and Brun preserved fifty of his father's short creations "in prose and verse," most of which consisted of a short prose introduction followed by a stretch of doggerel. Some pieces were handwritten, some typed; some were present in both forms. It does not appear that any of these pieces were ever published. On most of the work, the author was specified as "Art Ensign," less often as "Lute Ensign." Lute had organized the pieces into two categories: Romance and Pathos, and Dialect and Jazz. A few of these works were engaging, for example, "Absent-Minded," a good-natured rhyme about middle-aged forgetfulness, and "Woman Be Fair," in which Lute took society to task for regarding unmarried mothers as criminals and sinners, while excusing the men who'd also tasted fruit forbidden outside of marriage. Unfortunately, a greater number of his creative efforts were heavy-handed treatments of ethnic minorities, particularly blacks and Italians. A modern audience would likely not be amused by "A Dago's Conception," where an Italian worker rejoiced when the "Black Hand" kidnapped his spendthrift wife and threatened to kill her if her husband did not pay a ransom. Just as off-putting would be "A Desperate Darky's Prayer," the second paragraph of which informed the reader, "As a general rule, these swamp niggers are particularly dull, ignorant and extremely credulous, some are surprisingly so."

Brun's idolization of Joplin and his great admiration for other black musicians stands in impressive contrast to his father's apparent attitude. Could this have been a matter of generational rebellion? More likely, Brun's mind-set was in sympathy with that of the Reverend Dr. Marvin Albright, 100 years later; Dr. Albright closed his invocation at the 1999 dedication of the Scott Joplin Memorial Park in Sedalia by referring to Joplin as "one who spoke the universal language of the heart."

Not that Brun was above composing doggerel, as shown in the "Hal's Pal" chapter of *When the Ragtime Kid Grew Old*, when The Kid filled the back of an envelope with his wry reaction to Don Blanding's performance on Hal Nichols' radio show. Brun's poetic venture, "Cavalcade of Jazz," or "The Two-Four Beat," dated February 1, 1949, and available from the author for twenty-five cents, was a short promotional piece in rhyme, professionally printed as part of a flyer titled "Louis Chauvin and the Cavalcade of Jazz." On the back page, Brun dedicated the flyer "to these great Jazz Pioneers for their contributions to the Cavalcade of Jazz: Tom Turpin, Scott Joplin, Louis Chauvin, Tony Jackson, Jelly Roll Morton, Buddy Bolden, W.C. Handy, Zez Confrey, Geo. Gershwin." Handy was listed twice, so one of the entries was covered with a strip of opaque tape.

The left inner page of the leaflet featured the photo of Chauvin that Bill Russell apparently snagged for Brun from the St. Louis Republican Club. Above the picture is written "LOUIS SHOUVAN," and the caption reads, "'Only Known Picture of Louis Chauvin.' Taken at the turn of the Century." Then, Brun wrote a brief encomium for the tragic pianist.

The greatest natural pianist of them all. In almost everything written about him his name is spelled "Chauvin," which is wrong. His true name is

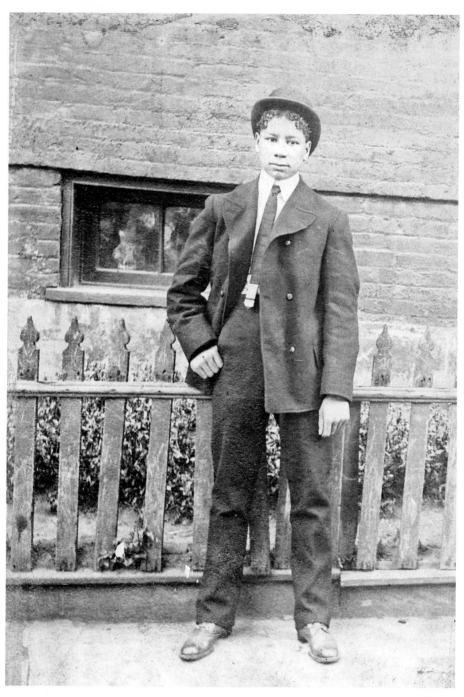

Photograph of Louis Chauvin ("Shouvan") with its cardboard and paper backing, possibly pulled off a wall of the Republican Club (previously Tom Turpin's Hunting and Shooting Club in St. Louis) by Bill Russell (Brun Campbell Archive).

Shouvan. He was an improvisor and piano virtuoso, and outranked Tom Turpin and Scott Joplin. He could not read or write music, and many of his original tunes and syncopations were transcribed by Tom Turpin and Scott Joplin without any due credit. Louis Shouvan was the greatest ragtime pianist, and it was he who advanced the idea that ragtime was a pool of many men's ideas, and that the tune should be considered as belonging to the man who was capable of putting the music down on paper, even though he did not compose it.

Brun's assessment of Chauvin's performance skills jibes with the opinions of other ragtime pioneers, but it would be difficult to agree with or refute The Kid's claim that Turpin and Joplin appropriated Chauvin's music. Might one or both of them have heard Chauvin play a theme here and there, and developed the fragments into full compositions? Yes, of course. But it's doubtful they stole entire pieces, though I suppose Chauvin might have offered his work at a set price, as Brun claimed Otis Saunders had been prone to do. We know Joplin tried for some time to get Chauvin to finish and publish a particularly lovely work he'd begun, and when it became clear that was not going to happen, the older man set himself to work with his young colleague, the outcome being "Heliotrope Bouquet," with Chauvin and Joplin credited as co-composers.

This flyer contains one of Brun's most puzzling inconsistencies, presenting as it does two spellings of his subject's name. Brun wrote elsewhere that the customary C-H-A-U-V-I-N was incorrect, that the correct spelling of the name was S-H-O-U-V-A-N, but he never did provide a source for the claim. According to David Reffkin, aside from Brun, only reclusive pianist-composer Bob Wright seems ever to have put forth support for the alternate spelling. The name was spelled in the usual fashion on the pianist's death certificate. In Rudi Blesh's August 29 notes of his interviews of Brun, the name appears as Chauvin, Shovan, and Shouvan. Reffkin suggests that both Brun and Wright might have seen the alternate spellings in an early article by Blesh, published before *They All Played Ragtime*. It's also possible that Brun provided Blesh with the idea, and Wright, reading the notes for the historian's book, got it into his head that Shouvan was the correct spelling. Despite the variations in Blesh's notes of his interviews with Brun, the pianist's name is spelled Chauvin throughout all editions of *They All Played Ragtime*.

On the right side of the leaflet, opposite the Chauvin material, is Brun's poem, through which he seems to present a new public attitude. During the early part of his revival activities, The Ragtime Kid was adamantly opposed to the manner in which jazz had supplanted ragtime, and preached a return to earlier, *better* musical forms. But with time, the tone from his pulpit changed, and he began to promote a return to ragtime that was based on the genre's position as progenitor of all jazz and jazz-related music that came after.

Why might this have happened? For one thing, Brun was recording piano performances on Lu Watters' West Coast label, and I imagine that Watters and his bandmen would not have taken kindly to Brun's dissing their primary musical form of choice. Roy Carew might have put a bug in Brun's ear, telling him that the magazines he hoped to publish in were basically jazz-oriented, and that they might tolerate ragtime articles, but only if they were written as proper historical pieces.

> Down in St. Louis, on Chestnut and Market Streets,
> That was the home of that old two-four beat.
> It was there Tom Turpin wrote "Harlem Rag,"
> While over at Sedalia, Mo., Scott Joplin wrote "The Original Rags."
> But when he wrote the "Maple Leaf Rag,"
> He put the two-four beat right in the bag.
> Louis Chauvin played piano on Chestnut Street
> And was the best of them all on the two-four beat.
> That beat spread to Memphis down to old Beale Street,
> And then down to New Orleans, to Rampart, Franklin and Basin Streets.
> When Buddy Bolden heard it he blew out a loud jazz call
> That rocked Lulu White's "Mahogany Hall."
> It put New Orleans jazz right on the ball,
> And made it the music of the Mardi Gras.
> Then up at Memphis Handy blew a fuse—
> For in 1912 he wrote the "Memphis Blues."
> That was good, so he wrote another, the St. Louis Blues."
> Now Zez Confrey, just to be a tease,
> Set a new pattern and wrote "Kitten on the Keys."
> Then George Gershwin got into a musical stew
> And sat right down and wrote "Rhapsody in Blue."
> So from Bolden to Gershwin it's been a musical treat,
> But it all goes back to the two-four beat."

It Has to Be Ragtime

by S. Brun Campbell

Scott Joplin's only white pupil and the original Ragtime Kid of the 1890's

A Second Call for a Truce

While the rhymes and rhythms of Brun's doggerel leave something to be desired, his sentiments and sense of history come through loud and clear.

In the last analysis, I think Brun was more a pragmatist than a man of unshakable principles. Once he was convinced he'd get more attention and respect for ragtime by shifting ground to show that ragtime, with its two-four beat, was the foundation for the wildly popular jazz and novelty music that came after, he'd have had no trouble adjusting his public stance.

As for Brun's claim, below his author line, that he was Scott Joplin's only white pupil—that's just plain wrong. Brun might well have been the master's first white pupil, but during Joplin's time in New York City, the composer had several young white students, including Martin Niederhoffer, who by all accounts admired Joplin fully as much as Brun did.

The reference to Tom Ireland's being 85 years old would date "It Has to be Ragtime" to 1950 or 1951.

Now that Ragtime Music, Two Beat, Dixieland Music, or whichever name you prefer to call it by, is becoming popular again, why for instance, should it be called "Dixieland Music from New Orleans," when the concrete evidence shows that it is Missouri Ragtime first put down on paper by the great, early Negro pianists and composers and pioneers of Ragtime. Tom Turpin of St. Louis, who put his first Rag, the "Harlem Rag," down on paper in 1896, and published in 1897; and over at Sedalia, Missouri, Scott Joplin put his first Rag down on paper, "The Original Rags," in the same year 1897, and it was published in 1899, by Carl Hoffman, Music Publisher of Kansas City, Mo. Now "Harlem Rag" and "Original Rags" were the first Rags ever written and published by Negro Composers of written Ragtime. No Rags or Dixieland Music was ever published by New Orleans Composers prior to Turpin's and Joplin's Rags, and copyright records will bear me out. What New Orleans Negro street bands played at the beginning of Ragtime was snappy march time, because, as W.C. Handy says, "New Orleans was still going through the musical revolution of the 1890's when Ragtime was born (written). The record shows that in September 1891, at Sedalia, Mo., there was formed a 12-piece Negro brass band called "the Queen City Negro Brass Band." Scott Joplin, the composer of the Maple Leaf Rag, played B-flat Cornet with this band in 1894–95, and this band was the first band to play written Ragtime. All their Ragtime Music was arranged by D.S. DeLisle, who arranged Tom Turpin's first Rag. This band was a uniformed band led by a snappy Drum Major. Some writers on New Orleans Music history claim that around the turn of the Century, Buddy Bolden's Band was the first New Orleans band to play ragtime. A prominent Negro band leader of today, who knew Bolden, said that he tried to play Ragtime. Tom Ireland, who played 1st Solo Clarinet with the Queen City Negro Brass Band, is still alive at Sedalia, Mo., and is now 85 years old, and has old Ragtime Arrangements that the old Queen City Negro Brass Band played in the 1890's. Now as to the historical importance that Sedalia, Missouri, played in early Ragtime Music's History, it was there that Scott Joplin wrote and had published his famous Maple Leaf Rag in 1899. This Rag is so perfectly constructed that it cannot be improved. It was this Rag that started the Musical Revolution of the 1890's, and changed America's dancing habits to the One-Step, Two-Step, Slow Drag, The Walk, Grizzly Bear, "Bunny Hug," Pony Prance, Texas Tommy, The Charleston, etc. Now New Orleans Jazz (Ragtime broken up) may have originated there, but Dixieland Music (Ragtime, I am sure, did not, for as I have stated, there are no copyrighted records to bear it out). But anyway, Missouri Ragtime and New Orleans Dixieland Jazz is fine music and I say, "Let's have a lot more of it."

Not the Best-Case Scenario: Scott Joplin and His "Maple Leaf Rag"

SCOTT JOPLIN & HIS "MAPLE LEAF RAG"
or a Music Fit for a King

by S. Brun Campbell
[handwritten]

Brun pitched the idea for a motion picture version of Joplin's life to many people. These pages appear to represent one of his proposals, beginning with lines of doggerel by Brun that segue into a short, superficial, error-filled Joplin biography which The Kid had requested and received from Lottie Joplin. The piece closes with a typo-studded "scenario," apparently Brun's notion of a movie musical based on the composer's life. It's not hard to guess whom Brun just might have had in mind to play the old white piano player in the opening scene.

There is a piece of music, titled "The Maple Leaf Rag."
Composed by the Negro Scott Joplin and is King of all the Rags.
It was first published in 1899, not just as a gag,
But, as a new kind of music, He put in the bag.
The Whole world went for it, like a kid for a "sway back" nag.
Rags were composed by the thousands, but none like the "Maple Leaf Rag."

Some musical historians say that Scott Joplin has been unjustly forgotten, and should have a memory tag.

They say that there would not have been much "Rag Time" music if it had not been for his "Maple Leaf Rag."

Scott Joplin may be forgotten, but his spirit still lives on, and the rtyhm of his music, will never be a drag.

I take my hat off to Scott Joplin, and his "Maple Leaf Rag," for when he wrote it, it became the King of Rags.

He died in 1917 at the age of 49, and was the great PIONEER of those good old Rags we all like to hear.

He has been forgotten by all but a few.

Do you remember him? I know that I do!

Joplin Biography

Furnished to Brun by Lottie Joplin

Aside from the superficiality and disorganization of the piece, the accuracy of information is highly subject to question.

Scott Joplin was born in Texarkanna Texas on Nov. 24, 1868.

When quite a young man he went to Sedalia Mo. to play a piano in a tavern where soon he became a favorite. The manager a musician began to take an interest in him. He commence to learn him cords and other things on the piano. Scott learned quickly and after a short time decided to go to a musical school. Soon after entering school he was playing his own compositions, getting along very well.

He decided to go to St. Louis, and soon every one was talking about his selections. There he had one published in 1899. This was the Maple Leaf Rag, which became the best ragtime number in the world.

All of the teachers and musicians called it the best number and used it as the example for Ragtime. Most all artist of variety played this number.

Many people asked him to come to Chicago, as he could get more money there and the city was larger and had more musicians.

He went to Chicago and the same success followed. He had published his first number with Stark and Son Publishers of St. Louis Mo. While in Chicago he published a few numbers there. After this he wanted to do something big. For over a year he talked of some of the things he would like to do. Then he moved to New York City where he could make more money, and met everybody in the musical world there.

In New York City he wrote many numbers and was very popular. By this time the Maple Leaf Rag was very popular and selling like hot cakes.

Scott wanted to write an opera, and did. He wrote an opera in 3 acts. Words, music, and orchestrated by him. Titled "Trumonisha" which was the best thing he ever did. If he could have lived to have seen it produced he would have been a very happy man as that was his chief desire.

Scott Joplin was King of all the ragtime writters of the world.

He went to Smith's School of Music in Sedalia Mo. which burned down about ten years ago. But the records were saved.

Scott Joplin was very original he loved harmony being particularly fond of the seventh cord. And his cords were different from other musicians. He was Scott Joplin at all times.

When Scott was a young kid, his family lived in a log cabin.

He use to spend four or five hours practicing every day until the old folks would catch him and chastise him. They preferred him to work. Although his father was a violinist.

But Scott was very persistent and still carried on. He married Miss Lottie Stokes who is now his widow Mrs. Lottie Joplin of 212 West 138th Street New York City.

Musical practice does not support Lottie Joplin's comment about her late husband's originality in harmonic development. As David Reffkin has pointed out, the seventh chord is extremely common in typical western harmony. However, Mrs. Joplin's statement brings to mind a passage in Smith's *The Jazz Record Book*: when Joplin returned to St. Louis after the 1893 Chicago World's Fair and played in low establishments to earn his living, he earned the nickname, "that diminished fifth man."

David Reffkin poses this suggestion: "A single tension-filled diminished chord in measure nine of 'Maple Leaf Rag' resolves to the tonic chord in measure ten. It is a particularly satisfying moment in the piece's opening. A diminished chord is built with the flatted fifth note of the scale, called a *diminished fifth*. Joplin's use of this structure within a driving rhythm would have been an attention-getter at the time. Some modern players start their performance at this point as an introduction, before returning to the usual opening, so this diminished chord is heard right off the bat. Perhaps Joplin did the same. It is reasonable to suppose he could have attained a short-hand nickname based on it.

"In the 1890s, ragtime composers typically did not work in strict isolation; sharing and developing their works in bars and other public venues was common practice. Brun frequently claimed Joplin had been working out the structure of 'Maple Leaf Rag' for many years before it was published. If that was true, the composer likely would have been experimenting with the diminished fifth during his time in St. Louis. A musically astute listener at one of the sessions might have picked up on the striking progression and tagged Joplin the 'diminished fifth man.' Thus, the nickname would be consistent with Brun's assertion that "'Maple Leaf Rag'" was Joplin's baby from the beginning."

Scenario Scott Joplin and His "MAPLE LEAF RAG,"
or "A MUSIC FIT FOR KING."

The place is small repectable cafe.

An old White piano player is seated at the piano playing the popular numbers of to-day. Finally he commenced playing his old favorite piece, "The Maple Leaf Rag." As he is playing it, a young couple comes over to him, and asks hime the name of the piece he is playing. (She says she likes it) He replies "It is the old 'Maple Leaf Rag'; and there is quite a story attached to the composer of it."

With eagerness the couple asks him to tell them the story of the composer. Story unfolds;

[Handwritten] Use Joplin's Biography here

A colored youth, age—practicing on an old broken down piano. A few years later, his Negro neighbors recognize his musical talent, and arrange to get him a better piano. A few years later, he compses his first musical number, (find out from his wife what the number was) marries a beautiful Colored girl; the Sedalia, Mo. Cakewalk days. (he put on the Cakewalks there). He composed several musical numbers before he finally composed the "Maple Leaf Rag" of 1899, which brought him fame and fortune, started the world on a Ragtime Jamboree (Show musicians and composers turning their talents to composing the new Ragtime music). Show Scott Joplin, (the Colored youth) now grown to manhood, receiving great popularity. Ragtime schools springing up all over America and Canada, with pupils learing to play the new music. Common gossip, back fence, etc.

Joplin continues to compose other musical numbers.

Show Gene Hawks, the great Ragtime piano player, leaving the docks at San Francisco in 1915 during the first World's Fair there, on his departure for Australia, to fill engagements there with his Ragtime piano playing. In Australia, playing to capacity houses, featuring the "Maple Leaf Rag." Show Les Copland, another great Ragtime piano player, featured with Al G. Fields Minstrels, touring Europe, and playing a command performance before the King of England (featuring the Maple Leaf Rag) playing Ragtime music Fit for a King. Joplin is forgotten and died year later.

Show the title of each of Joplin's compositions and Date composed on the screen in technicolor with an accompanying recording of that particular musical number, like for his Chrysanthemum number, showing a budding Chrysanthemum coming into full bloom. Use other numbers according. Finish picture with Scott Joplin's 3 piece Ragtime opera. Words and music and orchestration by him. [Handwritten] Show memorial for Scott Joplin.

I have, in my possession, These numbers by Scott Joplin: "The Maple Leaf Rag," "Pineapple Rag," "Fig Leaf Rag," "Gladiolus Rag," "Chrysanthemum," "Scott Joplin's New Rag," "Ragtime dance," "Paragon Rag," "Searchlight Rag," "Pleasant Moments" Waltz.

Here is a list of other of Joplin's Compositions: "Felicity Rag" "Nonpareil," "Cascades," "Easy Winners," "Entertainer," "Heliotrope Bouquet," "Elite Syncopations," "Swipsey" (Cakewalk) "Kismet Rag," "Peacherine Rag," "Strenuous Life," "Sunflower Slow Drag," etc., etc. Get rest or his compositions from Mrs Joplin.

Suggested by Mr. Brunnie Campbell

[Handwritten] Mrs. Joplin has opera in her possession.

The use of "Brunnie" seems odd in this context, though, as mentioned in *When Ragtime Was Young*, this was one of a number of nicknames Brun used in his childhood and as an itinerant pianist.

IV

Brun Campbell: An Appreciation

Anyone with interest in ragtime should have no trouble being grateful to Brun Campbell for his contributions to the field. Brun's account of his experiences as an itinerant pianist in the heyday of ragtime is the only extensive first-hand written report we have of that way of life. In addition, Brun's position as a major figure in the ragtime revival of the 1940s and 1950s came at considerable personal sacrifice. In a January 1951 letter to historian Mike Montgomery (a copy of which was kindly sent to me by Jon Milan, curator of the Montgomery Archive), Brun catalogued his later-life contributions to the field. He included mention of his ragtime compositions, commercial phonograph recordings, written accounts of early ragtime and its pioneers, but mentioned that he had never made any piano rolls. There were interesting details about the performance of the tune he came to call "Weeping Willow Rag," including the fact that he sought out "old pianos to get the old 'Front Parlor sound' of the 90s," and used his foot to hold the tempo. On other recordings, he removed the front of the piano and with his foot tried to produce the effect of a bass fiddle.

Brun's friend, musician Paul Lasswell, wrote in the May 1980 issue of *The Rag Times*: "he made a BIG CAREER plugging ragtime (and of course his own role as 'The Ragtime Kid'). All of the guys making a fortune out of ragtime now through records and personal appearances owe a tremendous debt to Brun Campbell. He kept it alive when it was very low in vitality and may have brought it back to life several times when it was almost dead." Though Lasswell's overall assessment of Brun's accomplishments is right on target, in point of specific fact, not many, if any, of the guys who played and recorded ragtime during the 1940s and early 1950s earned anything resembling a fortune.

Unfortunately, the bragging, embellishments, inaccuracies, and occasional outright falsehoods that stud Brun's accounts of ragtime history have lowered his standing in present-day ragtime circles. Even so, The Kid does have his enthusiasts. In an article titled "Brun's Boys," published in *The Rag Times* in 1980 and reprinted a year later in *Jazz Report*, George Willick wrote an informative and entertaining account of the influence Brun exerted on the music of the late Tom Shea, the late Trebor Tichenor, and David Thomas Roberts. In 1998, Jack Rummel took the group a step further with the release of a CD, *Brun's Boys*, featuring music by Brun, Tichenor, Roberts, Shea, and Rummel himself. In the liner notes, Rummel wrote, "On the musical tree of folk tradition, I see Campbell as a trunk, Brun's Boys as sturdy branches, and myself as an offshoot. But the Campbell influence is there. It is part of the fibre of each composer represented. I can feel it. I can hear it."

Brun enthusiasts look upon him as a missing link whose discovery, half a century after his heyday as a performer, had a tremendous influence on ragtime composers and performers. Trebor Tichenor, who for thirty-seven years taught Brun's music in his Washington University Ragtime History class, and who *St. Louis Magazine* named one of the five all-time most important St. Louis ragtime musicians, wrote:

"In an overall view of the world of folk ragtime, first there were the pioneers such as Brun, the itinerant pianists working wherever they could, and then came the hometown people throughout the region, writing and largely self-publishing their own rags. The early folk rag-era people (such as Turpin, Chauvin, and others) were never recorded. But then, along came Brun and his recordings, late in his life, recordings that hark back to that world. His was a hot, rhythmic, foot-stomping style, what you would've heard in the Sedalia and St. Louis sporting districts of the 1890s. We can hear familiar riffs, syncopations that would be used in a more disciplined fashion by Joplin and classic ragtime. Brun is our one precious link to the beginnings of the midwestern art of ragtime piano playing."

There also are Brun's Girls, and not coincidentally, the most prominent of these is Virginia Tichenor, Trebor's daughter. This is what Virginia remembers about her introduction to Brun Campbell and his music:

"When I was growing up and learning more about ragtime around age 12, my Dad talked to me about Brun Campbell. He said that Brun's recording of "Ginger Snap Rag" affected him deeply when he first heard it. If I remember correctly, he said that hearing "Ginger Snap Rag" was so powerful that it moved him to tears.

"I also felt that my father's version of Brun Campbell's "Chestnut Street in the '90s" was one of my father's signature pieces. It embodied everything that he loved about folk ragtime, yet he played it with his own characteristic Tichenor style. When I play that piece now, I actually hear more of my father than Brun Campbell, because I associate that piece so strongly with my father."

This from pianist Richard Egan, another of *St. Louis Magazine's* five most important Gateway City ragtime musicians:

"On a February night in 1976, while listening to Trebor Tichenor's Ragophile program, I was introduced to Brun Campbell's piano playing, an experience nothing short of a revelation. There was something in Campbell which was markedly different from what I had been hearing in the recordings of Joshua Rifkin and other Joplin interpreters, something closer to the earthy origins of music, almost primordial. I felt like my ear was treated to sounds like through a time machine, listening not into a radio's speaker but through a doorway of a boisterous, rugged brick saloon in that gently sloping valley between 17th Street and Jefferson Avenue."

Ragtime pianist John Petley wrote, "For me it began in 1985 at the annual Scott Joplin Ragtime Festival in Sedalia, MO. This was my first ragtime festival. I was hoping to try to develop my own piano style and had previously heard only a few recordings of ragtime played by various pianists, and was not sure if any of these could be considered an 'authentic' Midwestern style for the 1890's and early 1900's.

"I was walking down Ohio Street on the first day of the festival and in the distance heard an amazing rollicking piano sound coming from down on Main Street. As I got closer it sent a tingling sensation down my spine and put a huge smile on my face. This was the style I had been looking for. This had to be THE authentic 1890's bar room sound or at least what I imagined it would be. It was Sister Jean Huling playing Brun Campbell's music in her rough barrelhouse style and to me it was a revelation. I took out my small tape recorder and recorded as many of Brun's compositions as I could get her to play. What a joy!

"This actually formed the basis for my developing ragtime style and after almost wearing out the cassette tape, I began to look for other composers that had been influenced by Campbell's music. Pianists like Tom Shea, Trebor Tichenor, D.T. Roberts and Richard Egan to name just a few. At that time Richard was busy transcribing Brun's recordings so I was able to secure some early transcriptions from him. I continued studying and working hard on the Campbell sound, adding many of my own ideas to his, in a style that I think Brun himself might have approved of. Later, I found that while performing at festivals throughout the USA, I was consistently receiving a wonderful reception from audiences that could not seem to get enough of this rollicking piano style. I hope that it was also of some help to other younger ragtime pianists that might have a special interest in preserving this authentic style for future generations."

Pianist Terry Parrish, leader of the superb Elite Syncopators band, wrote, "I first heard Brun's playing back in the seventies, and once hearing his versions of 'Maple Leaf Rag,' then his own works, (especially 'Chestnut Street in the 90's,' 'Barbershop Rag,' 'Campbell Cakewalk,' 'Gingersnap Rag,' and 'Salome's

Slow Drag') I was entranced. Never had I heard such straightforward, relatively non-complex yet genuinely from-the-heart piano playing. His charming use of probably unintentional speeding up was what seemed like a Campbell trademark. I immediately decided to learn as many Campbell tunes as I could, but not with the intention of playing them exactly as he performed them. I quickly learned that the Brun style was not that easy to emulate ... never straying very far from what he was trying to say. Keep it basic, heartfelt, and with a continuous rhythm that takes you to those days beyond recall. If one can capture that wonderfully simple, intoxicating rhythm, you will have captured Campbell. To this day I still attempt to bring that marvelous sound to life once again! May his rags forever serve as a living testimonial to America's first really popular music."

Among the many outstanding folk ragtime compositions of the late Tom Shea is a piece titled "Brun Campbell Express," a salute to Brun's famous 1899 train ride from Arkansas City, Kansas, to Sedalia. In his liner notes for *Brun's Boys*, Jack Rummel quoted Trebor Tichenor: "Brun's style lives on in this runaway testimony to the folk blues. 'I still remember [Tom] playing [it] for us in 1964 and it just killed me it was so good,' recalls Trebor of this heady mix of 12- and 16-bar sections."

Also in the *Brun's Boys* liner notes, David Thomas Roberts acknowledged his debt to The Ragtime Kid, dating from a 1978 visit to St. Louis from his Mississippi home. "I was ... transported to the heart of the rural Missouri of my dreams. 'Barber Shop Rag,' 'Blue Rag,' and 'Ginger Snap Rag' initially affected me most. While rolling through the eastern Ozarks the next day, I began 'Kreole,' the spirit of 'Barber Shop' driving me, birthing a new day in my life as a ragtime composer."

After listing Brun Campbell as the first influence on her own work, ragtime pianist-composer Kathi Backus wrote, "I love the swinging, folk style of his music. Folk rag has always appealed to me and some of my favorite musicians today are the people that play that kind of style."

Richard Egan, Trebor Tichenor, and other ragtime historians have expressed the opinion that the singular, captivating quality of Brun Campbell's piano playing can be attributed to Brun's having retired from public performance in 1907 or 1908, and not going back onto a stage until the early 1940s. Therefore, he would not have had the need or even the opportunity to alter his playing style to please listeners whose tastes changed year by year. What 1943 audiences heard was a veteran ragtime pianist, playing music from the first decade of the twentieth century, and playing it the way it had been played *during that time* in the rough places in which it had been most popular. In his folio, Egan referred to Brun as a living time capsule. Paul Affeldt, who interviewed Brun and recorded him at the piano, commented, "I think Brun was akin to a human time machine when he wrote, when he talked, and most importantly, when he played."

However, given the evidence that Brun really never did stop playing ragtime piano in public, the reason for his singular playing style more likely related to his ego strength than to a hiatus from performance. Musically, The Kid seems to have been an extreme conservative who never abandoned his "Ragtime is where it began and ended" attitude. Whenever he might have played piano between 1907 and 1943, he'd have played to his own taste—played *his* idea of real ragtime—and if the audience didn't approve, well, that would've been just too bad.

It's worth noting that Brun's successes in reviving ragtime and the reputation of its King, along with his personal accomplishments as a performer and composer were due in part to a good deal of luck (along with a fair bit of persistence and shrewdness). He began to preach his gospel at precisely the right time, just as prominent musicians and historians were becoming interested in Joplin and ragtime and would be eager to talk to Brun to further their own investigations. In the process, they were able to promote The Ragtime Kid along with his teacher. Roy Carew and Lu Watters gave major boosts to Brun's campaigns, and the extensive mention Blesh and Janis gave him in *They All Played Ragtime* broadcast his name and aims to anyone interested in early American popular music.

Considering Brun's impatience, stubbornness, and fanaticism, barely modified by reflection and contemplation, I've wondered whether I would have liked him and whether we'd have become friends if I'd known him personally. Most of the time, I think yes to both questions, but I suspect he had a bit of a temper that might have been off-putting. And there would have been no way for me to get past his alleged physical violence toward women.

I've already pointed out that Brun needs to get big-time credit for his social attitudes, but it wouldn't be out of place to emphasize the matter. He grew up and spent his formative years at a time and in a place where the behavior of most whites toward blacks was reprehensible. Yet Brun always seemed to regard blacks as his equals, or even his superiors. All his life, he proudly told anyone who'd listen that he'd been Scott Joplin's piano student and that The King of Ragtime had conferred upon him the title of The Ragtime Kid. His associations with blacks seem to have been utterly free of racial prejudice, and he spent the last ten years of his life in a single-minded effort to restore recognition and respectability to a man who Brun felt had been unfairly stigmatized because of his race.

So in the last analysis, what should we make of Brun Campbell? Pupil of The King of Ragtime, piano "perfessor," tunesmith, ardent educator, spirited promoter, true believer. Impractical schemer, garrulous codger, embellisher, fabricator. Terrible barber, wife-beater. But Brun was hardly the only noteworthy musical artist with negative—even despicable—aspects to his character.

Brun was no legend in his own time, neither a great performer nor a great composer. But before almost anyone else, he recognized that Scott Joplin was a genius, a first-rate American composer, and he devoted the last ten years of his life to getting appropriate recognition for his hero. Was there an element of self-interest in his work? Yes, surely. But sometimes it's reasonable not to pay too much attention to motives. It took a personality like Brun's, with all its unbridled enthusiasm, narcissism, and low tolerance for frustration to achieve his ultimate degree of success. Brun never gave less than full measure, and many people today are grateful for the joyous music he composed and promoted. His unparalleled written accounts and recorded performances make it possible for us to experience his world without that annoying sensation of peering through a window darkened by 100 years of dust. My hat's off to The Ragtime Kid—just not for a haircut.

Brun sometimes referred to the itinerant pianists of his early years as "ragtime-playing fools," and in that regard, he was as black a pot as any of those kettles he so admired. We're fortunate now to have the opportunity to let our minds' eyes and ears take us to that little barbershop at 711 Venice Blvd., where we can settle into a chair, knock back a deep swallow from the glasses of whiskey the old "perfessor" pushes into our hands, and appreciate the greatest ragtime fool of them all as he spins his delightful yarns around us.

V

Recalibrating Brun:
The 1940s Musical Compositions

By Richard Egan

Richard Egan, pianist, composer, historian, author of the folio *Brun Campbell: The Music of "The Ragtime Kid,"* is an eminent authority and interpreter of Missouri ragtime. In the following pages, Rich will analyze and comment upon Brun Campbell's musical compositions and revisit his earlier opinions regarding both Brun's contributions to ragtime and his influences on composers and musicians who've come after The Original Ragtime Kid of the 1890s. Note to the general reader: this chapter includes musical terminology and notated examples, but Rich writes in a way that does not rule out the lay reader.

For most of the six decades following the death of Brun Campbell, the idea prevailed among ragtime scholars that his work was strictly a body of sound, that he did not write musical notation, that perhaps he could not write musical notation. Paul E. Affeldt, who knew Campbell during Brun's final years, and who released Campbell's recordings on LP in 1962–3, wrote that "as far as I know he never wrote down any of his rags."[1] I believed this until the early 1990s, when Trebor Tichenor provided me with a copy of Brun's "Barrel House Rag," which had been given to him by New Orleans jazz historian William Russell, who had inherited the manuscript from Roy J. Carew, a mentor and associate of Campbell.

"The Barrel House Rag" is an alternate title for "7–11 Rhythm," quite possibly named for the address of Brun's barber shop at 711 Venice Blvd. The manuscript, copyrighted on October 27, 1943, as "7–11 Rhythm," features a bold hand-printed underscored blocky title, "7–11 RHYTHM" still legible but scratched out and replaced with a cursive "The Barrel House Rag." This was typical of Campbell's nonchalance toward naming his pieces. Many of the rags that he recorded were apparently unnamed; the task of assigning titles was later handled by Affeldt.

(Another example of Campbell's nonchalance: On a 78 rpm record found among Brun's possessions, he had changed the title of "Grandpa Stomps" [also known as "Grandpa's Stomp"], replacing it with "Weeping Willow Rag" in honor of Scott Joplin. Never mind that Brun's raucous and unorthodox "Weeping Willow" had absolutely no similarity to Joplin's stately classic rag. I doubt there had been any serious forethought in making this tribute. Likely, the change represented a statement of sentiment direct from the heart of the impetuous disciple.)

From the early 1990s until 2011, "The Barrel House Rag" seemed to be the anomaly in Campbell's work. How odd it was that he chose to notate only one of his rags, and one which never surfaced on any formal or informal recording of his playing! Should we have been so complacent in assuming this to have been his sole foray into notation? We now realize that this assumption was shortsighted. Larry Karp's acquisition of eight additional scores has proven that Brun did indeed notate more than one composition. Like "The Barrel House Rag," these eight additions represent a different body of work from his recordings, with the exception of a similar passage at the beginning of both "Sapphire 'Blue' Rhythm" and the recorded "Slow and Easy."

The handwritten scores among Karp's acquisitions date from 1943 to 1945, during Brun's initial phase as a ragtime revivalist. He apparently deemed that writing scores, copyrighting them, and seeking performers as diverse as Happy Perryman and Sophie Tucker, was the path to recognition and perhaps riches. Possibly disillusioned by his dealings with music publisher Irving Siegel, he changed course in 1945, the year that his first article, "Sedalia.... Missouri: Cradle of Ragtime" appeared. From that point on, he evidently ceased notation and instead opted to write about ragtime, to promote his self-proclaimed prominence in the genre, and to record.

Popular lore has long suggested that Campbell retired from music in 1908 (though recent evidence suggests that actually occurred in 1907) and that his style didn't change thereafter. Jasen and Tichenor wrote that the West Coast label "discs show him playing the same way he did in the original era as a Folk ragtime performer."[2] Affeldt stated that he was "stuck in a time warp and we received a slice of early times."[3] I wrote that "Campbell was a folk musician, a time warp (the Rag-Time Warp?) from another era and place who had not been affected by later styles of music."[4] WRONG! It is time to recalibrate Brun Campbell.

Of the eight recently discovered scores, only one is an instrumental rag (and a bluesy rag at that). The others comprise a variety of blues and sentimental love songs that occasionally include 1940s-style elements. During the era of the peak popularity of Western Swing and songs such as "Don't Fence Me In" by Bing Crosby and the Andrews Sisters, Brun was promoting his song

V. Recalibrating Brun •

"I'm Paying as You Said I Would Some Day" as "cowboy or hillbilly swing."[5] He was definitely not stuck in a 1908 time capsule.

These new discoveries also demonstrate that Campbell's musical knowledge was broader and more sophisticated (though erratic) than had previously been understood. He actually knew how to notate, and he knew something about music theory.

Why were we duped? Why did we perceive Brun as living in a time warp from the ragtime era? Perhaps it's because of the rustic sound quality of his recordings, coupled with the simple, irascible spontaneity of his pieces. Perhaps his rags embodied how we later listeners envisioned saloon ragtime of 1900. There was a definite crudeness to his style, but perhaps it was more a result of having been recorded in his sixties after decades of handling his barber's scissors had stiffened his fingers, coupled with the fact that he was playing on less-than-stellar instruments in less-than-optimal conditions. His execution as a pianist was more rudimentary than his conceptualization of his music, and sections of his scores prove greater musical comprehension than we may have previously considered possible.

Let us examine these recent discoveries more closely:

The Rag

SAPPHIRE "BLUE" RHYTHM

Copyright: 1943

Structure: A B A B' C A D E F A

Typical of Brun Campbell rags, "Sapphire 'Blue' Rhythm" is characterized by an unorthodox and occasionally formless structure. Its six sections move through three keys, beginning in E-flat and remaining there until the fourth section, where it modulates atypically to the dominant key of B-flat. (Normal progression would modulate to the subdominant key of A-flat.) Another key change occurs sixteen measures later, again to the dominant key of F. After these sixteen measures, the rag passes back into B-flat before concluding with the first E-flat theme. Despite being in three different keys, the entire piece employs just five chords (plus their sevenths). These harmonic simplicities are typical throughout Campbell's music, typical of the blues, and, to a lesser degree, typical in folk ragtime literature.

Not typical of Campbell performance are right-hand passages that prove difficult for an average pianist to execute. The C strain in particular contains long phrases of sixteenth notes featuring parallel thirds:

Brun Campbell, "Sapphire 'Blue' Rhythm," C strain, measures 1–3.

Since these passages are significantly more difficult than the execution heard in his recordings, this adds weight to the idea that Campbell might have been a more formidable performer as a young pianist than he was later in life.

To ease the reading and study of these examples, I have performed the task of typesetting. Campbell's orthography is distracting and often difficult to follow. As an example, here are the same three measures:

Brun Campbell, "Sapphire 'Blue' Rhythm," same three measures, Campbell's orthography.

"Sapphire 'Blue' Rhythm" opens with an ascending pattern that is essentially the same as the first theme of his recorded "Slow and Easy."[6] After eight measures, a second theme arises out of the first motif to form a variation. The first section recurs, followed by a variation of the first variation.

Use of variations in folk ragtime is not uncommon. Jasen and Tichenor referred to variations being a part of "the Folk school of improvisatory playing."[7] Rags employing variations include Tom Turpin's "Harlem Rag," Euday Bowman's "Twelfth Street Rag," and Campbell's own "Essay in Ragtime."

In mentioning Turpin, the third strain borrows the melody of Turpin's "St. Louis Rag" third strain, but at the point where Turpin's rag progresses to the relative minor chord, Campbell digresses to the II chord. (Moving from the I to II chord is a common pattern in Campbell rags.) The third strain concludes with a melodic pattern that concludes many Campbell strains, a Campbellesque trademark or cliché:

A listener familiar with Campbell's recordings will note a prominent

Brun Campbell, "Sapphire 'Blue' Rhythm," C strain, measures 15–16.

"swing" in his playing style—he holds the first note of a melodic phrase for a longer period of time than the second note, the pattern repeating with the third note being longer in duration than the fourth, etc. This swing is known as "dotted rhythm," and Campbell presents us with a notated dotted rhythmic line in the fourth strain. Examine the dots after the 16th notes followed by 32nd notes, indicating that the dotted 16ths should be held three times longer than the 32nd notes:

Brun Campbell, "Sapphire 'Blue' Rhythm," D strain, measures 1–2.

It seems odd, however, that this is the only section of the score that features the dotted rhythm, when much of the piece seems to cry out for a gentle swing. Why did Campbell want to emphasize the prominence of the swing at this point? Was this simply another example of his general impulsive, illogical thought process?

After a meandering and lackluster fifth strain, a blues appears as the sixth strain. It is an atypical blues, however, in that it contains thirteen measures instead of the customary twelve. How does this happen? After the first four-measure line, there is a pause of sorts, a "breather" in the form of a one-measure descent which leads to the second four-measure line. Brun employed the identical "breather" or extra measure in his recording of "Rendevous Rag," final strain, twelfth measure, which converted a sixteen-measure strain into one of seventeen measures.

The opening eight measures return to conclude the rag. While far from perfect, "Sapphire 'Blue' Rhythm" provides a window into the compositional mind of Brun Campbell. This piece proves that many aspects of his later performances were typical of his thought process and composition, confirms that many characteristics of his performance were indeed central to his musical persona, and indicates that he may have been more capable pianistically as a younger man than his later-life recordings demonstrated.

The Blues

HE'S THAT HARD HEARTED REVENUE MAN

Copyright: 1944

Structure: Intro, Verse, Chorus (repeated)

Lyrics:

Verse: "Don't make no diff'rence if I'm in a jam
    and have to borrow on the Morris Plan,
    I get that notice from the revenue man...
    I drink my liquor and drink beer from a can
    but I can see the footprints of the revenue man
    It won't do no good to go to another land...
    For you'll run right into that revenue man,
    I guess I shouldn't jump into the frying pan,
    For all that dough goes to Uncle Sam."

Chorus: "He's the revenue man, He's the revenue man,
    I work all the time, as hard as I can,
    And there he is... holding out his hand...
    If you don't pay him, you'll land in the can,
    He's always after me where ever [sic] I am
    HE'S THAT HARD HEARTED REVENUE MAN."

This is a blues song in E-flat, written out fully with a staff for voice and complete two-handed piano accompaniment. To be performed at a "moderately slow tempo," an eight-measure introduction is followed by a twenty-four-measure verse and sixteen-measure chorus. The texture for piano is thick and rich, and indicates that Brun was fully adept in his comprehension of the blues idiom.

Filler notes, which add pianistic texture to the endings of each phrase in the verse, portray Campbell as a knowledgeable composer of blues features. For example, at the end of the first phrase is:

Brun Campbell, "He's That Hard Hearted Revenue Man," Verse, measures 7–8.

Musicians who are intimately familiar with Campbell's recordings might be amazed that he would think to write out a musical phrase employing parallel tenths—the A-natural, B-flat, and G in the right hand are paralleled by the F-sharp, G, and E-flat in the left hand, each left-hand note being ten steps below the right-hand notes. Not only is this a fairly sophisticated passage to conceive, there are no parallel tenths, or anything approaching parallel tenths, in Brun's recorded music.

Furthermore, at the end of the second phrase, is a line of parallel sixths:

Brun Campbell, "He's That Hard Hearted Revenue Man," Verse, measures 15–16.

Beginning with the G in the right hand and B-flat in the left hand, the notes in the phrase are six steps apart, again indicating a touch of sophistication in Campbell's blues compositional conceptualization.

The lyrics are characteristic of many pop songs of the 1940s, though Brun will never achieve a place in history as a high caliber lyricist.

YOUR SWEET MAMA'S HEADIN' FOR ANOTHER TOWN

Composer Credit given as "Irving Siegel and Brun Campbell"

Copyright: 1943 by Brun Campbell. Copyright assigned to Irving Siegel in 1945.

Structure: Verse, Chorus (repeated)

Lyrics:

Verse: "I married you, you said you'd be true,
    But you're just no good, so I'm telling you,
    I'm going to sue, I'm going to sue,
    And get everything that belongs to you,
    Now I'm free, so can't you see,
    I'm TNT, you're poison to me,
    I've got a boyfriend, with money to lend,
    And he's goin' to be my ever lovin' friend.

Chorus: "You had me, You lost me, You're the meanest man in town,
    And I'm through with you, Yes through with you, Goin' to leave you at
    sundown, for YOUR SWEET MAMA'S HEADIN' FOR ANOTHER TOWN."

This blues is the one known publication resulting from Brun's ill-conceived relationship with the publishing hustler Irving Siegel. In the key of A-flat, it contains one sixteen-measure verse and one twelve-measure chorus. Pathetically published as one page in the typewritten, mimeographed *Studio News Magazine*, the score contains nothing but the melodic line for voice. There is no piano part or harmony. However, since it is a basic blues, an average musician might be able to extract the chords from the simple blues melody. The verse progresses through a typical I-II-V-I pattern; the chorus is a standard blues progression.

Although Siegel receives top billing in the composer credits, the manuscript and copyright certificate both bear Brun's name, and the lyrics and melodies appear to be vintage Brun Campbell. It is doubtful that Siegel played any role in the writing of the piece, but rather, extracted credits from Brun as additional payment for the publication, such as it was.

The Love Songs

Mama's Little Baby Doll

"Copyrighted" handwritten at bottom of p. 1 (No Date)

Structure: Introduction, Verse, Chorus, Verse, Chorus (repeated)

Lyrics:

Verse: "Even if you are a Waac or even if you are a Wave, or
even if you are a Spar or you may be just a soldier boy with scars,
Even if you're in a plant or even if you're making cars,
Mother thinks of you all day, at night she sings a song so soft and sweet."

Chorus: "You are MAMA'S BABY DOLL even if you are six feet tall
and she loves you in the summer, spring and fall,
For she nursed you when you were oh so little and so small
for you're only MAMA'S LITTLE BABY DOLL."

Verse: "When you marched away to war, you see, you want to keep our country
free and to help all other lands to keep their dear and their precious homes
and liberties,
And when you come marching home to me after our great victory,
Then you'll kneel at mother's feet and have her sing a song so soft and
sweet":

When Irving Siegel wrote Campbell "to congratulate you on your ability
to choose commercial subjects,"[8] this song may have topped the list in Siegel's
mind. "Mama's Little Baby Doll" finds Brun striving to achieve commercial success via a combination of war subjects ("just a soldier boy with scars") and a
mother's love.

The song, in the key of B-flat, opens with a "clever" imitation bugle call
in an introduction with tempo marked "Moderato," followed by a verse marked
"Ballad Tempo." The chorus, however, is marked "Moderato" again, which I
believe would be significantly quicker than the ballad tempo, so I am not certain
how Brun perceived the tempo modulation. In his final letter to Siegel, he
described the piece as having a "good Dance rythm."[9]

The verse features the standard Campbell progression of moving from
the I to the II chord, while the chorus ventures through I-VI-II-V-I. At the end
of the chorus, on the final "doll," there is a modulation from I to the subdominant minor and back to I (B-flat–E-flat minor–B-flat) for a nice emotional
effect rarely heard in Campbell's music.

You Are Mama's Baby Doll

Not copyrighted; no date

Structure: Introduction, Verse (repeated)

Lyrics:

Verse: "When a babe you used to creep,
    Mother would rock you to sleep
    Singing you a little lulaby,
    She'd tuck you in your little bed,
    so tender and neat,
    And kiss your little bare feet."

Verse: "You are mama's baby doll
    even if you're five feet tall,
    She loves you in summer, spring and fall,
    She nursed you when you were oh
    so little and small,
    For you're only mama's baby doll."

When you're on a roll, why not keep a good thing going? An abbreviated version of "Mama's Little Baby Doll," this opens with a two-measure introduction which is nothing more than the final two measures of the song. The melody is the same melody as the chorus of "Mama's Little Baby Doll," same chord progression, same subdominant minor. Only some lyrics have changed.

Most likely, this song preceded "Mama's Little Baby Doll," and Campbell fleshed out the other song with additional construction and commercial subject material.

You Are the One I Want the Rest of My Life

Copyright: 1944

Structure: Intro, Verse, Chorus, Verse, Chorus (repeated)

Lyrics:

Verse: "I am so lonesome and blue, lonesome and blue,
    I dream about you, I dream about you,
    I think about you the whole day thru,
    Just only you, ... And if you
    ever leave me, ever leave me,
    I'd grieve for you, I'd grieve for you,
    So hold me tight, and let me hear you say":

Chorus: "I love you like no other boy

could ever love a girl
And I will always love you, my precious pearl
You've got my head in a whirl,
And if you'll only be my darling wife
I'll be happy the rest of my life,
YOU ARE THE ONE I WANT THE REST OF MY LIFE."

Verse: "Why do you treat me so mean, treat me so mean,
I'm going to scream, I'm going to scream,
so darling come clean, I'm on the beam
just for sweet you, ... You are my
heavenly dream, heavenly dream,
I'd die for you, Don't be so mean,
So hold me tight, and let me hear you say":

This song, marked "Moderato (Not Fast)" and in the key of C, makes use of harmonic effects found in its contemporary pop songs, and among Campbell songs is the most sophisticated and greatest departure from the norm.

The chord progression is standard, but there are elements rarely found elsewhere in Campbell's music. For example:

Brun Campbell, "You Are the One I Want the Rest of My Life," verse, measures 9–11.

In the second half of the second measure above (the tenth measure of the verse), the C chord not only becomes a C7 but the appearance of the D turns the chord into a C9. The subsequent chord in the treble features a G-sharp, which is an augmented fifth not heard elsewhere in Campbell literature. Then, at the beginning of the next measure, the left hand plays a tenth interval beneath an F6 chord, common in the 1940s but unheard of in Brun.

Elsewhere in the song are some nice little filler "runs," making this an interesting piece to study. It's too bad that the lyrics were not written by a more imaginative, less cliché-driven lyricist.

The Love Songs of Harold A. Campbell

Two of the eight songs in the Campbell collection are credited to Brun's younger brother, Harold (born 1891). The musical notation appears to be Brun's, and there is no discernible stylistic difference between the two brothers' output. Were Harold's name not on the sheet music, I would not be able to differentiate between this and the other Brun Campbell commercial songs. Could it be that Harold invented the words and sang the melody for his older brother to write down and harmonize?

DREAM IN MY ARMS

Not copyrighted; no date

Structure: Introduction, Verse, Chorus (repeated)

Lyrics:

Verse: "The orchestra's been playing 'hot' for lots of feet,
But Maestro knows that hearts in love like music 'sweet,'
The tune they're playing seems to be saying—
but let my heart repeat":

Chorus: "DREAM IN MY ARMS … let your dear eyes close,
DREAM IN MY ARMS, you're a beautiful rose,
This magical hour … love gives me a flow'r,
Your first blush of love you disclose,
DREAM IN MY ARMS ... your garden of love,
Your rosebud charms certain tulips dream of,
My two lips near you, a kiss light as dew,
For a DREAM IN MY ARMS of love…"

Composer credit is given as: "Words and music by Harold A. Campbell (SPA)." The acronym indicates that Harold was a member of the Songwriter's Protective Association. Eight of his songs copyrighted in 1940 are listed in the Catalog of Copyright Entries: Musical Compositions,[10] and there are compositions from other years as well. The titles of the 1940 Harold Campbell songs include "Egg in a Love Nest," "Crying in My Beer," and "Over Rangoon Was the Moon."

Written in A-flat with a tempo marking of "Moderato (Dreamily)," this is a typical cliché-driven Campbell love song, regardless of which brother composed it. A four-measure introduction leads to an eight-measure verse that follows the V-I-II-V chord progression. That opens into a sixteen-measure chorus that adheres to Brun's typical I-VI-II-V-I pattern whose only departure is the final line "DREAM IN MY ARMS of love," which modulates from I to the sub-dominant minor and back to I (A-flat–D-flat minor–A flat).

Guess Who's In Love

Not copyrighted; no date

Structure: Introduction, Verse, Chorus (repeated)

Lyrics:

Verse: "What is this thrill that comes to fill my heart tonight?
    My eyes a-glow should plainly show my heart's delight,
    Now what's the answer, Sweet miss romancer? (OR: Mister romancer?)
    A kiss if you guess right":

Chorus: "GUESS WHO'S IN LOVE... look at me and guess, (OR: hold me, dear, and guess,)
    GUESS WHO'S IN LOVE, what do my eyes confess?
    Who thrills at your touch? Who loves you so much?
    Who yearns for your tender caress?
    GUESS WHO'S IN LOVE, who's love is so true?
    GUESS WHO'S IN LOVE, so in love with sweet you,
    Don't you realize my heart's in my eyes?
    Darling GUESS WHO'S IN LOVE with you"

Except for the lyrics, this song and "Dream In My Arms" are identical. Had Brun lived in the age of computers, he could have used the "copy" and "paste" tools instead of performing the laborious task of notation with pen and ink. The piano parts differ only twice in the entire score, where a right-hand phrase of "filler" eighth notes has been moved an octave lower, into the left hand, and followed by a left-handed tenth in place of a single bass note.

I'm not certain whether "Dream In My Arms" or "Guess Who's In Love" was written first. Perhaps a negative reaction from a publisher (or impartial critic) for the first piece inspired the brothers to keep the melody but insert lyrics that they thought would improve their chances of selling.

These collaborations lead me to wonder about the relationship between the brothers. Did Brun ask Harold, the SPA-member songwriter, to collaborate with him to write popular songs, and maybe also lend credence to his credentials? Or did Harold, sympathetic toward his brother's strained financial situation, offer to help Brun out? It's entertaining to wonder which brother had the upper hand in the department of coercion. Who had the stronger influence in putting his brother up to this? Or were they two heads on the same Campbell coin?

More intriguing is the question: What did songwriter Harold think about the notoriety that brother Brun was to achieve a few years later?

Conclusion

Brun Campbell was indeed in the minority of ragtime-era pianists to survive into the 1940s and beyond, and he remained close to his ragtime roots. Again and again he demonstrated a deep love of ragtime, and devotion to Scott Joplin. And his performance style was impulsive and unorthodox, much in character with our expectations of a Midwestern saloon pianist. But was he truly stuck in a time warp? His commercially directed songs from the 1940s and his promotion of them show that Campbell was attempting to be relevant, and make a buck, in the mid–1940s. In addition, we must account for the constant parade of blues elements in his music.

The popular blues genre was a later development than ragtime. Although a smattering of twelve-bar strains infiltrated ragtime, and Campbell was possibly familiar with these strains during the first decade of the twentieth century, the blues' popularity didn't explode until 1912. W.C. Handy, who lived in the Mississippi Delta during the 1900s, stated that he did not become aware of primitive vernacular blues until 1903.[11] If the African-American Handy was not familiar with the blues until then, it is unlikely that Campbell, who was spending most of his time far west of delta country, would have incorporated them into his playing until later, well after he "retired from active playing in 1908."[12]

In Campbell's recorded repertoire, there are no fewer than ten different twelve-measure strains, including two in his beloved "Chestnut Street in the 90s," which has been performed and recorded more often than any other Campbell piece in the past half-century. Even in strains that are not twelve-measure blues, we find "blue notes" such as the minor third and minor seventh to be prevalent. Examine the opening of "Chestnut Street in the 90s":

Brun Campbell, "Chestnut Street in the 90s," introduction, measures 1–4. Transcription by Richard Egan.

The very first note, the D-flat, is the minor third in a B-flat chord. The left-hand chords include the A-flat, or minor seventh of the B-flat chord. This is merely one of constant examples in his music which indicate that the blues was a persistent stream upon his compositional consciousness. Were these blues elements as ubiquitous when he played in 1900? We will never know, but I have my doubts. More likely, the blues infiltrated his music gradually over the decades between 1900 and 1950. While he may have been stuck in a time warp, it was an evolving time warp. His loud, crude, stomping style may indeed be authentic to some saloon players in 1900, but the Campbell who recorded in the second half of the 1940s had added later influences to that earlier style.

Brun Campbell was indeed a significant figure in the ragtime revival, and his spontaneity in performance was perhaps a throwback to a 1900-era saloon pianist, but to state that there is a high degree of unadulterated ragtime purity in his music would be a stretch.[13] He was an American man living in the 1940s, familiar with music of that era, attempting to find his place both historically and contemporaneously within the context of that era. This may be the most important musical lesson of his newly discovered handwritten compositions.

* * *

I first heard Campbell's music on February 20, 1976, while listening to Trebor Tichenor's program *Ragophile*, which aired on KWMU radio for an hour each week. Why is that date etched in my memory? Because it truly was a revelatory experience, the dawning of a new epoch in my life. In those muffled and scratchy strains of "Chestnut Street in the 90s" I heard primordial raw power and droning forces of a Midwestern truth which, despite my two-year love affair with ragtime, had not been conveyed to me previously. I rapidly succumbed to obsession, and sought all of Campbell's available recordings.

In 1985, I was invited into the Tichenor home. When Trebor asked if there were any rarities in his collection of sheet music that he could copy for me, only one thought came to mind: Were there any manuscripts of Brun Campbell? Trebor shook his head and said that he and the others created versions of Campbell's music after listening to the recordings.

Instead of feeling let down, I became energized, driven to learn some Campbell pieces myself. But I needed notes on paper, so I began listening carefully to Campbell's recordings and commenced putting dots on lines. Transcribing was a task I had never done before. I didn't understand the nuances of musical notation, and the process was painstaking. Nonetheless, by 1986 I was able to play a half-dozen Campbell rags at the St. Louis Ragtime Festival on the Goldenrod Showboat. Encouraged by others, I plodded along with the transcription process. By 1993, the known works were complete and, with

Barry Morgan's patient typesetting and assistance, a folio was published. I was informally inducted into the loosely defined circuit of players influenced by Campbell known as "Brun's Boys."

Now, with Larry Karp's acquisition of Brun's collection, and Larry's thorough research, we have much more material, information, and understanding about this multifaceted character. The more I've learned about Brun, the more I've wondered how I would have reacted to him had our paths crossed. What would I have thought of his narcissism, his cockiness, his conniving ceaseless self-promotion, not to mention his commercial forays? I may have actually disliked the man. Occasionally, such thoughts have led me to wonder if it has really been worth the time and effort to have devoted such a sizable portion of my life and identity toward this ragged man and his ragged music.

In the end, however, I recognize my innate captivation with the rawness, the ruggedness, the powerful force that his music connotes. His is a voice in a cacophony of voices that are relevant to the American sound, the American soul. Like life on the continental plains—weather-beaten, wrinkled, rough, defiant—the music is not so much in a time warp but timeless. And for the sheer timelessness, power and excitement that is endemic to Brun Campbell, I have decided to embrace the man and be proud for having shared in a part of his story. I really have no choice but to continue forth as a loyal and undeniable member of "Brun's Boys," and I will do so without regret.

Notes

1. Paul E. Affeldt, "Brun Campbell," *Rag Times* (May 1982): 4.
2. David A. Jasen and Trebor Jay Tichenor, *Rags and Ragtime: A Musical History* (New York: Seabury, 1978), 25.
3. Affeldt, "The Saga of S. Brun Campbell," *Mississippi Rag*, Vol. 15, No. 3 (January 1988): 4.
4. Richard A. Egan Jr., *Brun Campbell: The Music of "The Ragtime Kid"* (St. Louis: Morgan, 1993), 11.
5. Brun Campbell, letter to Irving Siegel dated April 3, 1945.
6. "Slow and Easy" as played by Campbell may be heard in CD format on "Brun Campbell: Joplin's Disciple," Delmark DE-753, track 26.
7. Jasen and Tichenor, *Rags and Ragtime*, 50.
8. Irving Siegel, letter to Brun Campbell dated March 31, 1945.
9. Brun Campbell, letter to Irving Siegel dated April 4, 1945.
10. *Catalog of Copyright Entries: Musical Compositions, First Half of 1940* (Washington, D.C.: Library of Congress Copyright Office, 1940), 513, 680, 759, 760, 780, 801, 810, 812.
11. W.C. Handy, *Father of the Blues: An Autobiography* (New York: Macmillan, 1941), 74.
12. A broadly stated, often-repeated myth. This quote is from: Jasen and Tichenor, *Rags and Ragtime,* 52. There are many instances in the current book where Campbell himself would appear to confirm that he did retire from music in 1907–8, and other instances that would appear to be contradictory.
13. Richard Egan admits to having made contradictory statements to this argument, as recently as earlier in this book. This is his current argument.

Appendix 1

Musical Works by Brun Campbell

In true folk music tradition, Brun did not write down most of his compositions, works he developed from strains he'd played during his itinerant-pianist days—some of which incorporated themes taken from other pieces of music. Brun didn't even assign titles to the majority of his compositions; most of the tunes that have come down to us courtesy of Paul Affeldt's circa–1950 recordings were titled by Affeldt. Neither did Brun copyright most of the music. In 1993, when Richard Egan transcribed it for his folio, *Brun Campbell, The Music of "The Ragtime Kid,"* he copyrighted his own arrangements of the pieces.

But Brun (and his brother, Harold) were certainly looking to make a buck or two from musical compositions, so The Kid named and copyrighted some of the tunes, perhaps the ones he felt had the greatest chance of commercial success.

In the collection of Brun's effects was a folder titled "Songs." Most of the papers in this folder were covered with lyrics, written in Brun's hand, of well-known popular tunes of the day. Brun might have used these to help him through vocals during his public performances. However, four of the pieces appear to be Brun originals: their content and style are similar to lyrics of his other 1940s tunes, and there's no evidence that anyone else had composed them. Brun also wrote out lyrics for two tunes in a letter to Irving Siegel, dated April 3, 1945.

Of particular interest among the loose leaves in the Songs folder is a short segment of lyrics from *Blue Monday Blues*, a one-act opera by George Gershwin with lyrics by Buddy deSylva. This work was written for *George White's Scandals of 1922*, but the producer pulled it from the show after only one performance. In subsequent years it was revived under other names, but without any great deal of success. Today it is regarded as a landmark piece, a truly American operatic venture and a predictor of what was to come from Gershwin, including *Rhapsody in Blue* and *Porgy and Bess*. But in the 1940s, the piece was not at all well known, and the fact that Brun wrote out a page of lyrics stands as an indication that The Kid's musical knowledge and interests extended well beyond ragtime, and that black-themed music continued to engage him over the years.

One of the loose leaves in the Songs folder was titled, "Take it Off the G String and Play it on the E String." Barbara Stanwyck had starred in a 1943 movie, *Lady of Burlesque*, adapted from Gypsy Rose Lee's mystery novel of 1941 (probably written with help from author Craig Rice), in which Gypsy herself played a detective who solved the murders of strippers who'd been strangled with their G-strings. In the movie, Stanwyck sang the Sammy Cahn-Harry Akst tune, "Take it Off the E String, Play it on the G String." Brun likely would have known about the movie, perhaps even seen it, and I wondered whether he'd decided to capitalize on the Gypsy connection by reversing the strings, and composing a parody. But what I'd taken as cleverness was only classic Brun carelessness. The lyrics on the page in the folder are those of the original song, which is unfortunate. It would've made a good story, and it just might have made Brun a little money.

Informally Recorded Compositions

(Works recorded either in Brun's barber shop or garage
by his visitors, primarily Paul Affeldt)

"BC" indicates that Brun himself specified the title; "RE" designates titles assigned by Richard Egan during the production of his folio. All remaining titles were made up by Paul Affeldt. Unless otherwise stated, copyright is held by Richard A. Egan, Jr.

Barber Shop Rag
The Barrel House Rag (Public
   Domain) [BC]
Blue Rag
Brun's Slow Drag
Campbell Cakewalk
Chestnut Street in the 90s [BC]
Essay in Ragtime [BC]
Fragment
Frankie and Johnnie Rag [BC]
Ginger Snap Rag [BC]
Grandpa Stomps [BC]
Lulu White
Reminiscences

Rendevous Rag
Salome's Slow Drag [BC]
Salome's Slow Drag No. 2, referred
   to as "Salome's Slow Drag (Alter-
   nate Take)" on Delmark release
   [RE]
Short Rag
Slow and Easy
Tent Show Rag
Unnamed Strain, referred to as
   "Unknown No. 2[qm] on Del-
   mark release [RE]
Variations on a Theme by Joplin
   [RE]

The *Joplin's Disciple* CD also includes an Unknown No. 1 and Unknown No. 3. These tracks are not in the Egan folio because they were not available to the author at the time he was transcribing and publishing that work.

Unrecorded Compositions

COPYRIGHT REGISTRATION AND MANUSCRIPT

(For) Your Sweet Mama's Headin' for Another Town
> Published in *Studio News Magazine*, April 1945, p. 25, as having been written by Irving Siegel and Brun Campbell, copyright 1943 by Brun Campbell, copyright assigned 1945 to Irving Siegel, Music Publisher

He's That Hard Hearted Revenue Man

I'm Paying as You Said I Would Some Day
> Although the copyright certificate states that the music and lyrics were copyrighted by Brun, only lyrics could be found for this tune.

Mama's Little Baby Doll

Sapphire "Blue" Rhythm

7–11 Rhythm
> There's some uncertainty about this one. Brun copyrighted a tune with this title in October 1943, perhaps having chosen the name because of the street address of his barber shop and the implications of the numbers in shooting dice. However, on the manuscript, the title has been crossed out and replaced in Brun's hand by "The Barrel House Rag," and it's by this name that it appears in the Egan folio. Perhaps Brun thought that it was a catchier name, with more sales potential. It would be surprising if he gave any thought to the copyright implications.

You Are the One I Want the Rest of My Life

MANUSCRIPT ONLY

You Are Mama's Baby Doll (not the same tune as Mama's Little Baby Doll)

COPYRIGHT REGISTRATION ONLY

The Last Time I'll Ever Fall in Love

BY HAROLD A. CAMPBELL (MANUSCRIPTS ONLY)

Dream In My Arms

Guess Who's In Love
> These two tunes share a common melody, but have different lyrics.

Lyrics Only

I'm Paying as You Said I Would Some Day

[From a letter to Irving Siegel, April 3, 1945]

You told me that you loved me, and would love me till you died.
But you knew when you said it, you were telling me a lie.
You were the Big Black Spider and I was the little fly.
So don't pretend let's just say good bye.
-Cho-
Many years have passed away
Since you said I'd have to pay
and I wonder where my darling is today
for I love you more than I can say
and I'm sad both night and day
For "I'm paying as you said I would some Day."

Let Me Come Back Home

[Also in April 3 letter to Irving Siegel]

See that sleet and snow
My Baby's mad and told me to go.
She took all my jewelry and all my Dough
Black both my eyes and cut up my cloths
But I'll love that woman where ever she goes.
-Chor-
Baby don't make me roam
Say you'll let me come back home
You can have the beer, I'll take the foam
I'll buy you chicken and big T-Bone
But baby "let me come back home."

You Turned Your Back on Me

[From Songs Folder]

You told me that you loved me
But you turned your back on me.
You ran away with another
and took your heart away from me.
I loved you then,
But you turned your back on me.
Now go your way and leave me be
For I have another who ain't poison to me.
You had your chance
But you chose another.
But he quit you like you quit me.
Now you're between the devil and the deep blue sea.

While I am single and fancy free.
And Baby! You ain't never going to get another Chance,
To turn your back on me.

Dear Bob

[From Songs Folder.] Other tunes by this title exist, but they are of later composition and entirely different content. There is no clue as to Bob's identity in *When Ragtime Was Young* or in any of Brun's shorter written pieces.

Dear Bob

It doesn't seem long since we were in school
We fiddled around darned near broke every rule
Now there is tears in my eyes, I sort of feel like a fool
Still I miss you.

Dear Bob

The days seem so long and I feel so blue
I'm not sure just why but think maybe it is you
I think of those silly things that we used to do
Then I miss you
If you ever should feel
That you are all alone
And this is the end
Stop for a minute my friend
Think of me praying saying

Dear Bob

It's been lots of fun more fun than in years
The laughs we've enjoyed will ring in my ears
The thought of you far away will always bring tears cause I'll miss you

Dear Bob - - -

Untitled Lyrics

[From Songs Folder]

Oh well, oh well I feel so fine today
(Repeat)
Because the man who loves ("loves" is crossed out) sends me is coming
home to stay.
Got man over there
Got man over here

But the man over there oh lu baba la la
The man I love is built for speed, he's got everything his mama needs.
He now thrills me in the morning
thrills me in the night
That way he loves me makes me scream with might.
Coming in like a tiger
Out like a lamb
Starts lovin me
I harlou [?] oh ho
Lu baba Lulu

Tunes Brun Claimed to Have Composed but for Which There Is No Known Music, Lyrics or Recording

Front Parlor Piano (A Blue Slow Drag)
Memory Room Rag
Ricardo's Rag

A special case: Brun recorded a tune he called "Weeping Willow Rag, in memory of Scott Joplin." One of Joplin's rags was in fact named "Weeping Willow," but this lyrical composition bears no relationship beyond its name to Brun's hard-driving piece. Worse, Brun's "Weeping Willow" was simply a renaming of his well-known tune, "Grandpa Stomps," or as he sometimes called it, "Grandpa's Stomp." (There's also a "Weeping Willow Rag" by Harry Augustus Fischler, which bears no resemblance to either Joplin's or Brun's tune.) Given that Brun was looking for every link to Joplin he could exploit, and since the renaming of "Grandpa" likely predated Affeldt's recordings of Brun at the piano, The Kid might have figured it would be easier to rename an existing work than to compose a whole new one, and no one would ever pick up on it.

Appendix 2

Writings and Recordings

Written by Brun, Chronologically

Campbell, S. Brunson, and R.J. Carew. "Sedalia, Cradle of Ragtime, Part 1." *The Record Changer* 4, no. 3 (1945).

Campbell, S. Brunson, and R.J. Carew. "Sedalia, Cradle of Ragtime, Part 2." *The Record Changer* 4, no. 4 (1945).

Campbell, S. Brunson. "Preserve Genuine Early Ragtime." *The Jazz Record*, 1946.

Campbell, S. Brunson. "They All Had It." *The Jazz Record*, 1946.

Campbell, Brunson. "The Amazing Story of the Silver Half Dollar and the Ragtime Kid." *Venice Independent*, October 24, 1947.

Campbell, S. Brun, and R.J. Carew. "How I Became a Pioneer Rag Man of the 1890s." *The Record Changer* 6 (1947).

Campbell, S. Brunson. "Ragtime Begins." *The Record Changer* 7 (1948).

Campbell, Brun. "Ragtime (Silk Stockings, Short Skirts, Silk Blouses, and Velvet Jackets)." *Jazz Journal* 2, no. 4 (1949).

Campbell, Brun. "Early Great White Ragtime Composers and Pianists." *Jazz Journal* 2, no. 5 (1949).

Campbell, Brun. "From Rags to Ragtime and Riches." *Jazz Journal* 2, no. 7 (1949).

Campbell, S. Brun. "The Music of Scott Joplin." *New Orleans Jazz Club Newsletter* 1, no. 6 (1950).

Campbell, S. Brun. "Euday L. Bowman and the 'Twelfth Street Rag.'" *Jazz Journal* 4, no. 1 (1951).

Campbell, Brun. "More on Ragtime." *Jazz Journal* 4, no. 5 (1951).

Campbell, S. Brun. "From Rags to Ragtime, a Eulogy." *Jazz Report* 6 (1967).

Campbell, S. Brunson. "The Ragtime Kid (An Autobiography)." *Jazz Report* 6, 1967–68 (1968).

Campbell, S. Brun. "Two Beat Music Is Very Much Alive! (A Letter to Floyd Levin)." *The Rag Times*, 1970.

Written by Others

Affeldt, Paul E. "Brun Campbell." *The Rag Times*, 1982.

Affeldt, Paul E. "The Last of the Professors." *Jazz Report* 3, no. 1 (1961).

Affeldt, Paul E. "The Saga of S. Brun Campbell." *The Mississippi Rag* 15, no. 3 (1988).

Anderson, J. Lee. "Evolution of Jazz." *DownBeat*, 1950. (Three-panel cartoon strip with extensive captions).

Carew, Roy, and Don E. Fowler. "Scott Joplin: Overlooked Genius." *The Record Changer*, September 1944, October 1944, December 1944.

Edwards, "Perfessor Bill" "Sanford Brunson Campbell." http://www.ragpiano.com/comps/campbell.shtml. Accessed July 5, 2015.

Egan, Jr., Richard A. *Brun Campbell: The Music of "The Ragtime Kid."* St. Louis, MO: Morgan, 1993. "Famous Ragtime Personalities Flood S. Brun Campbell, 'Ragtime Kid,' Now Living in Venice, with Yule Cards." *Venice Evening Vanguard*, January 7, 1952.

Hanley, Peter. "World War I Draft Registration Cards 3." Ragtime–Blues–Hot Piano. http://www.doctorjazz.co.uk/draftcards3.html#ragdc. February 2009.

Hanney, Delores. "Scott Joplin's Disciple." *Venice Historical Society's Journal* 26 (Winter 2012).

Hoefer, George. "'Twelfth Street Rag' Story Told for the First Time." *DownBeat*, 1951.

Jones, Casey. "En Los Dominios Del 'Jazz.'"*Ricordiana (Buenos Aires)*, no. 2 (1951).

Kay, George W. "Ragged but Right." *The Record Changer* 9, no. 3 (1950).

Lasswell, Paul. "Some Thoughts about Brun Campbell and Ragtime." *The Rag Times*, 1980.

Levin, Floyd. "Another Letter from Brun." *The Rag Times*, 1971.

Levin, Floyd. "A Brun Campbell Letter." *The Rag Times*, 1971.

Levin, Floyd. "Brun Campbell, the Original Ragtime Kid of the 1890s." *Jazz Journal* 23, 1970. Reprinted as "Brun Campbell," in *The Rag Times,* 1971.

"Looking Backwards. Round the 'Houses' with Brun Campbell." *Jazz Journal* 2, no. 6 (1949).

"Once Ragtime King of Market St. Immortalized in Fisk Library." *St. Louis Argus*, June 4, 1948.

"Ory Greets the 'Ragtime Kid.'" *DownBeat*, 1948 [photo with caption].

Robinson, Lester L. "Original Ragtime Kid, Now Venice Resident, Plays Part in Jazz Revival." *Venice Evening Vanguard*, December 8, 1951.

Thompson, Kay C. "Reminiscing in Ragtime: An Interview with Brun Campbell." *Jazz Journal* 3, no. 4 (1950).

Willick, George C. "Brun's Boys." *Jazz Report* 10, no. 2 (1981).

Commercial Recordings

Note: There is little documentation on Brun's own recordings. The 78 rpm discs are from sessions between approximately 1947 and 1950. It is unclear which were commercially "released," as opposed to simply being pressed and perhaps duplicated for limited distribution, presumably soon after the recordings were made.

78 RPM, 10-INCH
(See note above.)

Echoes No. 1A & 1B
> 1A: 12th Street Rag–Brun Campbell & his ragtime piano
> 1B: Grandpa Stomp–Brun Campbell & his ragtime piano
> (In pen, on label, in Brun's handwriting: Weeping Willow Rag composed by Brun Campbell. In pen on label: 12th St. Rag). The handwritten titles are correct.

Brun Recording Company–1 side
> Memorial Record–The Maple Leaf Rag, 1899, by Scott Joplin (colored). Played by Brun Campbell as taught him by Scott Joplin in 1899 – first white pianist to play it.

Brun Recording Company–2 sides
> Side 1: Maple Leaf Rag, Recorded from Hand Played Piano Roll, Played by Scott Joplin. Recorded by Brun Campbell, Joplin's only White Pupil of the 1890s. The first white pianist to play "Maple Leaf Rag"
> Side 2: Salome Slow Drag

78 RPM, 10-INCH ALBUM
(See note above.)

Ragtime, Vol. 3. West Coast Recordings
> Brun Campbell & Lu Watters.
> Contains WCR 112: Brun, "Maple Leaf Rag," Watters, "Original Rags"; WCR 113: Brun, "Chestnut Street in the 90s," Watters, "Easy Winners"; WCR 114: Brun, "Essay in Ragtime," Watters, "Maple Leaf Rag."

LP

The Professors, Vol. 1, Brun Campbell and Dink Johnson (ESR 1201), 1962.
> Brun Campbell recordings (all on side 1 in playlist order; original composers noted): Maple Leaf Rag (Scott Joplin), Barber Shop Rag, Salome's Slow Drag, Fragment, Brun's Slow Drag, Short Rag, Essay in Ragtime, Slow and Easy, Blue Rag, Lulu White, Reminiscences.

The Professors, Vol. 2, Brun Campbell, Euday Bowman, and Dink Johnson (ESR 1202), 1963.
> Brun Campbell recordings (all on side 1 in playlist order; composers noted): Interview with Brun (spoken word), Ginger Snap Rag, Tent Show Rag, Grandpa's Stomp, Frankie and Johnnie Rag (based on a traditional melody), Campbell Cakewalk, Rendevous [sic] Rag, Twelfth Street Rag (Euday Bowman).

CD

Joplin's Disciple (Delmark 753), 2001.

"Master" and "alt" notations are part of the playlist; composers noted: Interview with Brun (spoken word), Essay In Ragtime (master), Essay In Ragtime (alt), Ginger Snap Rag (master), Ginger Snap Rag (alt), Salome's Slow Drag (master), Salome's Slow Drag (alt), Fragment (alt), Fragment (master), Frankie and Johnny Rag (master; "Johnny" sic), Frankie and Johnny Rag (alt; "Johnny" sic), Lulu White (master), Lulu White (alt), Blue Rag, Unknown #2, Unknown #1, Short Rag, Unknown #3, Tent Show Rag, Talk (spoken word), Grandpa's Stomp (master), Grandpa's Stomp (alt), Brun's Slow Drag, Campbell Cakewalk, Rendevous [*sic*] Rag, Slow And Easy, Twelfth Street Rag (master; by Euday Bowman), Twelfth Street Rag (alt #5, by Euday Bowman), Twelfth Street Rag (alt #6; by Euday Bowman), Barber Shop Rag (master), Barber Shop Rag (alt), Maple Leaf Rag (Scott Joplin), Reminiscences, Brun Reads Homage To Joplin (spoken word), Introduction to Maple Leaf Rag (spoken word), Maple Leaf Rag (Joplin piano roll; roll notation is part of the playlist; roll is presumably included for reference; composition by Scott Joplin; it is not a Brun Campbell "performance").

Note: In addition to the above entries, there are some questions as to other possible commercial recordings by Brun. He sold rights to his privately produced masters of "Ginger Snap Rag," "Twelfth Street Rag," "Frankie and Johnnie Rag," and "Salome Slow Drag" to Ray Boarman, proprietor of the Yerba Buena Music Shop in Oakland, who intended to produce records of these tunes bearing the label of the Yerba Buena Music Shop. However, David Reffkin states that to the best of his knowledge they were never issued.

Essays in Ragtime CD
By David Reffkin

When author Larry Karp contacted me about the idea for a biography of Brun Campbell, it took only moments for me to propose a recording to complement the book. For readers of musical biography, it is rare to have at hand a definitive recording of the composer's collected works. This book, in turn, complements the recording. *Essays in Ragtime* features performances by American Ragtime Ensemble, my group vocalists Carol Ann Parker and Sean Sharp, solo pianist Richard Egan, and even Brun Campbell himself.

None of Brun's works were published in his lifetime. In fact, only a few were written down. The piano pieces were initially learned through Brun's informal recordings of the late 1940s. Richard Egan published a folio of transcriptions made from the records, which included a few unfinished pieces and fragments. My orchestrations, based on the folio and manuscripts, and created in the style of period arrangements, bring an extra dimension of texture and depth to selected titles. Richard Egan, a specialist in the folk ragtime style of the Midwest, plays the remaining instrumental works. The vocalists join the Ensemble in the first recording of recently discovered songs com-

The *Essays in Ragtime* cover.

posed by both Brun and his brother, Harold Campbell. Bonus tracks round out the disc with a few of Brun's historic 78 rpm recordings and a 1948 tribute to Brun by radio broadcaster Hal Nichols.

Essays in Ragtime is a production of Rivermont Records, a company that honors musicians of the past and present with new recordings and reissues of the highest quality. The attractive 32-page booklet offers my extensive commentary about the composer and music, illustrated with images selected mostly from the Brun Campbell Archive. Executive Producer Bryan Wright assembled all materials into a finished product that realizes the original vision—a definitive recording that complements Larry Karp's story of Brun Campbell.

For further information about *Essays in Ragtime* (BSW-2236), and the entire Rivermont Records catalog, visit www.rivermontrecords.com.

Appendix 3

When Ragtime Was Young and *When the Ragtime Kid Grew Old*: Brun's Organizational Variations

In the three cartons of materials I organized into a Brun Campbell archive, there were seven versions of Brun's experiences as an itinerant ragtime pianist during the early years of the twentieth century. Five were titled *When Ragtime Was Young*; two were called *The Original Ragtime Kid of the 1890s*. It's not clear whether Brun had intended to compose two books or if he just had trouble settling on a title. Perhaps having given his *When Ragtime Was Young* manuscript to Rudi Blesh, he might have had second thoughts, and set out to reorder his work under a different title. Whatever the case, though chapter titles in *The Original Ragtime Kid* are different from those in *When Ragtime Was Young*, much of the content of the two books is similar or identical.

Brun approached writing in the same manner he approached life in general: when they'd handed out enthusiasm he was first in line, but by the time they got to distributing patience, deliberation, organization, and common sense he'd long since left the room. It appears that when he finished one version of his memoir and did some minimal rewriting, he started over, retelling the individual episodes and putting them into different sequences. Though some of the chapters in different versions of the stories share titles, the content varies, at times in substance, often in details. A striking feature was how often Brun was off by a single unit of time—one day, one year—whether between different accounts of a particular story or in regard to the occurrence of a specific historic event. The stories of his childhood and adolescence followed a reasonable time line, but Brun provided little temporal sequencing to frame his adventures as an itinerant pianist. This could have been due to his apparent narcissism: it might not have occurred to him that readers would have difficulty if sequences of events did not make sense.

Brun's incapacity to rework a piece of writing in the interest of effectively presenting all aspects of an event, and his inability to resolve inconsistencies of content, also might have had their roots in his narcissism and his poorly integrated personality. Some cognitive deficits also might have been at play, whether due to inborn factors or to several decades of hard living.

These three lists summarize the organization of the books.

When Ragtime Was Young *(Five Versions)*

Variations 1, 2 & 4 are similar. No. 2 looks like the earliest definitive attempt, which seems to have been edited to 4, then finalized in 1. The three chapters missing in 1 are present in 4. No. 3 might have been an entirely separate venture, less of a memoir, and focusing more on the general early history of ragtime.

1–Probably intended as a final copy. Brun's name appears at the top left of each page, and there is a specified word count, "about 18,000." 57pp

    Ch 1: The Original Ragtime Kid of the 1890s
    Ch 2: The Ragtime Kid Goes West
    Ch 3: [Missing]
    Ch 4: Treemonisha (by RJ Carew)
    Ch 5: Ragtime
    Chs 6 & 7: [Missing]

2–Seems like an earlier version of 1. Different order of chapters.

    Ch 1: The Original Ragtime Kid
    Ch 2: Scott Joplin
    Ch 3: Treemonisha (RJ Carew)
    Ch 4: Ragtime
    Ch 5: Early Great White Ragtime Composers and Pianists
    Ch 6: Looking Backward
    Ch 7: The Ragtime Kid Goes West

3–In this version, Tom Ireland, who was born in December, 1865, is referred to as being 83, which would date the work to 1948 or 1949.

    Preface–The First 5 Published Rags
    Ch 1: New Orleans Ragtime (Probably written by Roy J. Carew)
    Ch 2: The Evolution of Ragtime (Includes a history of Sedalia)
    Ch 3: Early Great White Ragtime Composers and Pianists
    Ch 4: Ragtime in the Red Light Districts
    Ch 5: The Ragtime Kid
    Ch 6: Scott Joplin
    Ch 7: Cavalcade of Jazz–The Two-Four Beat (poem)

4–(Hand-edited copy)

Ch 1: The Original Ragtime Kid of the 1890s
Ch 2: The Ragtime Kid Goes West (Moved up from Ch7 in Version 2)
Ch 3: (Originally 2): Scott Joplin
Ch 4: (Originally 3): Treemonisha, by RJ Carew
Ch 5: (Originally 4): Ragtime
Ch 6: (Originally 5): Early Great White Ragtime Composers
Ch 7: (Originally 6): Looking Backward

5–Part handwritten, part typed and hand-edited. Not separated into chapters. Probably a preliminary effort where a handwritten copy was later typed up, then edited in Brun's hand.

The Original Ragtime Kid of the 1890s
(Two Versions)

1
Author's Note
Ch 1: A Silver Half-Dollar Returns
Ch 2: A Pioneer Rag Man of the 1890s: S. Brun Campbell tells R.J. Carew
Ch 3: Ragtime Begins. P 11 [missing]
Ch 4: Ragtime Piano Playing Contests
Ch 5: Tom Turpin, James S. Scott, W.C. Handy
Ch 6: Bands That Helped Make Ragtime Famous
Ch 7: From Rags to Ragtime and Riches
Ch 8: Some of the First White Composers of Ragtime
Ch 9: The First Ragtime Circuit
Ch 10: A Hop Head's Dream of Paradise

2
Autobiography
Multiple dedications
Ch 1: A Silver Half-Dollar Returns
Ch 2: A Pioneer Rag Man of the 1890s: S. Brun Campbell tells R. J. Carew
Ch 3: Ragtime Begins
Ch 4: Ragtime Piano Playing Contests
Ch 5: Tom Turpin, James S. Scott, W.C. Handy
Ch 6: Bands That Helped Make Ragtime Famous
Ch 7: [Missing]
Ch 8: Some of the First White Composers of Ragtime. p. 28 [missing]
Ch 9: The First Ragtime Circuit
Ch 10: Interesting Items–Letters, Radio Script and Scott Joplin Memorialized

Chapter Titles Used in the Different Versions of Brun's Two Basic Manuscripts

When Ragtime Was Young

TITLE	VERSIONS IN WHICH THE TITLE IS USED
The Original Ragtime Kid of the 1890s	1, 2, 4
The Ragtime Kid Goes West	1, 2, 4
Treemonisha (by Carew)	1, 2, 4
Ragtime	1, 2, 4
Scott Joplin	2, 3, 4
Early Great White Ragtime Composers and Pianists	1, 2, 4
New Orleans Ragtime	3
The Evolution of Ragtime, Including a History of Sedalia	3, 5
Ragtime in the Red Light Districts	3
The Ragtime Kid	3
Cavalcade of Jazz	3

The Original Ragtime Kid of the 1890s

TITLE	VERSIONS IN WHICH THE TITLE IS USED
A Silver Half-Dollar Returns	1, 2
A Pioneer Rag Man of the 1890s	1, 2
Ragtime Begins	1, 2
Ragtime Piano Playing Contests	1, 2
Turpin, Scott, Handy	1, 2
Bands That Helped Make Ragtime Famous	1, 2
From Rags to Ragtime and Riches	1
Some of the First White Composers of Ragtime	1, 2
The First Ragtime Circuit	1, 2
A Hophead's Dream of Paradise	1
Interesting Items–Letters, Radio Script and Scott Joplin Memorialized	2

Appendix 4

Transcripts of Hal Nichols'
Memories 'N Melodies Radio Shows

Former bandleader and musician, radio host Hal Nichols gave Brun his initial push toward reviving ragtime and memorializing Scott Joplin. Nichols featured written material and recordings by Brun on several of his daily half-hour *Memory Room* radio shows which originated in Long Beach, California.

Among Brun's effects are transcripts of four of these programs, dated October 14, 1943, March 17, 1944, July 12, 1944, and April 6, 1948. The October 14, 1943 show is represented by a carbon-copy transcript of the entire program; transcripts of the other three shows are selective partial copies, containing only the material related to Brun's contribution, approximately half the program in each case. An acetate recording of the April 6, 1948 show is also in Brun's collection. Comparing the printed script with the acetate shows Nichols did not adhere rigidly to his written preparation. In the transcript below, on-the-air changes by the host are presented in brackets.

Nichols employed the breezy style of the typical 1940s radio personality: this was classic radio entertainment of the time, diversion rather than documentation. In light of current knowledge, the material was full of gloss-overs, errors in both personal and professional information, and apparent straight-out whoppers, most of which could not be pinned with certainty on either Nichols or Brun. Did Brun's mother really burn his copies of Joplin's music, including the pen-and-ink manuscript of "Maple Leaf Rag"? Given how jealously Lottie Joplin guarded her late husband's work, how might Brun have come by this material in the first place? What was the real story behind the alleged scratch on the record of "Memory Room Rag" that prevented its being played on the air, and what ever happened to that record? With whom was Brun engaged in making, let alone "completing," arrangements for the production of a motion picture version of *Treemonisha*? Just how much interest did Wendell Willkie really have in memorializing Scott Joplin? How much and what kind of support did Brun receive from the Duke of Windsor? What event or whose initial opinion caused *Treemonisha* to be considered unplayable?

Best to relax, suspend judgment, and read this material as part of a historical promotional project whose goals were nothing less than admirable, but where means to ends were concerned, anything went.

MEMORIES 'N MELODIES, THURSDAY, OCTOBER 14, 1943
I dedicate this script to
my friend S.B. Campbell
Sincerely,

KFOX
Hal Nichols

THEME: (UP AND FADE)

SOUND: (CLOCK CHIMING HALF HOUR)

ANNCR:
   It's time for another pleasurable visit with Hal Nichols in the Memory Room! Folks, put aside your worries and cares for a half hour or so and join the Memory Room gang in a half hour of MEMORIES 'N MELODIES. All over southern California, thousands of "dial-twisters" are comfortably ensconced close by the radio-side, with the lights turned low and the volume turned up and more than likely sipping a cup of fragrant after-dinner coffee, ready to enjoy thirty minutes of recorded melody of the past, punctuated here and there by a few informal comments from our Memory Room maestro himself. And now let's switch controls over to Hal's place where MEMORIES 'N MELODIES is ready to begin.

HAL:
   Good evening, folks. Yes, this is Hal Nichols, the Memory Room maestro in person, ready to present a musical greeting to all of you MEMORIES 'N MELODIES fans. I'm glad you decided to join us again tonight, and I think I can assure you that you're in good company. We have a real bunch of folks in the Memory Room family and a mighty sizeable bunch, too. I think you're going to like the program Nosey and I have picked out for your listening enjoyment tonight. It contains music of all kinds— and all good, too. To get the musical ball rolling, I have a nice little medley on tap for you.

   [The first half of the program consisted of popular and patriotic selections, with interspersed informal comments].

HAL:
   And here we are at the half-way point in MEMORIES 'N MELODIES, and that means intermission time. Tonight I have another "song story" for you, and I believe it's about the most interesting one yet. The background material for this "Story Behind the Song" came not from my own Memory Room files but from one of you members of the Memory Room family, Mr. S.B. Campbell. Mr. Campbell is a musician himself, having specialized in ragtime piano in the old days and is still an ardent devotee of that unusual and fascinating type of piano music introduced and made popular by such outstanding negro artists as W.C. Handy, who composed the "St. Louis Blues," Scott Joplin, writer of the "Maple Leaf Rag," and many others.
   Mr. Campbell is at this time actively engaged in a movement to erect a memorial

to Scott Joplin for his many contributions to the field of music, and we wish him all success. But it is another once-famous negro composer with whom our "Song Story" concerns itself tonight. The name of this composer, James A. Bland, may not mean a great deal to you, but his composition, "Carry Me Back to Old Virginny" certainly will. Mr. Bland also wrote "In the Evening by the Moonlight," "Oh, Dem Golden Slippers" and many other famous songs. As Mr. Campbell relates, the story of James A. Bland is unique and tragic. Though famous during life, death meant obscurity to this gifted southern negro, and for many years, Stephen Foster was popularly given credit for Bland's masterpiece, "Carry Me Back to Old Virginia." Recently, however, after a long and weary search, Bland's grave was discovered in Merion, Pennsylvania and he was officially given credit by Dr. Kelly Miller, Dean of Harvard University, Dr. Francis Cooke, editor of "Etude" Magazine, and Theodore Presser of Philadelphia for his immortal melody. As a young man, Bland wanted to become a minstrel, but, oddly enough, the fact that he was a real negro rather than one of the burnt-cork variety was against him.

"Carry Me Back to Old Virginia" was his first published song and a great hit from the beginning. In 1902, Bland was honored by having that song chosen as the state anthem of Virginia. At the present time a movement is under way to erect a suitable memorial to this great folk musician over his simple, unmarked grave. We wish it all success. Before we listen to "Carry Me Back to Old Virginia," I want to thank Mr. S.B. Campbell for going to the trouble of supplying me with this information. It was very generous and thoughtful of him, and I'm sure I speak for all you Memory Roomers when I say that tonight's "Song Story" is one of the most interesting we have yet heard. And here is James A. Bland's famous song, "CARRY ME BACK TO OLD VIRGINNY."

MUSIC: CARRY ME BACK TO OLD VIRGINNY

[The remainder of the program consisted of the playing of popular songs, along with an offer to listeners for "the latest Memory Room souvenir gift ... a folder of poems and articles for you dog-lovers."]

Mr. S.B. Campbell this is the Scott Joplin Story
used on March 17, 1944

Last night I told you that I had something special to tell you about on tonight's MEMORIES 'N MELODIES program. Well, it's halftime right about now, and I'm going to take the next few minutes to talk about that special subject. Most of us old timers are kind of partial to the type of music known as "ragtime." And, naturally, we're anxious to see that the fellows who pioneered this kind of music—which eventually grew into "jazz" and the popular music of the present day—get full credit for their work. One of the greatest ragtime piano players and composers of all time was Scott Joplin, writer of the "Maple Leaf Rag" and many other ragtime songs. One of our Memory Room listeners—himself an old time musician—has long been a fan of Scott Joplin's. This man is Mr. S. Brunson Campbell of Venice. Having been in on the ground floor himself in the early days of ragtime music, Mr. Campbell was in a good position to know who the great musicians of all time were. He says that without doubt, the "Father of Ragtime" was Scott Joplin. In order to bring to Scott Joplin the recognition and acclaim which he rightfully deserves, but which he did not receive during his lifetime, Mr. Campbell has started a movement to erect a memorial to this great negro composer for his fine work. I am happy to say that plans are proceeding successfully on Mr. Campbell's very worthy project. Many famous people have given encouragement to Mr. Campbell, among them W.C. Handy, composer of the "St. Louis Blues" and considered to be the "Father of the Blues," Paul Whiteman, and even such personages as the Duke of Windsor and Wendell Willkie. I learned of their interest in the project from Mr. Campbell and also from a recent headline article in the musician's trade magazine *DownBeat*. For the benefit of some of you folks who may not be familiar with Scott Joplin, let me pass on a few biographical notes on the "Father of Ragtime," supplied to me by Mr. S. Brunson Campbell. Joplin was born in Texarkana, Arkansas [crossed out] Texas, and was encouraged by his parents to take piano lessons at an early age. But young Scott became so enthusiastic about piano lessons—unlike most children—that he finally became so absorbed in his music that his parents actually had to discourage him. He spent all his time on his music, and would show very little interest in anything else. As music was not a very profitable occupation in those days, his folks thought it would be better if young Scott would not spend all his time at the keyboard but would try to learn a trade or some other means of making a living. But the boy was not to be discouraged. He kept right on playing, learning all he could, making a living by playing here and there. It was while he was playing an engagement at a tavern in Sedalia, Missouri that the manager noticed what exceptional talent Scott had. Even at the expense of losing this talented performer, the Tavern manager encouraged Scott to take up the study of music in a serious way and induced the young negro to study piano at a local music school "The Smith School of Music"; soon Joplin had progressed to the place where he had the ability to work out his own Revolutionary Musical ideas with ease and dexterity. It was then that he began composing experimentally on the thing that later became known as "ragtime." The serious critics describe ragtime as "kind of music characterized by a strongly syncopated melody, superimposed upon a regularly accented accompaniment." Well, those are mighty big words to describe music with a swing to it, aren't they? But it was a real innovation in music, an innovation out of which has grown jazz, swing, boogie woogie, and all the rest of the modern musical styles. After leaving Sedalia, Scott Joplin had his first hit, the "Maple Leaf Rag," published. The tune caused a sensation in musical circles, and Joplin played engagements in St. Louis, Chicago, New York, and many other large cities. After a career during which he made many other fine contributions to the library of modern music, Joplin died in 1917. Due to the excitement of the First World War and other reasons, Joplin's contributions to the field of contemporary music were largely left unrecognized. Mr. Campbell hopes to right this wrong. Oddly enough, as Mr. Campbell tells me in a recent letter, "Maple Leaf Rag" was not Mr. Joplin's favorite number. For his own amusement, the composer used to play his "Easy Winners" and his "Fig Leaf Rag," numbers quite different from the famous "Maple Leaf." Mr. Campbell spent many years collecting Scott Joplin's music and at one time had a complete collection of all his compositions, including the original pen and ink manuscript of "Maple Leaf Rag." But in 1922, Mr. Campbell's mother accidently burned these manuscripts, valuable manuscripts which, because of the death of the negro composer five years before, can never be replaced. Among these selections were copies of the more than thirty ragtime hits written by Scott Joplin and the music to a three act operetta written entirely in ragtime. I have a list of these compositions, many of which you'd recognize instantly, had I time to read it for you. We sincerely hope that Mr. Campbell and his friends will succeed in bringing belated recognition to this some-what obscure negro musician who contributed so much to American folk music and the popular music of today. Many great figures of the musical world have admitted their indebtedness to Scott Joplin. Isaac Goldberg, in his book, *Tin Pan Alley*, said of him: "Scott Joplin was 20 years ahead of his time and has been unjustly forgotten." Well, I'm sure the efforts of Memory Roomer S. Brunson Campbell will rectify that injustice. At some future date, I hope to feature the music of Scott Joplin on one of our MEMORIES 'N MELODIES programs.

TUESDAY, July 12, 1944

As I hinted a little earlier in the program, tonight's "Contributor's Night" inter-mission feature is a little bit—in fact, quite a bit—out of the ordinary. As you know, we usually read scrapbook items of one kind or another sent in by the MEMORY ROOM gang, poetry, philosophy, after-dinner stories, and things like that. Well, tonight I'm going to take a night off and let someone else do the work. No, I haven't a guest artist in the MEMORY ROOM—not in person, anyway. But I do have one by recording. You regular members of our gang have heard me mention S. Brunson Campbell's name numerous times on MEMORIES 'N MELODIES in connection with ragtime music and the eminent Scott Joplin, who was the originator of that type of music. Mr. Campbell has devoted a great deal of time during his life to study and research on ragtime rhythms, their origin and growth and so on. An accomplished musician himself, he learned rag-time piano playing as a boy from the originators of the music themselves. In recent years, he has headed a movement which has as its aim the recognition of these early greats of popular music. Particularly Scott Joplin. Latest reports on the movement indicate that it is going very well—thanks largely to Mr. Campbell—and that a suitable mon-ument to Scott Joplin will be erected as soon as materials are available after the war. Mr. Campbell has always been anxious to preserve ragtime music in its original form. To this end, he has corresponded widely with Scott Joplin's widow and other persons who had access to some of these early manuscripts and has amassed a considerable collection of them. He had a complete collection at one time which was destroyed by fire. But, Mr. Campbell wasn't satisfied just to have the music in manuscript form; he also wanted to have it in recorded form, played in the original way. Musical styles change, you know, and it isn't unlikely that a certain style may be lost completely unless it is carried on by actual sound as well as by notes. So, Mr. Campbell has started making a number of records privately, playing some of them himself and having others played by expert piano players carefully coached by him. Tonight, we are going to have the pleasure of hearing a couple of these privately made recordings. The first one I'm going to play is Scott Joplin's "Fig Leaf Rag," a kind of companion piece to his famous "Maple Leaf Rag." It is played by Mr. Paul Lasswell, and is ragtime music in its purest form. An interesting thing about this number is that as far as is known, this is the only recording of this song in existence. Mr. Campbell went to a great deal of trouble to obtain the only manuscript of it from Mrs. Scott Joplin. It was her favorite number of all her husband's many compositions. And, now let's listen to this fine example of real old ragtime rhythm. The "Fig Leaf Rag."

(FIG LEAF RAG)

Well, how did you like that? It certainly was the real McCoy, all right. And, now I have another recorded piano contribution to our special "Contributor's Night" feature for this evening. This recording is played by Mr. S. Brunson Campbell personally. It isn't an old number—in fact, it was written especially for this program—but it is done in exactly the same style as the original ragtime. It is called the "Memory Room Rag." In the "Memory Room Rag," you may notice a passage familiar as a passage in the "12th Street Rag." This was originally written by Mr. Campbell in 1903 and later became part of the other number. Just for old time's sake, Mr. Campbell incorporated it into the "Memory Room Rag." And, here it is, a ragtime number composed especially in honor of the MEMORY ROOM program, by S. Brunson Campbell and played by him, the "Memory Room Rag."

(MEMORY ROOM RAG)

I think you'll agree that the "Memory Room Rag" is really a grand bit of work, and I want to thank Mr. Campbell for his generous gesture in dedicating it to our program and making the recording for us. I also want to tell you about another thing Mr. Campbell is promoting. It isn't widely known, but Scott Joplin was a serious musician of great talent. In addition to his rags and other compositions, Joplin also composed a three act opera, based on Negro music and having as its theme the negro's struggle against superstition and ignorance. I have read the story of the opera and looked over the music for it, and it appears to be of a very high quality. With the consent of Mrs. Joplin, Mr. Campbell is in the progress of completing arrangements for this opera to be made into a motion picture. The name of the opera is *Treemonisha*, and it takes place in Arkansas on a plantation in the early days. There are 27 numbers of all kinds—solos, duets, choruses, quintets, and so on—in the work, and it should make a very fine musical picture. I want to compliment Mr. Campbell on his endeavors in putting this project over and wish him all success. I know all the members of our MEMORY ROOM group join me in that. I also want to thank Mr. Campbell for the fine ragtime recordings. I know you've enjoyed hearing them on tonight's "Contributor's Night" program. Perhaps we'll have the pleasure of having more of them on the program in the future as Mr. Campbell's work in preserving early musical styles continues.

A Broadcast over KFOX, Long Beach, Calif by
the owner—Hal Nichols

(COPY)

SONG STORY NIGHT ON HAL'S MEMORY ROOM
APRIL 6th, 1948

When Memory Roomer S. Brunson Campbell set out to establish a memorial for his old friend and one time teacher Scott Joplin, composer of the "Maple Leaf Rag," a few years ago, we determined to give him all the encouragement we could. From my own experience, I realized it would be a difficult task to obtain proper recognition for this old time Negro musician who was the "Father of Ragtime," who led the way for the Berlins and Gershwins and other great composers of [in] the modern idiom to follow.

That was because Scott Joplin was a modest sincere hardworking musician who cared more for music than [for] glory. He spent a large part of his life in the small town of Sedalia, Missouri, where Mr. Campbell met him and studied under him as a boy. Joplin learned harmony, counterpoint and the fine[r] points of the art of music at the Smith College of Music in that city. Joplin was no ordinary piano thumper but a real trained musician of great talent. His ragtime opera "Treemonisha" is so difficult and intricate that musicians are still unable to play it.

Scott Joplin wrote the first real ragtime number approximately fifty [sixty] years ago, "Original Rags," it was called. Many other rags followed it [it omitted] in the Nineties and shortly afterwards of which "Maple Leaf Rag" was the greatest and best known. Memory Roomer Campbell collected all of Joplin's rags and many other mementos of Joplin's career into a private collection. And in addition Mr. Campbell has spent years in attempting to get Scott Joplin properly recognized as one of the great[est] musical innovators of his time. It has been Mr. Campbell's lifelong ambition to see a memorial erected to his old time piano instructor.

Well, I am [I'm] happy to announce on behalf of Mr. Campbell, that his ambition is to be finally realized. No, the memorial won't be one of granite or bronze—-much better than that. It will [It'll] be a memorial more useful and lasting, more alive and vital. Thanks to Mr. Campbell's efforts, Scott Joplin will be accorded a place of honor in the Library of Fisk University of Nashville, Tennessee, alongside of George Gershwin and other notable men of music. After considerable correspondence with the Trustees and officials of the University, Brun Campbell has agreed to turn over his entire private collection of Scott Joplin mementos to be put on display as a Scott Joplin Memorial on the grounds of the University. The collection includes original copies of some thirty-six Joplin compositions, including the opera *Treemonisha*, as well as many other items such as pictures of Scott Joplin and his piano, places where he played, bands of which he was a member, and so on. Also included is a complete biography of Scott Joplin, written by Mr. Campbell himself and edited and approved by Mrs. Joplin, whom, I believe [know], is still living. Joplin himself died in 1917 [April 4, 1919, which is 29 years ago Sunday].

Well, I know all of you who love ragtime will be pleased to know that Mr. Campbell has realized his ambition and that Scott Joplin's contribution to the music of America has been finally recognized and his name perpetuated for posterity. And now, to climax our brief review of how this came about, I'm going to play a recording of "Maple Leaf Rag," Joplin's most famous, played by Mr. S. Brunson Campbell in the way Scott Joplin taught him to play it, the true ragtime style. Here it is, and I hope you enjoy it for old time's sake, the "Maple Leaf Rag."

Appendix 5

Interview of Cecil Charles Spiller by Galen Wilkes, January 26, 1992

Cecil Spiller was a recording engineer and ragtime fan who was well-acquainted with Brun Campbell during the ragtime revival years of the 1940s and 1950s. Without Spiller's efforts, it's doubtful that we'd have many, if any, recordings of Brun's piano playing.

Historian, composer, and performer Galen Wilkes interviewed Spiller during the 1980s and 1990s about his experiences with Brun. The recordings introduce new information about Brun, and also extend previously-known information.

Most interesting, though is the manner in which Spiller's narration complements Brun's, giving the reader a strong sense of how conversations and interactions between the two men must have sounded. Like Brun, Spiller at times raised more questions than he answered. The stories he told sometimes contradicted Brun's accounts in *When Ragtime Was Young*, as when the recording engineer seemed to replace Buffalo Bill with Billy the Kid. Some of Spiller's information is clearly wrong: history amply states that the big Land Rush was not in St. Louis, but in Arkansas City. And—again, like Brun—Spiller tended to ramble, starting a story, then jumping to another. For this reason, I have edited the original interview in the interest of reader comprehension.

GALEN WILKES: Okay, we'll get started here.

CECIL SPILLER: Mm-hmm (affirmative).

GALEN WILKES: Cecil, when did you first meet Brun Campbell?

CECIL SPILLER: I can't hear you. What?

GALEN WILKES: Oh. Cecil, when did you first meet Brun Campbell?

CECIL SPILLER: Okay. Well the first time that I'd met Brun, it was in Ocean Park. They were putting on some dances with Kid Ory, and during intermission, this fellow came from out of the audience and set down and started to play the piano. When he did, everybody was amazed at how good he was. So then, after he played a few things, I went up and asked him who he was, and he said he was Brun Campbell, The Ragtime Kid. And I talked to him further on it and made a casual acquaintance before Ory came back on and played.

Brun stayed around, and I asked him where he lived, that I'd like to come down and maybe record him. And I'd heard of Brun Campbell. Nesuhi Ertegun did a record of him, with I think somebody else. So then he gave me the address, and then the next opportunity I had, I went down to see him in this barbershop he had on Venice Boulevard. And, it was quite interesting. I came in and he was cutting a guy's hair, or something like that. He immediately stopped and sat around and talked about ragtime, I said, well go ahead and continue your business and then we'll talk about it. So, fine. So there's some other customers who are in there, and he had this piano in back of his barber shop, there. And he goes back and he wants to play something

I said, "What about your customers?" "Oh," he says, "they can wait." So, then I had an old disc-recorder that I built up at the time, and I went down and recorded him. And one of the problems was to get him to ever complete something. Like on some of these acetates that we have here, he only played a little bit and then he stopped and say, "Well, I want to do something else." I'd say, "Brun, go ahead and play something."

This particular acetate, here, is one that he did play complete and it was the "Twelfth Street Rag," which was issued on some of the Paul Affeldt recordings. And later when we used some larger acetates, we got all of the stuff together that Paul had issued, and I dug back through the files and tried to contact other people (who might have had material recorded by Brun).

Dave [unintelligible], who was one of the sponsors of these Ory sessions had made a couple of recordings, and he came down to the Rendevous Ballroom there, I believe, it was Saturday night, and that, I think, was 1947, 48. I believe that was the time that all this was taking place. And then I talked to Les Koenig who had *Good Times Jazz* and I said, "Look, this guy is a legend. Let's get him into a studio and make a recording of him."

So, Les said, "Well, fine." So we go over to Hollywood, there, to his studio in the bottom of the Pantages Theater. They have a concert grand, beautiful piano down there. Brun sits down, and hits a couple of notes, "I can't play on that thing. The action is too stark. Stamp on it." And, so that blew that session. And so I told him, I said, "There's another fellow I know down here in Santa Monica that has a recording studio. Maybe we can get him down there and record . But Brun doesn't like this piano either. So we did a little interview, we talked to him about it. Les Koenig was kind of a strange guy, a little bit kind of temperamental. And he said, "Well, I can't waste all the time. This guy, is too much of a problem. We can't get a piano that he likes. I said, "Well, we just find an old upright . That's what he's used to playing and the action is loose on it. Why can't we go down to his barbershop?"

And that was just the time that tape was coming in and Les did have a tape machine, but I never could get him interested again to try to do it. So I did as much recording as I could. And then, we put out a 78. Brun wanted to get it out, so we went ahead and financed. Of course, those days it didn't cost much to get a 78 out.

Then, we had a guy print some labels for us. And we didn't know at that time that the labels had to be a special paper, because when they put them in a press, they will tear. So, the first batch of these records, a lot of them came out where the label was torn on it. Then we learned that you had to have a special paper for them. And I think that record was "Frankie and Johnny" and the "Tiger Rag." And then whenever I had an opportunity, I'd record him.

And after my experience with him, he'd want me to come down to get a haircut every week. If I didn't show up on this particular night and day, he'd call me up and say, "You're due for a haircut." I said, "I don't get a haircut, maybe once a month." And he's, "Come around now, " he says, "I have some other stuff and sheet music and things I want to show you."

So, he had this tremendous collection of sheet music there, and he said, "What am I going to do with it?" I said, "Well, Fisk University was doing a lot with ragtime, and so on. Why don't you send a bunch of it back to them where it'll be taken care of." At that time I had a couple of kids, and I was afraid the stuff would get torn up. He had quite a lot of music. He was around... He was 78 or so when he passed on. I believe he got a heart attack. I heard about it afterwards. The family, incidentally, didn't like his ragtime. They didn't particularly like the music. They had a little spinet piano, belonged to his daughter in the house. And they didn't want him to play on that. They didn't like him playing that on that piano, there.

I don't think they particularly liked me because I was encouraging him in all of this ragtime thing. So I was not notified. And I heard about later from somebody else that knew about, that he passed on.

So I went down to see the family, and I asked them about all this music, sheet music and stuff that he had a lot of it all pinned up over the barbershop and, they said, "Oh, all that junk we just took it out and threw it away and just burned it," or something. So I was glad that at least we did get that stuff back to the Fisk University.

GALEN WILKES: Now, where was the ballroom where you met him? Where was that located?

CECIL SPILLER: That was located in Ocean Park. There was a big Lick Pier in Ocean Park, actually on the borderline between Ocean Park and Santa Monica. And, it was called the Rendevous Ballroom. It was a kind of an old, dilapidated ballroom, and it was a question of whether it was in Santa Monica or Ocean Park. They called it Santa Monica Ocean Park.

Well, Lick Pier was probably another quarter of a mile up further where they had the big ballroom. They had another ballroom where the black musicians performed on Lick Pier, because at that time everything was strictly white and in the main big ballroom down there, it was white only, and the black ballroom, there, was down at the other end of the pier. And I worked, for Words and Music Company, and the shop right on Pier Avenue, there.

And this other ballroom down there. Jelly Roll Morton played there in 1936, I believe it was. And, I was able to go down there after I got off work and hear him, his band. Mostly, it was blacks that were down there.

GALEN WILKES: Huh?

CECIL SPILLER: Don't want to ramble on, here, too much. [laughs]

GALEN WILKES: Okay, okay. Now, how old was Brun at the time when you first met him?

Cecil Spiller: Well, he must have been up of 65 or so, I think, at that time. I don't think he really knew exactly how old he was. Oh, he said he was first started playing when he was 14. He started playing down in New Orleans. That's what he says, but Brun tells a lot of different stories, and not all of them coincide together. He started playing in these houses that they had with the swinging doors, the double-door, and one madam there, and she would lean out over the door and hustle business. And he played piano in the back of this place. This was probably 1914 or so. And then he got on the river, came up on the river boats to St. Louis.

He was playing in various places up in St. Louis, and he tells a story about looking for a job. And he goes into this place and he said, "You got a job for a piano player?" And the guy says, "Well, yeah. But you gotta be pretty good," he says, "they shot the other piano player that was in here." And Brun didn't think anything about it and he found out it was actually was true, that this is what happened. And then also, I think I may have related to you a story about how Billy the Kid came into this place, and wanted Brun to play the same song, I don't remember the name, over and over again. And he said he just kept on playing it over and over again. He said this lasted all through the evening. Course, he said, not one person [laughs] [unintelligible] was tired of hearing that number. And he said this went through until dawn the next day.

Then he said that Billy the Kid just threw him silver dollars all the time when he would play. And then he said he went outside and Billy said, "Take all those dollars and throw them up in the air." And he did. He said that Billy shot and hit the silver dollar, and put a dent in it from the bullet. Brun said that he had the silver dollar and flattened it out again. Then he said he was kind of down on his luck and spent the silver dollar.

And then he said, one time down in his barbershop, a fellow came in and gave him a silver dollar to cut his hair, and the silver dollar had the indent of a bullet on it! And he claimed this was the same [laughs] silver dollar that turned up! But Brun was prone to some exaggeration.

GALEN WILKES: Amazing.

CECIL SPILLER: Actually, it was true or not.

And then he said he was back to St. Louis when they had the grand land-rush. When they lined all these wagons up and shot a gun in the air and then the people just took off, whatever land they could get to was theirs. And according to what he said, people were trampled to death and everything else because all these people just dashed out there. And after he was in his period of coming out here to California he ran a pretty straight business with the barbershop and he'd married this lady. This lady was a very straitlaced type of average American that had their kind of values, and she knew nothing about Brun's background.

He also tells about, in this St. Louis period, where he worked as a madam's boy, and he lived, apparently, with this madam there, and she kind of supported him, and so I asked him about it. I said, "Well, did you hustle business for her like being a pimp or something?" And he's, "Oh, no, I didn't do that, of course." Found he did, like Jelly Roll Morton. That was kind of what they did. They went out and hustled for them. So his part about this, of course, his family being respectable [laughs]. Was fairly interesting, though, that they had, in more recent years, been kind of more interested in him and his music, and they came down to the old Music Hall [Galen Wilkes says Cecil was speaking of the Old Town Music Hall, in El Segundo, CA]. It'd be the daughter and I don't know, the mother. His wife is probably pretty old now. But the daughter was interested in it.

Then, of course, when, when they heard about the music itself that Paul Affeldt was putting out, they immediately got dollar signs in front of their eyes and figured there was a lot of money being made. And I tried to explain to them that none of us had really made anything out of it at all, we did it more of a labor of love.

GALEN WILKES: I imagine—is his widow still living?

CECIL SPILLER: What?

GALEN WILKES: Is Brun's widow still alive?

CECIL SPILLER: I don't know. I don't know whether she is or not. Now, ask...Phil Kaufman.

GALEN WILKES: She'd probably be over a hundred, or something.

CECIL SPILLER: Yeah, I doubt it. But the daughter, the daughter, I'm sure, she's still alive.

GALEN WILKES: Uh-huh.

CECIL SPILLER: But they had very little recollection of anything about him or his music at all. They were not receptive to it, at all. Because she was a probably a church-going type of a person. But ask, be sure and ask Phil about it. He may have the address. But, I don't think there's really much information that she could really give you.

GALEN WILKES: Do you recall any of the tunes that Brun was playing when you first met him?

CECIL SPILLER: I don't remember them. Most all of the tunes we had duplicated on the Paul Affeldt material. You could get the list of the tunes there. But down at the Rendevous Ballroom, I believe he played "Maple Leaf" and "Twelfth Street" down there. And he, we were talking about those rags, and he always claimed that most of the people played them way too fast. That the "Twelfth Street" and the "Maple Leaf Rag" was supposed to be played at a little slower tempo.

GALEN WILKES: Now, where did the titles to the pieces he recorded come from?
    Cecil Spiller: The what?

GALEN WILKES: Where did the titles to the pieces he recorded for Paul, where did they come from? Those titles?

CECIL SPILLER: Well, some of the things were Brun, and I think it's just things that he thought up. All the rags were strains from other things in there, and ... he claimed that Louis Chauvin was the greatest ragtime player of all times. And he said they used to have those ragtime contests down there where these different musicians would all come together and they'd applaud whoever won.

And he said that Jelly Roll Morton would never play if he knew that Louis Chauvin was going to be there because Louis Chauvin was probably one of the greatest, and a lot of the music that Scott Joplin put out, Brun claims that this was music that was originally composed by Louis Chauvin and according to what Brun said, Chauvin was not a trained musician and couldn't write it up. So that apparently Scott Joplin took a lot of that stuff and put his name on it. And that's what Brun claims. I don't know how true that is.

GALEN WILKES: Mm-hmm (affirmative). Did Brun read music?

CECIL SPILLER: Oh, yes…

GALEN WILKES: He di-

CECIL SPILLER: … yes. He had apparently had music lessons and so on. Yes, he did. He had some musical background, there. I don't know where he got it because he claimed he ran away from home when he was about 14, is what he said. And that's where he developed the name, The Ragtime Kid. He certainly did have some formal…

GALEN WILKES: Mm-hmm (affirmative).

CECIL SPILLER: … education.

GALEN WILKES: All the pieces that he recorded and that you saw him play, were they all played by memory?

CECIL SPILLER: Yes. He never played from any sheet music, at all, as far as I know. It was all from memory.

GALEN WILKES: Uh-huh. And did he every play from any sheet music at the barbershop?

CECIL SPILLER: No, he never played from the music. He had the music up there but he never played from them. And even the recordings, he never played the same thing twice the same. He was like most of those musicians, he'd kind of improvise to himself. And of course he had that tremendous left hand. He played terrific.

Then, one of the things that I had to watch with him, was that he was like Jelly Roll Morton when they made the Library of Congress things, is the stomping of the foot on the mic stand and the thumping. Right away I noticed him, because he was there stomping with that foot, So I got the mic away from him because I'd figured this was going to happen without all of the Jelly Roll stuff.

GALEN WILKES: What did you think of his style of playing?

CECIL SPILLER: I loved it. I was really just so impressed with it . It was such a relaxed, carefree type of playing. And that's kind of a piano player's kind of music that I like, and well, it's like Paul Lingle was one that was that type of piano, and of course, Jeff Stacey is another really relaxed type of piano, and … It's one of the things that happen like with a lot of the jazz ragtime festivals that they have when Jim Turner and Zimmerman play and … Zimmerman, finally, is playing much more relaxed on it. And Jim Turner, of course, we're very good friends, and Jim has a very formal education. I said, "Jim, you gotta play relaxed on it." Waller, of course, was very relaxed. I love, of course, Fats Waller, the way he played.

And that was the thing what I think ragtime is all about. And even that matter, the whole thing of the jazz and New Orleans and all the type of jazz, and people say, why do you love it? Because of the relaxed feeling. That's why I feel that so many times you get these musicians at a studio and, well like the one time with ... I worked with Les Koenig for a while and he was going to record George Lewis, and he comes in the studio and all the lights are flashing and he says, "Take one. Take two." And these guys come unglued. So the way that I like to see them record is have these fellows hang up and just play for fun where they're not thinking about it. That's why I think live performers is the only way that ragtime or jazz should be played and played to people.

GALEN WILKES: Uh-huh. Were all the cuts issued of Brun?

CECIL SPILLER: Everything that we've had, as far as we could tell. I went through some of this stuff again, and Paul has another album of stuff, the final one that he had. But all the stuff available of anybody that has a Brun, it's been all out. Even the short things are incomplete, we did for posterity.

GALEN WILKES: Right.

CECIL SPILLER: There's this young fellow, Roberts, by the name of Roberts [Galen Wilkes says that Cecil was referring to David Thomas Roberts], that's been quite a disciple of his, and we had put out a record for him and he was greatly influenced and plays so much like Brun he's a one of the very few that has done it. We got one record out, but the guy is literally impossible to try to work with. He wants everything note-perfect and wanted to do a lot of editing of anything in there. He doesn't realize that, the thing is, sure they play a few wrong notes, but it's the relaxed feeling of the music that they had, and he ... I did one session for him.

GALEN WILKES: Uh-huh. Were Brun's recordings made in the barbershop?

CECIL SPILLER: Beg your pardon?

GALEN WILKES: Were Brun's recordings made in the barbershop?

CECIL SPILLER: Well, in the back of the barbershop. The barbershop itself was in the back, right in the back. There was a cleaning establishment next to it, but they had a little place in the back, and this piano was in the back part of the barbershop. And then he had a piano in his garage, where he went over and apparently practiced a lot. And, we did record some of the stuff over there, too because it was just an old upright that he loved.

GALEN WILKES: Mm-hmm (affirmative). Was there any memorabilia in the barbershop?

CECIL SPILLER: Well you mean, ... well just some sheet music, and some pictures and stuff that he had, which Paul has most of the pictures. Of course, I took several pictures of him, and, one that I think I have up in the house, of him in the barbershop looking at the sheet music. I think I have an extra copy ... look, I saw it the other day. If I remember, you could have a copy of...

GALEN WILKES: Ah.

CECIL SPILLER: But that was him standing back, looking at this music.

GALEN WILKES: Uh-huh. Did he have anything hanging on the walls?

CECIL SPILLER: Oh, yes. He had a lot of the music on the wall. But that was the stuff that I referred to that they destroyed, just took off ... but there was nothing really rare. He had a bunch of rags and other stuff ... a whole bunch of it went back to Fisk

University, and this other stuff was like, oh, "Twelfth Street," a bunch of other things like that. He claims that he personally knew W.C. Handy, knew him quite well. Brun said he wasn't really much of a piano player. Of course, that happens lots of times, a lot of composers [laughs] aren't necessarily good musician. But that was about all that he had.

Then he had this, of course, the book that Rudi Blesh did of all the old players. *They All Played Ragtime*, which is a pretty good account with most of the stuff about Brun there.

GALEN WILKES: Right. Could you tell us the story about when Brun was shaving some customer and he mentioned something about ragtime, and you said he shaved the guy's mole off, or something?

CECIL SPILLER: [laughs] Well this was when I was there, one time, I was waiting for him. And well he just nicked the guy's ear, just a little bit. Nick on the ear when he was shaving. I always made a habit that I was always clean-shaved before I went down, I didn't want to [laughs] be like Van Gogh and lose an ear [laughs] in the situation there. He cut the hair, fine, but no shaving, because he just really became transformed when anybody would talk about ragtime, which of course was his whole life. Apparently, he had been down there in Venice for all those years and just been a mere barber, cutting hair

GALEN WILKES: Did Brun have any pupils or people that he showed how to play ragtime, or maybe taught them anything? Did he have anybody come to him?

CECIL SPILLER: No, I don't believe so. I don't believe he ever taught any of them, but he would always stress that they needed to have a strong left hand and not to play too fast. He said that was one of the misconceptions of it, of ragtime, to play too fast.

And that was, of course, one of the things down at the old Music Hall to say that I felt that many of them played the music way too fast. What it was, was just not according to what he meant it to be.

GALEN WILKES: Mm-hmm (affirmative). Who were some of the other ragtime people that Brun knew? He knew Joplin?

CECIL SPILLER: Scott Joplin, and then, of course, Louis Chauvin, and then, Turpin. Ben...

GALEN WILKES: Tom Turpin?

Cecil Spiller: Tom Turpin. Yeah. Tom Turpin, who he thought was great. Jelly Roll Morton, he said, was a very good piano player but he felt that that he wasn't in a league with Tom Turpin or Louis Chauvin. But this Louis Chauvin is the one that he thought a lot of him, but apparently there was never any recordings that were made of, of him. Nobody could ever uncover any of that stuff. Of course, that would be in that 1914 to 1920 period, apparently when that took place.

GALEN WILKES: Yeah, well, Chauvin died in 1906.

CECIL SPILLER: Where?

GALEN WILKES: He died in 1906.

CECIL SPILLER: 1906?

GALEN WILKES: Yeah.

CECIL SPILLER: Well, it must been before the World War…. Well, you see this is some of the stuff that doesn't jive, because if he would've met him, which he claims he did, he must have had to have been older than 14 when he when he was playing in the houses of prostitution back there. So then there's the War period. between World War I and what he did at that particular time. I don't know. Paul has been writing and trying to do a history of Brun, as much as he can. And he says he's been interviewing as many people, himself, Dave, and so on, about trying to get all these stories to jive, you see. I know Paul would be only too glad to let you have that stuff.

GALEN WILKES: Hmm. Okay. What was Brun's personality like?

CECIL SPILLER: Very jovial. Very unassuming type of person. Not stuck-up and saying "I am the greatest" or anything else like that. But he was what I felt was a very, very humble player. He never came on like Jelly Roll did, because Jelly Roll was supposed to be very egotistical, and…. But, no, Brun wasn't. He was a very, very, very nice, nice person. Very nice person to be around [laughs].

GALEN WILKES: Did you get to talk or meet Jelly Roll at that concert, at all?

CECIL SPILLER: No, I really didn't. I just knew that he was playing. I really wasn't that much into the New Orleans type of music, but I just went over and listened to it because it was a lot of other different bands that come over there.

GALEN WILKES: Uh-huh. What became of Brun's things after his death?

CECIL SPILLER: His what?

GALEN WILKES: What became of Brun's possessions after his death?

CECIL SPILLER: Well, the only things, the possessions, that we were interested in were his sheet music and any of the photographs that he had. Fortunately, I had all the photographs and copied most all the pictures that he had. Made copies, all of them. But that was the only thing. As I say, when I went down to see them, I was very nice about it, said I was very sorry to hear about him passing on. And I said he thought an awful lot about all that music he had up on the wall down there, and they said, well, all that stuff we just threw it away. That's what they said, and so nothing I further I could try to do about it.

So I did go over by the barbershop and there was nothing on the walls. Whoever went in there apparently had taken all the stuff off the walls. And they were chatting, they were kind of redoing it. I don't think it was going to be a barbershop anymore.

GALEN WILKES: Mm-hmm (affirmative), I'm out of questions. Anything else you would like to add about Brun?

CECIL SPILLER: No, I think we've pretty well covered most everything about him. It was just unfortunate that we couldn't have had more things done. I tried to do as much as I could. He would stop playing some of these things and jump along on something else … yeah. But, certainly the only person who's ever played anywhere's near like him, Roberts, is the only one. He's the only one that's really took up and kind of followed in his footsteps, the way he played.

GALEN WILKES: Mm-hmm (affirmative).

CECIL SPILLER: So, maybe that answers about everything that I have.

GALEN WILKES: I think so.

Appendix 6

Brun Campbell Family Tree

Brun Campbell Pedigree (courtesy Bob Resta)

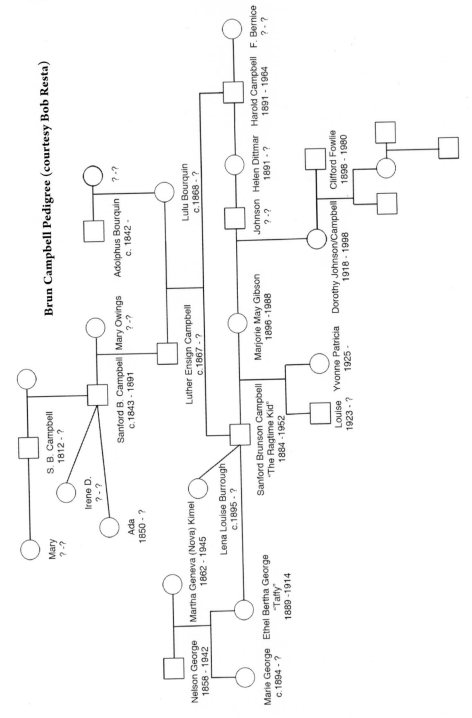

Index

Affeldt, Paul 47, 57, 67, 188–189, 191–192,
214; *Joplin's Disciple* (CD) 46, 71, 114, 206,
209, 214, 216; projects 88, 207, 232, 235
Alexander, Melford 22, 157, 159, 166–167
Allison, Kansas 10–13
Allison Breeze 12
Allison Times 12
Arkansas City, Kansas 14–21, 24–25, 28–30,
32, 35–36, 39, 48, 53, 58, 60–64, 145, 155,
188, 231
The Arkansas City Traveler 58, 60, 63
The Arkansas Kid 26, 42–43, 49
Armstrong, Louis 143
Armstrong-Byrd Music Store 20–21, 109,
149, 160, 168
Asbury, Herbert 45
Atchison, Kansas 16
Avery, Ray 133, 140, 146

Backus, Kathi 188
Barbary Coast 39, 44; businesses 37, 40–43,
46–49, 132, 172; history 41, 45; *see also*
San Francisco, California
Barber, Charles E. 69
barbershop quartets 11, 15, 27
"Barbershop Rag" 187–188; *see also* Campbell, Brun
"Barrel House Rag" 191–192, 208–209;
birth 1, 9; *see also* Campbell, Brun
Bates, Katharine Lee 51–52
Berkey, Charm H. 32, 53
Berlin, Edward A. 71, 112, 153–154
Berlin, Irving 1, 146, 299; "Alexander's Rag-
time Band" 3, 83, 87, 100
Billy the Kid 231, 234
Biloxi, Missouri 34
Bland, James A. 78–79, 225
Blanding, Don 82–83, 175
Blesh, Rudi 2, 4, 95, 137–139, 141, 153, 219;
Circle Records 137; *They All Played Rag-*

time 2, 4, 23, 47, 132, 135–136, 139, 143–
144, 177, 189, 238
"Blue Rag" 188; *see also* Campbell, Brun
Boarman, Ray 140, 216
Bolden, Buddy 175, 178–179
Bontemps, Arna 90, 94; Fisk University
library 89, 124–127, 129–130; *They Seek a
City* (aka *Anyplace but Here*) 89, 104, 108–
109, 116–117, 134
Boone, John William ("Blind Boone") 157,
165
Borneman, Ernest 115–116, 149, 151
Boswell, W.C. 111–112, 116
Bowman, Euday 194, 213, 215–216; *see also*
"Twelfth Street Rag"
Bradbury, Ray 133
The Brun Campbell Archive *see* Karp, Larry
"Brun Campbell Express" 188
"Brun's Boys" 206
Buffalo Bill 32, 34, 38, 231
Buffalo Bill's Wild West Show 32, 34
Burrough, Lena Louise 60, 62–65

clothing 27, 29–31, 49, 51, 55, 73, 89, 148,
158, 166–167
Campbell, Adolphus 12
Campbell, Brun: as barber 2, 29, 62, 64–67,
71, 75, 133, 146, 238; "Cavalcade of Jazz"
135, 174–175, 220, 222; children 2, 54, 61,
65–66, 75, 107, 235, 242; in Colorado
Springs, Colorado 49–52; death 147, 233;
"From Rags to Ragtime and Riches" 98,
121, 213, 221–222; as Joplin's pupil 2–3,
22–23, 71, 90, 92, 109, 116, 129, 135, 138–
140, 143, 145, 147, 149, 160, 168, 173, 179,
189–190, 227, 229; in Kansas City, Missouri 52–53; list of works 207–212; mar-
riages 2, 54, 59–67, 75, 104, 145, 234–235,
242; musical style 48, 92, 129, 135, 138–
140, 149, 166, 169, 186–189, 191–201,

204–206, 235–239; "My Girl Taffy" 39, 54, 58–63; "The Original Hot Men of the 90s" 117–119, 123, 156–169; *The Original Ragtime Kid of the 1890s* 5–7, 131, 141, 148, 219, 220–222; personality 4–5, 11, 25, 29, 31, 34, 38, 46, 49, 62, 75, 86, 123, 189–190, 192, 206, 219–220, 232–233, 239; promotion of Scott Joplin 72–147, 172–173, 180–181, 216, 223–230; "Ragtime in the Red Light Districts" 54–58, 169–172, 222; revivalist period 2, 6, 64–147, 173, 179–180, 192; runaway to Sedalia, Missouri 3, 20–21, 23, 139, 145, 236; in San Francisco, California 40–49; supposed performance gap 27–28, 38, 53, 57, 59, 64, 67, 144–145, 172–173, 188, 192; in Tulsa, Oklahoma 2, 27, 54, 60, 63–65, 144; *When Ragtime Was Young* 5–6, 9–64, 66–67, 69, 74, 110, 120, 123, 130–141, 148, 156, 169, 174, 184, 219–220; in Wichita, Kansas 38, 53; *see also* "Barbershop Rag"; "Barrel House Rag"; "Blue Rag"; "Campbell Cakewalk"; "Chestnut Street in the 90s"; "Dallas Blues"; "Essay in Ragtime"; "Ginger Snap Rag"; "Grandpa Stomps" (aka "Weeping Willow Rag"); "He's That Hard Hearted Revenue Man"; "I'm Paying the Way You Said I Would Some Day"; "I'm the Singing Cowboy"; "Let Me Come Back Home"; "Mama's Little Baby Doll"; "Memory Room Rag"; "Rendevous Rag"; "Salome's Slow Drag"; "Sapphire 'Blue' Rhythm"; "You Are Mama's Baby Doll"; "You Are the One I Want the Rest of My Life"; "You're Going to Pay on Judgment Day"
Campbell, E. Simms 104, 109–110, 115, 118, 123, 146
Campbell, Harold 4, 29–30, 242; background 65, 202; compositions 202–204, 207, 209, 217; "Dream in My Arms" 202–203, 209; "Guess Who's in Love" 203
Campbell, Lulu Bourquin 11–12, 24, 28–31, 65, 141, 174, 223, 227, 242
Campbell, Luther Ensign 11–15, 18, 24–29, 65–66, 141, 174–175, 242
Campbell, Sanford Brunson (Brun's grandfather) 10–14, 23–24, 242
"Campbell Cakewalk" 187; *see also* Campbell, Brun
Cantor, Eddie 56
Carew, Roy 4, 6, 97, 107, 116, 122, 124–125, 137, 146, 170, 173, 178, 189, 191; Tempo-Music Publishing Company 94, 119; writings 9, 85–86, 95–98, 103, 107–110, 115, 118–120, 128, 130–131, 134, 136, 156, 163–169, 173, 214, 220

"Carry Me Back to Old Virginia" 78–79, 225
Charters, Ann 72
Chauvin, Louis 38, 46, 95–96, 131, 132–135, 139, 150, 155–160, 164, 166, 167–168, 175–178, 186, 235–238; "Heliotrope Bouquet" 127, 131, 162, 177, 184
Cherokee Strip 14–20, 24
"Chestnut Street in the 90s" 47, 130–131, 139, 186–187, 204–205, 208, 215; *see also* Campbell, Brun
Chicago, Illinois 1, 100–101, 108, 121, 127–128, 132, 141, 159, 163–172, 181–182, 226
Chicago Herald American 121
City Hall Barber Shop 2, 7, 66, 71–78, 105, 133, 144, 146, 191, 232–239
Civil War 13
Compton, Glover 47
Confrey, Zez 72, 175, 178
Copland, Les 183
Colorado City, Colorado 50–52
Colorado Springs, Colorado 49–52
Coyote Kid 50
Cripple Creek, Colorado 51
C.W. Hodges (barber shop) 64–65

"Dallas Blues" 93; *see also* Campbell, Brun
Daniels, Charles (Neil Moret) 150
David, "Piano Price" 47
DeLisle, D.S. 164, 179
deMille, Cecil B. 86–87
Denver, Colorado 52, 57, 79
Dockstader, Lew 29
Dorsey, Thomas Andrew 125
Doubleday and Company 132
DownBeat 22, 84, 129, 145–146, 214, 226
Downtown Wichita 199–120
Duck, Lem 44–45, 49
Durling, E.V. 121, 146

Eccles Disc Recordings 87, 106–108, 118, 133
Echoes 133, 140, 215
Egan, Richard 6, 33, 46, 92, 152–153, 186–188, 191, 214; transcriptions 88, 205–207, 216
El Cerrito, California 122
El Reno, Oklahoma 24–28, 42, 60, 155
El Reno Land Lottery 24
Elman, Dave 80–82
Encyclopedia of Music for Pictures 72
Ertegun, Nehusi 232
Esquire 109–110, 117–119, 123, 156, 169
Esquire's Jazz Book 110, 118, 123
"Essay in Ragtime" 118, 130–131, 194, 208, 215–216; *see also* Campbell, Brun
Essays in Ragtime (CD) 216–217; *see also* Reffkin, David

Evans, George 29
Ewen, David 123

Fisk University 71, 96, 125, 129, 233, 237–
238; Joplin archive acquisition 71–72, 89,
124–132, 139, 172, 229, 233
Fort Smith, Arkansas 64
Fort Worth, Texas 57
Fowler, Don E. 86, 95–96, 108, 214

George, Ethel Bertha 24, 30–31, 35, 53–54,
57–64, 242; divorce 60–62
George R. Smith College *see* Sedalia, Mis-
souri
Gershwin, George 71, 87, 96, 125, 129, 175,
178, 207, 229
Gibson, Marjorie May 60–62, 65–66, 75,
104, 144, 242
Giles Brothers 33
"Ginger Snap Rag" 140, 185–188, 208, 215–
216; *see also* Campbell, Brun
Good Times Jazz 232
"Grandpa Stomps" (aka "Weeping Willow
Rag") 133–134, 192, 208, 212, 215–216;
see also Campbell, Brun
Grauer, Bill 130
Grinstead, Daniel 113–114
Gullickson, Gordon 108–109, 114–115, 130
Guthrie, Oklahoma 24, 32, 34

Hall, Moss 1, 178
"Hal's Memory Room" *see* Nichols, Hal
Handy, W.C. 4, 78–81, 99, 107–111, 115, 119,
123, 132, 146, 159–161, 167–169, 175, 204,
221–226, 238; compositions 80, 99–100,
104, 107–110; *Unsung Americans Sung* 80,
88–89, 95–96, 124; writings 82–84, 87–89,
95–100, 104–105, 108–111, 124–125, 130,
134, 147, 179
Hannibal, Missouri 139–140, 154
Happy Hooligan *see* Duck, Lem
Harney, Ben 71, 159, 167–168
Harrison, Arkansas 38
Hastings, Ida 22, 157, 166
Hastings, Jim 22
Hawks, Gene 183
Hayden, Scott 22, 38, 96, 116, 119, 150–151,
154, 157–160, 166–168
Heermans, Jerry 4, 33, 135–138
"Heliotrope Bouquet" *see* Chauvin, Louis
"He's That Hard Hearted Revenue Man" 75,
196–198, 209; *see also* Campbell, Brun
Hickok, Wild Bill 37
Hill, George Roy 72
Hill, Ted 31–32
Hoffman Music Publishers 150, 157, 165

Hogan, Ernest 163
Hollywood, California 87, 199, 122, 144, 147,
161, 232
Hominy, Oklahoma 42
The Hominy Kid 42, 49
"A Hop Heads Dream of Paradise" 131, 221
"How About You?" 172–173
Hug, Armand 141–142, 146
Huling, Sister Jean 187
Hutchinson, Kansas 15, 39–40

"I'm Certainly Living a Ragtime Life" 2
"I'm Paying the Way You Said I Would Some
Day" 101, 193, 209–210; *see also* Camp-
bell, Brun
"I'm the Singing Cowboy" 101–102; *see also*
Campbell, Brun
Ireland, Tom 71, 122, 127, 143, 179–180

Jackson, Tony 94–99, 159, 167, 175
James, Jesse 14, 26, 38, 162, 221
Janis, Harriet 2, 4, 47, 95, 132, 135–143
Jayhawk Press 119–120
jazz 1–2, 87, 98, 102, 104, 111, 115, 120–124,
128, 130, 133, 135, 141, 149, 155, 157–158,
166, 173, 177–180, 225, 236, 237; historian
Roy Carew 4, 6, 9, 85, 94, 191; misuse of
term 128, 144, 147; traditional 69
Jazz Journal 4, 32, 54, 98, 121, 128, 135–136,
138, 142, 148, 169, 213–214
The Jazz Record 173, 213
The Jazz Record Book 71, 182
Jazz Report 23, 185–186, 214
Jazzman 110
John, Al 38
Johnson, Charles 74; "Dill Pickles Rag" 52
Johnson, James Weldon 125
Jones, Irving 163
Jones, Richard M. 111
Joplin, Lottie 4, 87–90, 99, 103, 107–108,
115–128, 133, 143, 172–173, 183; Joplin
grave memorial 81, 83, 86, 117; Joplin man-
uscripts 75–78, 86, 90–95, 114–115, 125,
129, 181, 223–230; marriage status 75, 98,
122, 182
Joplin, Scott 2–3, 22, 38, 46–47, 60, 64–147,
154–169, 175, 177, 186, 189–192, 204, 208,
212, 220–222, 236, 238; "The Cascades"
124, 127, 138, 150; death 75, 100, 134, 151,
157, 165, 226, 230; "The Easy Winners"
85, 127, 161, 184, 215, 227; education 152–
153, 157, 165, 181–182, 226, 229; "The
Entertainer" 46, 127, 161; "Euphonic
Sounds" 76, 124, 127, 136, 162; "Fig Leaf
Rag" 85, 90, 127, 162, 184, 227–228; grave
69, 72, 89, 106, 116–117, 125, 129, 172–173;

list of works 125–127, 161–162, 184; The Maple Leaf Club 71, 122, 127; memorial 71–72, 77–87, 95–99, 103–120, 125, 129–135, 172–175, 184, 215, 222–230; "Original Rags" 21, 23, 127, 138, 140, 150, 157, 161, 165, 178–179, 215, 229; potential film biography 95, 116, 119–120, 124, 128, 180–181, 223–230; Saunders, Otis 20–21, 95, 109, 115–116, 122, 140, 145, 148–155; Scott Joplin Ragtime Festival 153, 187; silver half-dollar 23, 31, 53, 67–68, 139, 213, 221–222, 234; "Silver Swan Rag" 126; Stark, John 2, 84, 107, 109, 121, 151, 158–159, 162, 165, 167, 181; "Sunflower Slow Drag" 21, 119, 127, 138, 160–162, 184; "Swipsey" 21, 124, 127, 138, 161–162, 184; that diminished fifth man 182–183; *Treemonisha* 71, 76, 85–93, 103, 109, 114–115, 120, 124, 127–130, 142, 157, 162, 165, 182, 184, 220–230; *see also* "Maple Leaf Rag"
Joplin, Missouri 60
Joplin's Disciple (CD) *see* Affeldt, Paul
Jordan, Joe 150

Kansas City, Missouri 29, 52, 132, 143, 150, 154, 157, 160, 165, 168, 170, 172, 179
Karp, Larry 192, 206, 216–217; The Brun Campbell Archive 22, 26, 68, 71, 73, 91, 106, 126, 134, 176, 217, 219; Ragtime Trilogy 3
Kennedy Barber Shop 38, 65
Kerfoot Hotel 24–27
Kerr, Erskine 123–124, 146
KFOX 69, 73, 84, 136, 223–30
Kingsbury Encyclopedia of Country Music 101
Koenig, Les 232, 237
Krell, William H. 1

Lasswell, Paul 185–228
Leonard, Eddie 55–56
"Let Me Come Back Home" 101; *see also* Campbell, Brun
Levin, Floyd 67, 107
Lillie, Gordon *see* Pawnee Bill
Lingle, Paul 236
Littleton, Colorado 50
London Jazz Journal 149
Long Beach, California 69, 72–74, 223–230
Los Angeles, California 65, 69, 77, 90, 115, 144, 146
Los Angeles Examiner 144, 146
Lunceford, Jimmie 125

"Mama's Little Baby Doll" 90, 199–200, 209; *see also* Campbell, Brun
Manitou, Colorado 50–52

"Maple Leaf Rag" 1–2, 20–23, 27, 43, 69, 85, 94, 116, 127–128, 131, 135, 138–139, 143, 145, 148, 160–161, 168–169, 178–184, 187, 223–230, 235; composition 85, 119, 140, 148–154, 165, 182; copyright 76–77, 87; memorial 71, 86, 114–115, 173; piano roll 111–114, 135–136, 140, 216; publications 1–2, 84, 108, 134, 151–152, 180–181; recordings 69, 74, 78, 81, 87, 93, 96, 105–108, 111–120, 129–130, 153, 173, 215; titling 121; *see also* Joplin, Scott
Maricopa, California 57
Market Street *see* San Francisco, California
Marshall, Arthur 22, 38, 71, 95–96, 138, 150, 154, 157–160, 166–168
Marshall, Owen 150
McCook, Nebraska 13–14
"Melancholy Baby" 74
Melrose Music Company 76–77, 86–87
"Memory Room Rag" 88, 92–93, 223, 228; *see also* Campbell, Brun
Midway Dance Hall 43
The Mississippi Rag (journal) 57, 67
Mize, J.T.H. 140–141
Mobile, Alabama 38
Montgomery, Michael 185
Morath, Max 1
Morton, Jelly Roll 38, 94–95, 110, 119, 131, 159, 161, 167, 169, 175, 233, 235–239
Mullen, J.B. 120
Musicians Mutual Protective Association 96

Naas, Paul J. 77–78
Nashville, Tennessee 71, 89, 125, 129, 132, 173, 229
Nation, Carrie 53
Native Americans 10–11, 14–19, 24–25, 57; Apache 24; Cherokee 14–17, 24; Cheyenne 24, 27–28; Chickasaw 17; Choctaw 17; Creek 17; Indian Territory (Oklahoma) 15–18, 32, 42, 55, 57; Kaw 18; Kiowa-Comanche 24; Seminole 17; Ute 50
New Orleans, Louisiana 94, 104, 150, 213, 236, 239; Campbell, Brun 57, 220, 222, 234; as a center of ragtime 123, 155, 159, 167, 178–180; establishments 131–132, 146, 172; Russell, William 124, 131–132, 191
New York, New York 28, 42, 95, 107, 124, 143, 159, 167, 171–172; Handy, W.C. 80, 88–89, 161; Joplin, Lottie and Scott 75, 109, 127, 143, 151, 157, 161–162, 173, 179, 181–182; publications and musical organizations 132, 150, 162, 164, 226
New York World Telegram 109–110
Newkirk, Oklahoma 35–36

Nichols, Hal 72–97, 99, 105–106, 116–117, 136, 175, 223–30; "Black and Blue Rag" 72, 90; composer 72, 74, 79–80, 90; "Harmony Rag" 79, 90
Nicol, Duncan 37, 40–42
"No Name Rag" 46–47
Norton, George 74
Norwood, Zoe 111–114

Oakland Tribune 45
Oberlin, Kansas 9–14
Oberlin Herald 11
Oberlin Opinion 13
Oklahoma City, Oklahoma 19–21, 24, 36, 60, 109, 139, 145, 148–149, 155, 160, 168
Oklahoma Land Rush 14–19, 234
Old Town Music Hall 235, 238
Ory, Kid (Edward) 128, 165, 214, 231–232
Owensboro, Kentucky 34

Palmyra, New York 13–14
Paramount Pictures 87
Parrish, Terry 187–188
Patterson, Sam 150, 155
Pawnee Bill 17, 27, 64
Perrin, Syd 163
Perry, Robert 112
Perryman, Happy 101–102, 192
Petley, John 187
phonograph 1, 4, 6, 85, 92–93, 116, 120, 133, 135, 185
Pisco John's Bank Exchange Saloon 40–42, 132
Platter Chatter 111, 116, 173
Portland, Oregon 4, 135
The Professors (LPs) 46, 215
Pryor, Arthur 151
Pueblo, Colorado 52
Purcell's 46–48, 172

race relations 1–3, 15, 18, 22–23, 31–32, 46, 71, 80–83, 93, 96, 98–100, 103–107, 110, 142, 152, 163–164, 175, 189, 233
radio 1, 72–105, 115, 117, 129, 142, 175, 187, 205, 217, 223–224
The Rag Times 67, 107, 153, 185–186, 213–214
railroad 10–12, 16, 23, 25, 40, 49, 50–54, 58
The Record Changer 4, 9, 72, 86, 94–100, 104, 108–109, 115, 120, 127, 130, 138, 142, 148–151, 173, 213–214
Record Roundup 133, 140
Reffkin, David 21, 33, 47, 113, 128, 153–154, 162, 177, 182, 216–217; The American Ragtime Ensemble 216; orchestration 216; *see also Essays in Ragtime* (CD)

Remick, Jerome 33, 150
Rendevous Ballroom 102, 128, 232–235
"Rendevous Rag" 196; *see also* Campbell, Brun
Richmond, California 40
Rifkin, Joshua 72, 187
Roberts, David Thomas 186, 188, 237, 239
Roberts, Jay 46
Robinson, J. Russel 90, 96, 103, 128–129
Rochester, New York 10, 13–14
Roosevelt, Teddy 36–37, 81
Rose, Wally 69
Rosebud Club 131; *see also* Turpin, Tom
Rough Riders 32, 26
Rummel, Jack 185–186
Russell, Bill (Russell William Wagner) 124, 131–132, 137, 173, 175–176

"The Saga of S. Brun Campbell" 57, 67, 206, 214
St. Joseph, Missouri 11, 14
St. Louis, Missouri 52–53, 130–131, 205, 214, 231; as a center for ragtime 34–35, 67, 84, 89, 95, 108, 128, 137, 139, 150–188, 234; Joplin, Scott 89, 97–98, 103, 109–110, 150, 152, 157, 167–168, 181, 226; Turpin, Tom 119, 155–158, 161, 164, 166, 168, 176, 179; World's Fair 27, 66, 150
St. Louis Argus 130
St. Louis Magazine 186–187
"Salome's Slow Drag" 140, 187–188, 208, 215–216; *see also* Campbell, Brun
Sam Fox Publishing Company 90
San Francisco, California 41–51, 59, 62, 64, 120; Chinatown 42–46; Market Street 40; *see also* Barbary Coast
Santa Fe, New Mexico 16, 40, 52, 54, 58
Santa Monica, California 93, 102, 114, 128, 147, 232–233
Santa Monica Evening Outlook 147
"Sapphire 'Blue' Rhythm" 192–196, 209; *see also* Campbell, Brun
Saunders, Otis 20–21, 115–116, 139, 145, 148–154, 160, 165, 168; Oklahoma City, Oklahoma 21, 139, 148; Sedalia, Missouri 20–22, 95, 145, 149, 154–155, 160, 165
Sayers, Henry J. 131
Scott, James 38, 95, 150, 157–160, 166–168
"Scott Joplin: Overlooked Genius" 72, 94, 99, 108, 214
Sedalia, Missouri 1–3, 20–23, 31, 69, 71, 84, 95–96, 121, 133, 137, 139, 145, 147, 149, 152–153, 181, 186–188, 222; cradle of ragtime 96–98, 103, 121–124, 132, 143, 151, 154–169, 180; George R. Smith College 152–153, 157, 165–166, 182, 226, 229;

Hubbard School 142–143; see also "Sedalia, Cradle of Ragtime"
"Sedalia, Cradle of Ragtime" 97, 103–104, 108, 120, 173, 192, 213; see also Sedalia, Missouri
Sedalia *Democrat* 121–122, 143, 173
Shea, Tom 186
Siegel, Irving 100–102, 192, 199, 207, 209–210; "Your Sweet Mama's Headin' for Another Town" 93, 101–102, 198, 209
Simms, Dr. Bartlett D. 115, 149
"Slow and Easy" 194
Song Writers Protective Association 91
Sousa, John Philip 150
Spider Kelly's 46–47
Spiller, Cecil Charles 231–239
Spooner Dramatic Company 35
Stacey, Jeff 236
Standard Music Roll Company 112
Stark, John 2, 108–109, 121, 128, 142, 158–159, 167; locations 84; publications 2, 51, 162, 165, 181
Starr, Henry 37–38, 64
The Sting (film) 72
Studio News Magazine 101, 198, 209
Swanson, Adam 47

Taffy *see* George, Ethel Bertha
temperance movement 53
They All Played Ragtime see Blesh, Rudi
Thompson, Charlie 46
Thompson, Kay C. 32, 98, 146, 214
Tichenor, Trebor 186–187, 191–194, 205; commentary 33, 188; *Ragophile* 187, 205; Washington University 186
Tichenor, Virginia 186
Topeka, Kansas 16
Truman, Harry S. 81, 107
Tucker, Sophie 93–94, 192
Tulsa, Oklahoma 2, 27, 37–38, 54, 59–60, 63–66, 144
Turpin, Tom 38, 95, 115, 119, 123, 131–132, 135, 139, 150, 154–167, 175–179, 186, 194, 222, 238; "Harlem Rag" 119, 131–132, 156–157, 162, 164, 178–179, 194; see also Rosebud Club
"Twelfth Street Rag" 78, 92, 132–135, 140, 194, 213–216, 228, 232, 235, 238; see also Bowman, Euday
"The Two-Four Beat'" see "Cavalcade of Jazz"

Universal Studios 90, 103, 129

Van Alstyne, Egbert 28, 74
Venice, California 2–7, 32, 66–67, 74–90, 94, 101–107, 121–122, 130, 133, 142–146, 190–191, 226, 232, 238; history 66–67
Venice Evening Vanguard 66, 144, 146, 214
Von Tilzer, Harry 55, 119

Waggner, George 90, 103
Walker, Marie 140, 151–152, 154
Walker, Morton 140, 151–152
Walker, Ray 137–138
Waller, Fats 236
Washington, Kansas 9, 12
Watters, Lu 69, 120–123, 130–131, 135, 142, 178, 189, 215
"Weeping Willow Rag" see "Grandpa Stomps" (aka "Weeping Willow Rag")
West Coast Recordings 121, 131, 142, 215
Whiteman, Paul 79, 81, 84, 87, 128, 226
Who Is Who in Music 65–66, 140–141
Wichita, Kansas 16, 25, 38–39, 53, 120, 155
Wiley, Clarence 33, 136; "Car-bar-lick Acid" 33, 136
Wilkes, Galen 231–239
Williams, Clarence 104, 109–111
Williams, Harry 28
Williams, Tony 157–160, 165–168
Willick, George 185–186, 214
Willkie, Wendell 84, 87, 223, 226
Wilson, Alfred 150
World War I 214, 226, 239
World War II 74, 86–87, 90, 92, 97, 199, 227, 239

Yerba Buena Music Shop 140, 216
Yerxa, Ted 115
"You Are Mama's Baby Doll" 200, 209; see also Campbell, Brun
"You Are the One I Want the Rest of My Life" 90, 200–201, 209; see also Campbell, Brun
Younger, Cole 115
"You're Going to Pay on Judgment Day" 101; see also Campbell, Brun

Zimmerman, Richard 102, 126, 236